A BIO(
SKETC]
EARLY HONG KONG

Hong Kong University Press thanks Xu Bing for writing the Press's name in his Square Word Calligraphy for the covers of its books. For further information, see p. iv.

Echoes: Classics of Hong Kong Culture and History

Series General Editor: Robert Nield

The life of Hong Kong and its region has been explored in a vast number of books. They include ground-breaking scholarly studies of great standing, and literary works that shed light on people, places and events. Many of these books unfortunately are no longer available to the general reader.

The aim of the Echoes series is once more to make available the best of those books that would otherwise be lost. The series will embrace not only history, but also memoirs, fiction, politics, natural history and other subjects. The focal point will be Hong Kong, but the series will extend to places connected with the city or sharing some of its experiences. In this way we hope to bring a growing number of classic publications to a new and wider readership.

Other titles in the Echoes series:

Thistle and Bamboo: The Life and Times of Sir James Stewart Lockhart
Shiona Airlie

Power and Charity: A Chinese Merchant Elite in Colonial Hong Kong
Elizabeth Sinn

Chinese Christians: Elites, Middlemen and the Church in Hong Kong
Carl T. Smith

Edge of Empires: Chinese Elites and British Colonials in Hong Kong
John M. Carroll

Anglo-China: Chinese People and British Rule in Hong Kong, 1841–1880
Christopher Munn

City of Broken Promises
Austin Coates

Macao and the British, 1637–1842: Prelude to Hong Kong
Austin Coates

A Macao Narrative
Austin Coates

The Road
Austin Coates

The Taking of Hong Kong: Charles and Clara Elliot in China Waters
Susanna Hoe and Derek Roebuck

A BIOGRAPHICAL SKETCH-BOOK OF EARLY HONG KONG

G. B. ENDACOTT

New introduction by John M. Carroll

香港大學出版社
HONG KONG UNIVERSITY PRESS

Hong Kong University Press
14/F Hing Wai Centre
7 Tin Wan Praya Rd
Aberdeen
Hong Kong
www.hkupress.org

First published in 1962 by Eastern Universities Press Limited, Singapore.

© Marshall Cavendish International (Singapore) Pte Ltd (formerly operating as Times Media Pte Ltd) of Times Publishing Ltd, 1962

This edition published by Hong Kong University Press in 2005
Reprinted 2011

ISBN 978-962-209-742-1

British Library Cataloguing-in-Publication Data
A catalogue entry for this book is available from the British Library.

Printed and bound by Pre-Press Limited in Hong Kong, China

Hong Kong University Press is honoured that Xu Bing, whose art explores the complex themes of language across cultures, has written the Press's name in his Square Word Calligraphy. This signals our commitment to cross-cultural thinking and the distinctive nature of our English-language books published in China.

"At first glance, Square Word Calligraphy appears to be nothing more unusual than Chinese characters, but in fact it is a new way of rendering English words in the format of a square so they resemble Chinese characters. Chinese viewers expect to be able to read Square Word Calligraphy but cannot. Western viewers, however are surprised to find they can read it. Delight erupts when meaning is unexpectedly revealed."

— Britta Erickson, *The Art of Xu Bing*

To My Parents

Contents

LIST OF PLATES

INTRODUCTION TO THE PAPERBACK EDITION
G. B. ENDACOTT AND HONG KONG HISTORY

John M. Carroll

IN his preface to the first edition of *A Biographical Sketch-book of Early Hong Kong*, G. B. Endacott explained how he hoped his book would "in some measure have recaptured the flavour of the period, and give an idea of some of the characters who walked in Queen's Road a century or so ago." Even a brief summary of some of these characters will demonstrate the wide range of European personalities in early Hong Kong, the tiny colony that Britain acquired in 1841 to expand its commercial and political interests in China. In Chapter 1, we meet Captain Charles Elliot, the first administrator of colonial Hong Kong, who was later criticized both by British officials and European merchants for not extracting more from the Qing[1] government than this tiny, "barren island." Henry Pottinger, subject of Chapter 2 and first governor of Hong Kong, during the Opium War wanted to raze the city of Ningbo as a warning to its Chinese residents, but at a banquet marking the Treaty of Nanking (which ceded the island of Hong Kong to Britain "in perpetuity") sang English songs for Qing Imperial Commissioner Qiying.[2] Chapter 8 explains that William Caine, the first magistrate of Hong Kong, fought Hong Kong's rampant "lawlessness by a ruthless application of flogging with the rattan, with or without imprisonment." Though he was later reinstated, John Hulme (Chapter 9), the first chief justice, was suspended for drunkenness. Thomas Anstey, the "fearless, energetic and upright, but rather unbalanced" attorney general in Chapter 13, spent much of his career in Hong Kong "combating all the abuses, imagined or real, with which he thought the local government was riddled." Chapter 21 is on George Chinnery, the painter who according to popular legend went to China to escape from his wife, "the ugliest woman he ever saw in the whole course of his life," also spent some time in Hong Kong when he was not enjoying the Mediterranean tranquility of the Portuguese territory in Macau (where he is buried in the Protestant Cemetery). In Chapter 22 we meet, amongst "Some Other Foreigners," the only woman in Endacott's book: Harriet Baxter, the Anglican missionary and educator of Chinese girls, who accidentally almost shot a friend while out walking after dark.

---

1 "Ch'ing" in the Wade-Giles system of romanization used in Endacott's book.
2 "Ch'i-ying" in the Wade-Giles system, though Endacott uses the Cantonese pronunciation, "Kiying."

Born in 1901 in Beer, a small fishing port in South Devon in the west of England, George Beer Endacott liked to describe his own youth as "not unique, but still worthy of notice." The son of a railway worker, Endacott studied at Exeter and Oxford, where he read philosophy, politics, and economics. He taught history in British high schools until he joined the Royal Navy in 1942, serving as an interpreter with French forces in the Mediterranean. Just as it had been in the early colonial period, Hong Kong was a microcosm of Britain's changing imperial status when Endacott arrived there in 1946 to join the History Department of the University of Hong Kong as a lecturer (and remained the only faculty member in the department until 1952). In the early 1840s Britain was shifting from mercantilism to free trade, consolidating its occupation of India, and expanding its presence in Southeast Asia and China. Although Britain had recently regained control of Hong Kong from Japan when Endacott arrived, the local economy was in shambles, civil war loomed across the border in Mainland China, and the countdown to independence in Britain's largest colony, India, was well under way.

By the time *A Biographical Sketch-book* was published in 1962, the British Empire was being dismantled even more rapidly than it was expanding when the subjects of Endacott's book came to Hong Kong. A new group of colonial civil servants had arrived in Hong Kong. These were the "retreads" from the recently independent colonies. In Asia alone, India, Burma, Ceylon, and Malaya had all won their independence, while Singapore, where Endacott's book was first published, would in 1963 temporarily join the new nation of Malaysia. The writings of Karl Marx, Mao Zedong, and Frantz Fanon were galvanizing anti-colonial and anti-imperialist movements across the world, and Hong Kong was caught in the middle of the Cold War, even while depending on its giant neighbor just across the border — the new People's Republic of China — for food, water, and other resources.

Like most colonials, Endacott took the legitimacy of British colonialism in Hong Kong as given. Never in this book, for example, does he question the British motives or means for acquiring Hong Kong. In both *A Biographical Sketch-book of Early Hong Kong* and *A History of Hong Kong* (1958), which for decades remained the definitive English-language history of Hong Kong, Endacott praised Charles Elliot's remarkable restraint in the first Opium War. Note, for example, how Chapter 23 on the "Princely Hong" of Jardine, Matheson & Co., the largest of the European firms in South China, never mentions opium, which although not necessarily the underlying cause of the first Opium War was nonetheless its immediate cause. (Yet in Chapter 5 Endacott regrets the irony of how the liberal-minded John Bowring, who had been president of the Peace Society that advocated the peaceful resolution of international disputes, and who wanted more humane policies for the Chinese in Hong Kong, helped precipitate the second Opium War between China and Britain.)

Like many British merchants and politicians from the period he described, Endacott saw that war between Britain and China had been inevitable. "The old methods of solving disputes between the two countries were becoming no longer acceptable," he wrote in *A History of Hong Kong*, "and since the Chinese would not open diplomatic negotiations or recognize the British government as anything but normally tributary, it followed that any serious incident would easily lead to war. There was no acceptable alternative." The British acquired Hong Kong not for territorial empire but for commercial expansion in China: "A healthy trade demanded settled conditions, suppression of robbery, guarantee of contract and of impartial justice. Since the Chinese were thought to be unable to provide these conditions, the British had to provide them. This is fundamental to understanding any history of Hong Kong."[3]

Nor did Endacott make any attempt to hide his enthusiasm for the some of the early administrators of colonial Hong Kong, reflecting as they did "the virility of Victorian society." Although like "all pioneers" their methods were "rough and ready," Endacott writes in *A Biographical Sketch-book* how "their energy and enterprise must command admiration. " Although he discusses the crime and other problems in early Hong Kong, Endacott saw colonialism in Hong Kong as a process of trial and error in which principled men of action could eventually overcome obstacles, and as a stabilizing force in China. Early Hong Kong of course had its share of both "greedy self-seeking adventurers" and "men of high principle devoted to the public welfare." But, Endacott reassures us, "Brooding over all was the Colonial Office in London, vigilant in the detection of abuse and insistent that the interests of the Chinese be safeguarded." The fundamental task for early colonial administrators was establishing order within a frontier, and, given colonial Hong Kong's relative historical stability compared with that across the border in Mainland China, Endacott, like most colonial officials, believed that this fundamental task had been successfully completed.

This is not to suggest that Endacott was completely uncritical of the colonial record in Hong Kong. Although books such as *A History of Hong Kong* celebrate Hong Kong's economic prosperity and political stability, they also mention how the colonial legislature passed various ordinances that discriminated against the Chinese population of Hong Kong: until the late 1800s, Chinese could not walk on the streets after nine without a note from their employer and had to carry lanterns; legal punishments for Chinese were generally higher, while flogging was common since many colonial officials believed that poor Chinese preferred the colonial jail to life on the street.

Endacott's later scholarship became slightly less celebratory of British rule. Endacott's preface to *Hong Kong Eclipse* (1978), his account of the

---

3 G. B. Endacott, *A History of Hong Kong*, rev. ed. (Hong Kong: Oxford University Press, 1973), vii–viii, 13.

Japanese occupation from 1941 to 1945, noted that although the book had been intended as an official history, "this was not to be."[4] This comment has prompted speculation that the colonial government disapproved of the way Endacott discussed how poorly prepared the British had been for the Japanese invasion of December 1941. Endacott warned against making any rash judgments about Hong Kong's defenses without considering the obstacles — for example, the influx of refugees from China that drained the government's resources. But he also drew attention to the colonial regime's slow plans for air-raid defense, its reliance on weak artillery and old ammunition, as well as to the weakness of British intelligence, which seriously underestimated the size and quality of the Japanese forces. Endacott also included details of the Japanese occupation that may have been embarrassing to the Hong Kong government — how, for example, the Japanese went to great lengths to publicize and explain their policies to the Chinese of Hong Kong, and how they made some positive changes such as public health campaigns, medical and educational facilities for the poor, and agricultural schemes in the New Territories.

As Endacott explains in his preface to *A Biographical Sketch-book*, many of the chapters in this book first appeared as journal articles. Consequently, the book often reads more as an album of sketches or snapshots of these men (and with one exception, Harriet Baxter, they are all men) as they passed through Hong Kong, rather than as a complete collection of biographies. Because Endacott focuses almost solely on these men's time in Hong Kong, readers may sometimes wonder why they behaved the way they did. Yet Endacott's sketch-book approach effectively captures the overlapping colonial connections and networks within the British Empire and particularly in Asia. Colonial officials often moved from colony to colony, which could affect the way they interacted (or, as could often be the case, did not interact) with each place. Although the importance of such imperial connections would have been obvious to contemporary colonial officials and colonists, who would have read in the local press about developments in other colonies, they have often eluded historians of colonialism. Endacott shows how Charles Elliot, who had served in West Africa, the East Indies, and the West Indies, later served in the new Republic of Texas, and as governor of Bermuda and of Trinidad. Henry Pottinger, who before coming to Hong Kong had already "proved himself a man of action" in India, later became governor of the Cape of Good Hope, then of Madras. Before coming to Hong Kong, George Bonham, introduced in Chapter 4, had served in Sumatra and the Straits Settlements, of which he became governor at the age of 34. He, like Governor John Davis (Chapter 3), had started his career with the East India Company. Hercules Robinson (Chapter 6), appointed to restore confidence

---

4 G. B. Endacott, *Hong Kong Eclipse*, edited and with additional material by Alan Birch (Hong Kong: Oxford University Press, 1978), xiii.

after all the scandals under fourth governor John Bowring (who had not begun his career in the colonial service), had previously served in the West Indies and subsequently became governor of Ceylon, New South Wales, New Zealand, and the Cape of Good Hope.

Not only does Endacott tell us where these officials came from and where they went after Hong Kong, he also explains how their past shaped their actions and attitudes during their time in Hong Kong. Bowring, for example, entered government service reluctantly and late in life because of a failing business career. His Unitarianism and belief in the utilitarianism of Jeremy Bentham put him at odds with the European business community of Hong Kong from the outset. William Caine, who began his career as an army officer in India, brought "something of the East India Company traditions" to Hong Kong (which in contemporary code would have referred to Caine's loose morals, taking bribes, and strict administration of justice through the "discipline of the barrack-room").

A recurring theme in Endacott's book is the Hong Kong colonial government's reliance on a tiny handful of European linguists. One particularly intriguing and colorful of these "China experts" was Registrar General and Protector of Chinese Daniel Caldwell. The subject of Chapter 14, Caldwell was an interpreter married to a Chinese woman and suspected of both "shady transactions regarding brothels" and associating with pirates. Another so-called China expert was Charles Gutzlaff, the Lutheran missionary and Chinese secretary to the Superintendent of Trade. As Chapter 16 shows, Gutzlaff also served as an interpreter for opium traders, in exchange for using their boats to spread Christian scriptures and tracts, and who claimed to have become a naturalized Chinese citizen in Siam by adopting into a Chinese family there.

Readers familiar with the British colonial experience in India may be surprised by how little interest most British officials seem to have taken in Chinese culture. Certainly there were exceptions. Before coming to Hong Kong as governor, Endacott tells us, John Davis had been one of the few East India Company officials who bothered to study Chinese. Davis helped found the Hong Kong Branch of the Royal Asiatic Society, which continues today to promote interest in Hong Kong history. John Bowring believed that learning Chinese and maintaining more personal contact with local Chinese residents and officials in China would help him solve problems in Hong Kong and improve Anglo-Chinese relations — a task at which his predecessors had failed. Included in Chapter 17 among "Some Other Officials" is Thomas Wade, the linguist and diplomat who served as assistant Chinese secretary to the Superintendent of Trade. Wade later became Professor of Chinese at the University of Cambridge, where he helped devise the Wade-Giles system for romanizing Chinese. Also in this chapter is Samuel Fearon, the first registrar general, who later became Professor of Chinese at King's College, London. And most students of

Chinese history are familiar with James Legge, the great Scottish scholar, missionary, educator and "public-spirited citizen." Chapter 20 mentions how Legge was so committed to spreading Christianity yet maintaining good relations between Britain and China that, when he embarked upon a missionary expedition to Guangdong Province in 1861 during the Taiping Rebellion, he stipulated that no British gunboat should be sent to avenge his death if he were killed. After returning to Britain, Legge became Professor of Sinology at Oxford, where he continued to translate the Chinese classics until his death in 1897.

But such men were rare in Hong Kong. Whereas in India learning local languages and cultures was considered essential for conquering and controlling Britain's "Jewel in the Crown," most British officials in China and Hong Kong did not share this concern. Unlike in India, Europeans in China and Hong Kong communicated with Chinese almost completely in English or pidgin. Shortly after his arrival in Hong Kong in 1859 — very nearly twenty years after the British first occupied the island — Governor Hercules Robinson complained that not a single senior colonial officer in his new administration could read or write Chinese. When Robinson offered financial incentives to encourage officers to study Chinese, only three responded to his offer. Not until two years later, in 1861, did the British make plans for training (including Chinese language instruction) cadets for the Hong Kong Civil Service.

This lack of interest in Chinese culture among British officials and colonists has never been explained adequately. One possibility is that because Britain acquired Hong Kong primarily for commerce rather than for settlement, most Europeans in early Hong Kong were sojourners who had no intention of staying in the colony for more than a few years. The difference between China and India may also have been a matter of timing. Whereas in the late 1700s and early 1800s the East India Company encouraged its employees in India to learn local languages and customs, most of the traders in early Hong Kong were private traders who arrived after the East India Company had already lost its monopoly on the China trade. These private traders were interested mainly in making a quick fortune, rather than in learning about Chinese culture. By this time, even in India the old generation of British "Orientalists" interested in Indian culture had been replaced by the new "Anglicists," and the East India Company no longer promoted the study of Sanskrit, Arabic, and Persian. Finally, India may have been the exception rather than the rule. As D. K. Fieldhouse has argued, British colonial officials often had little knowledge of local conditions in their empire.[5]

This lack of local knowledge on the part of British officials and colonists should not, however, lead readers to accept uncritically the

---

5 D. K. Fieldhouse, *The Colonial Empires: A Comparative Study from the Eighteenth Century*, 2nd ed. (London: Macmillan, 1982), 246–247.

standard assumption that the early Hong Kong government for the most part left the Chinese population alone. Colonialism in Hong Kong did not involve the widespread slaughter or dislocation typical of many other colonies. And it is equally true that the British received help from all sorts of Chinese collaborators, and that colonialism offered many opportunities to Chinese in Hong Kong. But Britain nevertheless acquired Hong Kong primarily though a bloody war with China, and colonialism could be disruptive and bewildering for both indigenous villagers and newcomers from all over Guangdong province.

The early British vision of colonial Hong Kong was frequently called "Anglo-China." According to this vision, Hong Kong was to be not just what Henry Pottinger called the "great emporium of the East" but, in the words of historian Christopher Munn, "also a model of British good government, a living exhibition of European civilization, a meeting point between east and west, where the manners, institutions and technologies of both cultures would engage each other in a productive and beneficial way." Yet as we see in many of Endacott's chapters, the early colonial government faced great difficulties in transforming Hong Kong into more than a colonial outpost and opium center. The colony was plagued by economic depression, piracy, crime, and disease. Munn argues that, because the colonial government failed to help Hong Kong fulfill this vision of "Anglo-China" and was unable to obtain reliable help from the local Chinese leadership, until the late 1800s colonial rule "exerted a considerable impact on people's daily lives." As Hong Kong failed to become the "great emporium of the East," both the colonial government and European residents increasingly viewed the majority of Hong Kong's Chinese population as criminals. Hong Kong had one of the most top-heavy governments and largest police forces in the British Empire, a huge military presence, an elaborate system of monopolies and taxes, not to mention oppressive curfews and registration programs for controlling the majority Chinese population. With a criminal justice system that created new offenses applicable only to them, the Chinese in Hong Kong "lived under a constantly changing, labyrinthine system of intrusive regulatory laws and policing practices, which increasingly criminalized many daily activities and brought thousands of people into direct contact with the police and the courts."[6]

One of Endacott's greatest strengths lies in his ability to capture the frontier-like atmosphere of early colonial Hong Kong. Hard though it might be to believe today, Hong Kong in the early 1840s had all the rugged excitement of a gold-rush frontier town. Charles Elliot's proclamation in January 1841 that Hong Kong would be a free port attracted an influx of Chinese from the counties across the harbor, European merchants and

---

6 Christopher Munn, *Anglo-China: Chinese People and British Rule in Hong Kong, 1841–1880* (Richmond, Surrey, England: Curzon Press, 2001), 2–4.

missionaries, and adventurers of all nationalities. For many British colonial officials and European residents, the Chinese in Hong Kong represented the "scum of Canton." Robert Montgomery Martin (Chapter 10), the colonial treasurer who devoted his fourteen months in Hong Kong to proving that the colony was of no use as a trading center, described the Chinese population there as a "Bedouin sort of population, whose migratory, predatory, gambling and dissolute habits, utterly unfit them for continuous industry, and render them not only useless but highly injurious subjects in the attempt to form a new colony."[7] In Britain, Hong Kong came to be seen at best as a haven for European outlaws, deserters, adventurers, and speculators. A writer for the *Economist* noted in August 1846 how "Hong Kong is nothing now but a depot for a few opium smugglers, soldiers, officers and men-of-war's men."[8] Robert Fortune, an English botanist and adventurer who visited the island, wrote that whereas in the earliest days of the colony the foreign population had consisted of "generally most upright and honorable men," by 1845 the foreign population now formed a "very motley group."[9] Oswald Tiffany, an American visitor, described "these worthless adventurers" as "Scapegoats and scoundrels from the purlieus of London, creatures that only missed Botany Bay by good fortune." These "dock loafers, who had never at home put their heads into decent houses, would swagger along three of four abreast, elbowing quiet men out of the way, and replying to a word by a blow."[10]

A prominent theme in colonial rhetoric everywhere was that colonialism helped ensure peace and order. As Endacott's chapters show, however, this was not the case in Hong Kong. Early Hong Kong attracted all sorts of "lawless elements," both Chinese and European. Henry Pottinger wrote in January 1844 how "such is the expertness and daring of the lower classes of the already immense Chinese population on this island, that thefts and robberies are of frequent occurrence."[11] Some colonial officials were convinced that Chinese authorities in Guangdong deliberately deported vagabonds, vagrants, thieves, and other outlaws to Hong Kong, both as a way to get rid of criminals and to undermine the stability of the colony. Robert Montgomery Martin insisted that "Hong

7 "Report on the Island of Hong Kong," 24 July 1844, enclosed in Davis to Stanley, 20 August 1844, Papers of the House of Commons, 1857, session 1, vol. xii, reprinted in R. L. Jarman, ed., *Hong Kong Annual Administration Reports, 1841–1941*, vol. 1: 1841–1886 (Oxford: Archive Editions, 1996), 8.

8 Cited in E. J. Eitel, *Europe in China: The History of Hong Kong from the Beginning to the Year 1882* (Hong Kong: Kelly and Walsh, 1895; Hong Kong: Oxford University Press, 1983 reprint), 242.

9 Robert Fortune, *Three Years' Wanderings in the Northern Provinces of China, including a Visit to the Tea, Silk, and Cotton Countries: With an Account of Agriculture and Horticulture of the Chinese, New Plants, etc.* (London: J. Murray, 1847), 28.

10 Osmond Tiffany, Jr., *The Canton Chinese or The American's Sojourn in the Celestial Empire* (Boston: James Monroe and Company, 1849), reprinted in Barbara-Sue White, ed., *Hong Kong: Somewhere Between Heaven and Earth* (Hong Kong: Oxford University Press, 1996), 38–39.

11 Great Britain, Colonial Office, Original Correspondence: Hong Kong, 1841–1951, Series 129 (CO129), Public Record Office, London, CO 129/5/11, 30 January 1844, Pottinger to Stanley, reprinted in Steve Tsang, ed., *Government and Politics: A Documentary History of Hong Kong* (Hong Kong: Hong Kong University Press, 1995), 162.

Kong is viewed by the Chinese as a spot where adventurers and reckless characters may make something out of the English, and where burglars and robbers may resort with impunity, and live upon the profits of their villainy."[12] Martin also reported that "the European inhabitants are obliged to sleep with loaded pistols; frequently to turn out of their beds are midnight to protect their lives and property from gangs of armed robbers, who are ready to sacrifice a few of their number if they can obtain a large plunder."[13] Robert Fortune, the British botanist, claimed that the "town swarms with thieves and robbers."[14] J. M. Tronson, a British naval officer who visited the island as part of a voyage to China, Japan, and Russia, and later came from Bengal to command the British garrison, recalled how, "A part of the city named Tai-pin Shan, is inhabited by the Coolies, and by refugees and scoundrels from all parts of the empire . . . Some of the outcasts prowl about the island, and commit various depredations whenever they meet with defenceless people."[15]

Endacott is equally adept at showing the many other obstacles the British faced in settling their new frontier colony. Consider, for example, the predicament of Henry Pottinger, who faced the problem of distributing land. Elliot had allotted land by grant, but Pottinger was soon ordered to end this practice. Another problem was constructing a suitable form of government. Pottinger was charged with establishing a new Legislative Council and Executive Council as in other colonies. Local European merchants wanted some sort of municipal government, but they were determined that their Chinese counterparts not be included. Then there was the problem of taxes: officials at home thought colonies should be self-supporting, but colonists argued that in a free port they should not be taxed. How then was the colonial government to raise money for public works and a police force? An example of the further complexity of this problem surfaced in the summer of 1857 European critics blamed Governor John Bowring for not taking stronger measures to curb crime. Eager not to drive out the Chinese merchants, they argued, Bowring allowed them to pay lower police rates than the European merchants.[16] It thus comes as no surprise that several governors of early Hong Kong commented on the irony that it was their British countrymen, rather than their Chinese subjects, who were the most difficult to manage. As Endacott shows, tensions with local merchants were a perennial problem for Hong Kong administrators. Few foreigners in South China, we are told, were sorry to see Charles Elliot leave in August 1841. The reason why Henry

---

12 "Report on the Island of Hong Kong," 15.
13 "Report on the Island of Hong Kong," 9.
14 Fortune, *Three Years' Wanderings*, 27.
15 John M. Tronson, *Personal Narrative of a Voyage to Japan, Kamtschatka, Siberia, Tartary, and Various Parts of the Coast of China; in H. M. S. Barracouta, 1854–1856* (London: Smith, Elder & Co., 1859), 55.
16 *The Friend of China*, 29 July 1857.

Pottinger was so unpopular among foreigners in Hong Kong was that "he alone upheld the public interest in the face of self-seeking officials and merchants." Second governor John Davis was "hated" by Europeans in Hong Kong, "for whom he showed only contempt." When Davis left Hong Kong in March 1848 after resigning before his term was completed, no speeches or banquets were given.

Exacerbating these problems was the chronic shortage of manpower. The book jacket for the original edition of this book explained that the British Empire expanded so quickly in the early nineteenth century that "posts were being created faster than men of character and ability could be found to fill them." In his preface, Endacott explains how manpower was "sadly lacking, and that little attempt was made to organize a colonial service to overcome the deficiency. One of the astonishing things about the British Empire at that time was its unsystematic growth, and makeshift arrangements." Consequently, "recourse had to be made to whatever local men were available." Thus Pottinger, who frequently complained of being overworked, often had to give junior posts to men "of the adventure class, many from Australia, and other roving types." Pottinger was often criticized for not controlling crime, but he had to rely on a small group of locally recruited European soldiers and seamen. Preventing police collusion and extortion was also a problem, especially since the pay for policemen was so low.

All these problems and obstacles are embodied in the short tenure of John Davis, the second and, according to Endacott, "most unpopular" governor of Hong Kong. Only weeks after arriving in Hong Kong, Davis introduced the Registration Ordinance, a highly controversial scheme for registering the entire population that was later amended to apply only to lower-class Chinese. Davis then spent the rest of his time in Hong Kong trying to end the "administrative chaos" that had plagued the colony even before Davis arrived; levying taxes, controlling crime "arising from the influx of disorderly elements from the mainland," and fighting a protracted quarrel with Chief Justice John Hulme.

Like many historians of his era, Endacott regretted how we often forget that "history is made by men." Thus the founding of the colony of Hong Kong was "closely bound up with the career of Captain Charles Elliot." William Caine, the first magistrate of the colony, was an "outstanding personality" who "impressed his personality on the administration of law and order in the Colony." (Note, however, that Endacott does not slip into psychohistory. For example, although he tells that Charles Gutzlaff had an "unhappy upbringing under an unsympathetic step-mother," he does not pursue this any further.) But if the moral of Endacott's story is that men of action can shape history, one of the other morals is that such men are often disliked in their own time. Although Charles Elliot's conciliatory attitude during the Opium War proved that he was "undoubtedly a man of personality and strength of character," these same virtues brought him into conflict with European merchants in Hong Kong. Henry Pottinger was "too forthright and too decided in his opinions to be easy to work with." John Davis was a "man of strong character . . . an authority on the Chinese, keen in argument . . . urbane, bland, and self-assured." Thus we learn that George Bonham, third governor, was the first popular governor of Hong Kong. However, Bonham's popularity derived not from any programs or reforms but because his tenure coincided with a period of greater economic prosperity, and because most of the unpopular decisions had already been made by his less popular predecessors. Although Bonham realized that Hong Kong residents were taxed more lightly than those in Singapore, he refused to jeopardize his popularity by raising taxes. Bonham also deferred solutions to controversial problems such as flogging and branding of criminals. Thus Bonham "rarely got into trouble because he pursued no vigorous policy." Bonham's secret for success reminds one more of a Taoist sage than of a colonial governor: "Without exerting himself or showing much leadership, he showed friendliness, consideration, and a nice sense of what was better left alone."

More worthy of notice than this minor contradiction, however, is Endacott's term "men of action." As there is only one woman in Endacott's book, Harriet Baxter, we can assume that Endacott would not be impressed by the more modern "people of action."[17] With the exception of some European civilians in *Hong Kong Eclipse*, women rarely appear in Endacott's work. Even more unsettling given how the majority of Hong Kong's population has always been Chinese, noticeably absent from Endacott's book is any serious discussion of the Chinese population of early Hong Kong. The reason for this, he writes in his preface, is that during that time the Chinese were "sojourners only, as indeed they have been during the whole of the Colony's history until recently." Endacott was correct in that many colonial sources do not say much about the early Chinese population of Hong Kong. But the absence of these Chinese is a pattern found throughout his scholarship. At an academic conference in the mid-1990s at Hong Kong University one of his colleagues observed, only somewhat facetiously, that Endacott's work could lead readers to believe that the colony had no Chinese residents. In both *A History of Hong Kong* and *Government and People in Hong Kong, 1841–1962: A Constitutional History* (1964), we frequently read about "the Chinese," but never quite meet them, while at other times Endacott seems to include the Chinese mainly as the reason for Hong Kong's lack of political representation (in *Government and People*, Endacott argued that "Broadly the overwhelming Chinese character of Hong Kong and the need to protect their interests

---

17 A considerably fuller biography of Harriet Baxter can be found in Susanna Hoe, *The Private Life of Old Hong Kong: Western Women in the British Colony* (Hong Kong: Oxford University Press, 1991), chapter 11.

have been the main factors in the delaying the introduction of essentially Western ideas of political freedom."[18]) In *An Eastern Entrepot: A Collection of Documents Illustrating the History of Hong Kong* (1964), Endacott attributed Hong Kong's remarkable economic growth mainly to "British liberal economic policies, particularly free trade, and a strong laissez-faire spirit in administration which aimed at keeping the ring clear for free enterprise under the law administered impartially to all without fear or favour."[19] And although *Hong Kong Eclipse* remained the most thorough study of the Japanese occupation in English until the publication of Philip Snow's recent study, *The Fall of Hong Kong*, it too focused mainly on the European population of Hong Kong.

Like many European historians of Hong Kong, Endacott was restricted to English-language sources. There is no reason to doubt his declaration in the preface here that he was not trying to "belittle" the contributions of Hong Kong's Chinese residents. Much of the recent scholarship on colonies has rightly shifted from analyses of European colonists and indigenous elites to studies of "subalterns": workers, peasants, and women, for example. But understanding Hong Kong, or any colony, means also looking at its expatriate communities. Hong Kong was never comprised solely of Chinese and Britons. Like the treaty ports along the coast and waterways of China, and like most other cities in the British Empire, the colony was from the outset multi-ethnic. Apart from the British and the Chinese there were Eurasians, Indians, Portuguese from old families in the colony of Macau, Jews, other Europeans, Armenians, and Americans. Although Endacott does not discuss the Asian communities, his chapters introduce some of the other European nationalities in early Hong Kong. Charles Gutzlaff, the missionary and interpreter, originally hailed from Pomerania. Until 1851, the assistant harbour master was an Italian, while the colonial treasurer who succeeded William Mercer in 1854, was R. Rienacker, a German. The clerk of councils, Leonardo d'Almada de Castro, was Portuguese.

Focusing solely on the European community of Hong Kong, however, poses several dangers. First, it ignores how British colonialism was made possible by Chinese collaboration throughout Hong Kong's history. The British received help from Chinese in the Opium War, which gave Britain control over Hong Kong Island, and during the early development of the young colony. One example of these Chinese is Kwok Acheong, a boatman who supplied the British forces during the Opium War. After the British takeover, Kwok settled in Hong Kong where he became a successful comprador, or middleman, for the Peninsular and Oriental (P&O) Steam

18 G. B. Endacott, *Government and People in Hong Kong, 1841–1962: A Constitutional History* (Hong Kong: Hong Kong University Press, 1964), vii.
19 G. B. Endacott, *An Eastern Entrepot: A Collection of Documents Illustrating the History of Hong Kong* (London: Her Majesty's Stationery Office, 1964), ix.

Navigation Company. Like many of the British merchants in Hong Kong, Kwok tried his hand at many commercial ventures: he owned a bakery, tried briefly importing cattle to Hong Kong, ran a general merchants' firm, and started a line of steamships that sailed between Hong Kong, Canton, and Macau. By the late 1870s, Kwok had become a regional shipping magnate. He was a frequent advisor to the colonial government until his death in 1880. The Chinese were also responsible for building Hong Kong. As in many European colonies in East Asia, Chinese contractors, builders, and laborers completed all major construction work in Hong Kong. An example is Tam Achoy, one of the most successful contractors, who had worked for the British in Singapore as foreman in the colonial dockyards. Tam built some of the most important buildings in early Hong Kong, including the P & O Building and the Exchange Building for Dent and Co., one of the largest European firms. As Endacott explains in Chapter 10, the Exchange Building was later purchased by the government for use as the colony's Supreme Court. In return for his services to the British in Singapore and Hong Kong, Tam received land grants in the Lower Bazaar, the area where most of Hong Kong's new Chinese residents settled. Tam eventually became one of the largest Chinese businessmen in early Hong Kong, leading the *Friend of China* in 1857 to describe him as "no doubt the most creditable Chinese in the Colony."

Endacott's claim that the Chinese in Hong Kong were only sojourners must also be taken with caution. For this is a fiction that would dominate colonial discourse on Hong Kong until after World War Two, a convenient excuse for not introducing political representation and social welfare. Many Chinese in Hong Kong were no more sojourners than the British officials covered in Endacott's chapters. As the work of Carl Smith and other historians has shown, a group of more or less permanent Chinese residents began to emerge in the colony by the late 1850s, not because of the colonial government's efforts to attract wealthier and more "respectable" Chinese residents, but because of the chaos and destruction of the massive Taiping Rebellion that tore China apart in the 1850s and early 1860s. Whereas in the early years Chinese merchants had resided mainly in the squalid Chinese sections of Hong Kong, leaving their families back in their home villages or in Canton, by the 1850s and 1860s Chinese businessmen were beginning to buy or rent property for their wives and families from European owners in the more desirable parts of the main town. These new Chinese businessmen were soon establishing guilds, neighborhood-watch groups, and philanthropic associations — demonstrating the community spirit and urban consciousness that colonial officials hoped from their Chinese subjects. For these Chinese, the colony became a home rather than simply a place to get rich fast.

Furthermore, the same colonial records that Endacott used for his books contain evidence of how by the mid-1850s the Hong Kong government realized that the Chinese merchants were responsible for the colony's new prosperity. In 1855 Officiating Registrar-General Charles May (discussed in Chapter 15) informed John Bowring that the turbulent conditions on the Chinese mainland had brought many new Chinese traders to the colony, and that the local Chinese community was beginning to build houses of better quality.[20] In August 1857 Governor Bowring declared that the Chinese of the colony were "all concurring to render Hongkong one of the most prosperous and progressive of Colonies under the protection of the British flag."[21] In May 1863 Hercules Robinson, the last governor covered by Endacott's study, reported to the Colonial Office that, "It is the Chinese who have made Hong Kong what it is and not its connection with the foreign trade."[22] Hong Kong's new economic growth, sparked by the arrival of new Chinese capital and labor, moreover benefited local European merchants and attracted new foreign investment. This was perhaps most evident in the founding in 1864 of the Hongkong and Shanghai Bank, which would become the leading bank on the China coast for over fifty years and still plays a leading role in Hong Kong's economy. Although most of new bank's capital came local European, American and Parsi firms, Chinese capital was crucial from the outset.

Like the European community, the Chinese community of Hong Kong also found ways to express its approval of colonial officials' performance. One way was through strikes and boycotts, which characterized Hong Kong's colonial history from the start. Another method was the traditional send-off, which became a ritualized form of performance assessment. When Charles Gutzlaff left for England in October 1849, some 170 Chinese shopkeepers praised him with this address: "Since he came to this place his official character has been spotless as water, and not a cash even has he received as a bribe. We bear in grateful remembrance the influence he has exercised in turning men to virtue . . . he was truly 'a courteous, princelike man treating others as himself'."[23] When Governor George Bonham left the colony in April 1854 leaders of the Chinese business community presented him with a sentimental farewell address: "As merchants, whose avocation has led us to leave our native country and cross the seas, you have watched over and shielded us as a father would a child, and ever extended towards us the most affectionate regard."[24] When John Bowring left in May 1859, the European community ignored his departure. But the Chinese community, Endacott tells us, bade farewell with "presents and other indications of their high opinion of him."

---

20 CO 129/51, 4 July 1855, May to Bowring, 29–30.
21 1CO 129/64/125, 11 August 1857, Bowring to Labouchere, 88.
22 Robinson to Rogers, 21 May 1863, reprinted in Irish University Press Area Studies Series, *British Parliamentary Papers, China, 25: Correspondence, Dispatches, Reports, Returns, Memorials, and other Papers Respecting the Affairs of Hong Kong, 1862–81* (Shannon, Ire.: Irish University Press, 1971), pp. 62.
23 *Hong Kong Register,* 2 October 1849.
24 *Hong Kong Register,* 25 April 1854.

Another result of omitting the Chinese from Hong Kong's early history is that we never see how poorly many Europeans in Hong Kong treated these Chinese. Visitors to Hong Kong were frequently shocked by the local Europeans' scorn and disdain for the Chinese, noting how they would beat Chinese workers with sticks and umbrellas. In 1877 an Englishman complained after a short visit how British military officers treated all Chinese "as if they were a very inferior kind of animal to themselves."[25] Osmond Tiffany, the American visitor, recalled how the "Chinese suffered many indignities at Hong Kong," and how the "worthless [European] adventurers of the town took every occasion to disgust the Chinese, and did not even spare any portion of the better inhabitants."[26] It is also difficult to assess the validity of some of Endacott's claims without more evidence from the Chinese side. For example, we must simply take Endacott at his word that William Caine "won the respect of the Chinese too, for though he had a commanding personality which instilled respect, it was combined with dignity and impartiality."

G. B. Endacott died in 1971, leaving his last book, the history of the Japanese occupation, to be completed by his colleague Alan Birch. Both building upon and challenging Endacott's work, subsequent generations of Hong Kong historians have utilized research materials unavailable to Endacott and asked new questions about Hong Kong's early history. Theologian and historian Carl Smith has reconstructed a group of Chinese elites and middlemen generally missing in the work of Endacott and other colonial historians.[27] The late sociologist Henry Lethbridge explored issues of class and race that escaped the interest of historians in Endacott's generation.[28] In her study of the Tung Wah Hospital of Hong Kong, Elizabeth Sinn has shown how the relationship between the Chinese community and the colonial government in early Hong Kong was plagued by conflicting ideas about death and sickness.[29] Sociologist Chan Wai-kwan has applied a class analysis to early Hong Kong society, focusing on the making of the Chinese and European merchant classes and the Chinese working class.[30] Challenging the popular image of Hong Kong's history as one of stability, continuity, and political apathy, Jung-fang Tsai has painted a vivid picture of conflict, popular unrest, and nationalist activism in the

25 Cited in James Pope-Hennessy, *Half-Crown Colony: A Hong Kong Notebook* (London: Jonathan Cape, 1969), 53.
26 Tiffany, *Canton Chinese*, in White, *Hong Kong*, 38.
27 Smith, *Chinese Christians*, and *A Sense of History: Studies in the Social and Urban History of Hong Kong* (Hong Kong: Hong Kong Educational Publishing Co., 1995).
28 Henry J. Lethbridge, *Hong Kong: Stability and Change* (Hong Kong: Oxford University Press, 1978).
29 Elizabeth Sinn, *Power and Charity: The Early History of the Tung Wah Hospital, Hong Kong* (Hong Kong: Oxford University Press, 1989).
30 Chan Wai Kwan, *The Making of Hong Kong Society: Three Studies of Class Formation in Early Hong Kong* (Oxford: Clarendon Press, 1991).

colony from its founding.[31] Christopher Munn's recent study demonstrates how the early colonial government failed to transform Hong Kong into the much-anticipated "Anglo-China" where Chinese and European traders would flourish under British liberalism and impartial justice.

Some of the figures in Endacott *Biographical Sketch-book* have found their way into these new studies, often in considerably less flattering light. For example, Endacott writes that after being reinstated John Hulme went on to "gain the esteem of all sections of the community." According to Christopher Munn, however, Hulme was "notorious" for his "hostility" to Chinese defendants, and for the heavy sentences he awarded to non-Europeans.[32] Whereas Endacott describes William Caine, first magistrate of the colony, as severe but "dignified" and "impartial," Munn suggests that he, like many of the other officials in early Hong Kong — William Bridges, Daniel Caldwell, and W. H. Mitchell — received bribes. Although Endacott does not exonerate such men of all charges, he generally falls short of accusing them. We learn that Caine was often criticized for speculating in land, Caldwell was implicated in "too many questionable transactions" to ever gain a solid official position, and that Bridges was "typical of the adventuring class of Englishmen" of his time: strong, competent, and determined, but also "rather unscrupulous." And whereas Endacott sees harsh punishment and sentences as a necessary deterrent — or at least as products of their time — Munn, like many contemporary critics in early Hong Kong, argues that such methods not only contradicted official views of British impartial justice, but also failed to control crime and drove away more respectable, wealthy Chinese.[33] Whereas Endacott describes Charles Gutzlaff as a "brilliant linguist," Munn characterizes him as "deeply incompetent," arguing that his mistranslations of colonial government proclamations "provoked fatal clashes between government and people."[34] Munn similarly writes that Caldwell's inability to read much Chinese, and his weakness in the Hakka dialect spoken by many of Hong Kong's Chinese residents, "raises questions about his effectiveness as principal interpreter in the criminal courts."[35]

The Hong Kong of today — since July 1997 the Hong Kong Special Administrative Region (HKSAR) of the People's Republic of China — would be scarcely recognizable to a visitor from Endacott's sketch-book (who one hopes would certainly arrive in considerably less time than Henry Pottinger, who came to Hong Kong on the overland route via Suez

31 Jung-fang Tsai, *Hong Kong in Chinese History: Community and Social Unrest in the British Colony, 1842–1913* (New York: Columbia University Press, 1993).

32 Munn, *Anglo-China*, 175, 192.

33 Munn, *Anglo-China*, 113.

34 Christopher Munn, "Colonialism 'In a Chinese Atmosphere': The Caldwell Affair and the Perils of Collaboration in Early Colonial Hong Kong," in Robert Bickers and Christian Henriot, eds., *New Frontiers: Imperialism's New Communities in East Asia, 1842–1953* (Manchester: Manchester University Press, 2000), 17. A similar argument is made in Munn, *Anglo-China*, 65,

35 Munn, *Anglo-China*, 65.

in the "remarkably short time" of 67 days.) Yet significant continuities and legacies persist. A short walk from Queen's Road would reveal clues that our visitor would find hard to miss. Streets and roads such as Caine Road, Robinson Road, and Pottinger Street were renamed temporarily during the Japanese occupation (Queen's Road, for example, became Meiji Road), but they have not been changed since the transfer to Chinese sovereignty. A small handful of former colonial buildings have been preserved, including Flagstaff House, built in 1846 as the office and residence of the Commander of the British Forces in Hong Kong but now home of the Hong Kong Museum of Tea Ware; Government House, completed in the 1850s in a classical style but later renovated substantially during the Japanese occupation; and St. John's Cathedral, the Gothic-style Anglican cathedral built in 1849 that still plays an active role in Hong Kong's religious community.

As it did in the early decades of its colonial period, Hong Kong lacks a constitutional framework that satisfies both government and governed. And although he differs from the early colonial governors not just insofar as he is Chinese but because he has no prior political experience, Hong Kong's chief executive, Tung Chee-hwa, too has faced a series of crises from the beginning of his administration: the 1997 Asian financial crisis, which led to unprecedented unemployment; a protracted legal challenge to the new government's 1997 ordinance on proving "right of abode" status; the SARS epidemic in the spring and summer of 2003; demands for political reform; and low public opinion. Finally, as in the early years of colonial Hong Kong, the young HKSAR has developed its own rituals of performance assessment. A massive public protest on 1 July 2003, the sixth anniversary of the transfer to Chinese rule, forced Tung to withdraw proposed anti-subversion legislation, while an April 2004 survey found that public dissatisfaction with the Hong Kong government's handling of relations with the central authorities in Beijing was at its highest level since the 1997 transition. Just as ruling early colonial Hong Kong proved to be a harder task than its founders had envisioned, so may be ruling the new SAR.

FURTHER READING ON EARLY HONG KONG

Bard, Solomon. *Traders of Hong Kong: Some Foreign Merchant Houses, 1841–1899.* Hong Kong: Urban Council, 1993.

Carroll, John M. *Edge of Empires: Chinese Elites and British Colonials in Hong Kong.* Cambridge, Massachusetts: Harvard University Press, 2005.

Chan, Ming K., ed. *Precarious Balance: Hong Kong Between China and Britain, 1842–1992.* Armonk, New York: M. E. Sharpe, 1994.

Chan Wai Kwan. *The Making of Hong Kong Society: Three Studies of Class Formation in Early Hong Kong.* Oxford: Clarendon Press, 1991.

Crisswell, Colin N. *The Taipans: Hong Kong's Merchant Princes.* Hong Kong: Oxford University Press, 1981.

Faure, David, ed. *Society: A Documentary History of Hong Kong.* Hong Kong: Hong Kong University Press, 1997.

Fok, K. C. *Lectures on Hong Kong History: Hong Kong's Role in Modern Chinese History.* Hong Kong: Commercial Press, 1990.

Hoe, Susanna. *The Private Life of Old Hong Kong: Western Women in the British Colony.* Hong Kong: Oxford University Press, 1991.

Hoe, Susanna, and Derek Roebuck. *The Taking of Hong Kong: Charles and Clara Elliot in China Waters* (Richmond, Surrey, England: Curzon Press? 1999).

Holdsworth, May. *Foreign Devils: Expatriates in Hong Kong.* Hong Kong: Oxford University Press, 2002.

King, Frank H. H. *Survey our Empire! Robert Montgomery Martin (1801?–1868): A Bio-Bibliography.* Hong Kong: Centre of Asian Studies, University of Hong Kong, 1979.

Morriss

Munn, Christopher. *Anglo-China: Chinese People and British Rule in Hong Kong, 1841–1880.* Richmond, Surrey, England: Curzon Press, 2001.

Pope-Hennessy, James. *Half-Crown Colony: A Hong Kong Notebook.* London: Jonathan Cape, 1969.

Sayer, Geoffrey Robley. *Hong Kong: Birth, Adolescence, and Coming of Age, 1841–1862.* London: Oxford University Press, 1937.

Sayer, Geoffrey Robley. *Hong Kong 1862–1919: Years of Discretion.* Hong Kong: Hong Kong University Press, 1975.

Sinn, Elizabeth. *Power and Charity: The Early History of the Tung Wah Hospital, Hong Kong.* Hong Kong: Oxford University Press, 1989.

Smith, Carl T. *Chinese Christians: Elites, Middlemen, and the Church in Hong Kong.* Hong Kong: Oxford University Press, 1985.

Smith, Carl T. *A Sense of History: Studies in the Social and Urban History of Hong Kong.* Hong Kong: Hong Kong Educational Publishing Co., 1995.

Tsai, Jung-fang. *Hong Kong in Chinese History: Community and Social Unrest in the British Colony, 1842–1913.* New York: Columbia University Press, 1993.

Tsang, Steve, ed. *Government and Politics: A Documentary History of Hong Kong.* Hong Kong: Hong Kong University Press, 1995.

Welsh, Frank. *A Borrowed Place: The History of Hong Kong.* New York: Kodansha, 1993.

White, Barbara-Sue, ed. *Hong Kong: Somewhere Between Heaven and Earth.* Hong Kong: Oxford University Press, 1996.

PREFACE

THIS book had its origin in a desire to provide students with supplementary reading to a general history of Hong Kong, but it is hoped that it will be found of wider interest especially to those with a taste for the biographical approach to history. It is sometimes overlooked that history is made by men; one modern historian, G. M. Young, has reminded us that we should go on reading history until we hear people talking. This book is about people, and aims at showing the sort of people who lived in Hong Kong some hundred or so years ago. It covers roughly the first twenty-five years of the Colony's history from its founding in 1841 up to the governorship of Sir Hercules Robinson, 1859–65. This is a fairly well defined and compact period during most of which the Colony was the headquarters of the British Superintendent of Trade and Plenipotentiary in China, and these posts were held jointly with that of Governor of the Colony. The governors during this period were figures of some importance.

This restricted canvas is open to criticism, and a selection of biographies more representative of the whole of the Colony's history might have been thought more useful. The objection which prevented that course being taken was that the selection would have been much more arbitrary and might well have afforded space for no one except Governors. The shorter period allowed a wide choice of subjects and permitted more detailed treatment and intimacy. It is hoped that the book will in some measure have recaptured the flavour of the period, and give an idea of some of the characters who walked in Queen's Road a century or so age. Every effort has been made to ensure accuracy.

To those who, like the Duchess in Wonderland, are in need of a moral, it is that man-power to provide for the growing British commercial and political interests overseas in the earlier nineteenth century was sadly lacking, and that little attempt was made to organize a colonial service to overcome the deficiency. One of the astonishing things about the British Empire at that time was its unsystematic growth, and makeshift arrangements. Until schools and universities in Britain were expanded it was difficult to meet the demand for officials from home, and in the meantime the adventurer class had to be called in to the manifest enrichment of the biographer's work.

In history, it has been well said, we deal with saints and sinners, and in Hong Kong story, if there were greedy self-seeking adventurers, there were also men of high principle devoted to the public welfare. Brooding over all was the Colonial Office in London, vigilant in the detection of abuse and insistent that the interests of the Chinese be safeguarded.

Another astonishing thing is the virility of Victorian society. The men of that age pushed their way to every corner of the globe, and this book aims to show that part of the process which relates to Hong Kong. Their methods were rough and ready as with all pioneers, but their energy and enterprise must command admiration.

To the possible objection that few Chinese appear in the book, it must be remembered that at first the Chinese had no occasion to come to Hong Kong except on short visits for trade, and therefore no reason to bring their families. The Chinese were sojourners only, as indeed they have been during the whole of the Colony's history until recently, and it was not until toward the end period covered here, that Chinese families were coming to reside. It would be of great interest to trace the early history of the well-known Chinese of later years but more research from private sources would be needed for this, and in its absence the contribution of the Chinese to early Hong Kong cannot fairly be appraised. For these reasons, and without seeming to belittle that contribution, it has been judged preferable to confine these sketches to Europeans.

Chapters 1–5, 8, 9, 12–15, and 17–19 first appeared as a series of articles contributed to *Orient*. They have all been revised. Those in Part I dealing with the governors have been rewritten, in an attempt to show in more detail their personality and their contribution to the Colony. Some of the others have been treated more lightheartedly as persons. Ten new chapters have been added.

There is inevitably some repetition in a collection of biographical sketches, and in making some apology for the irritation thereby occasioned to the reader, I can only hope that the people I have written about will be sufficiently interesting in themselves to offer some compensation.

The select bibliography gives a broad indication of the sources used. The Hankow and Morrison Collections and the Far Eastern section of the Hong Kong University Library have been invaluable, and I am grateful to the University Librarian, Mrs. Dorothea Scott, and her staff for unvarying courtesy and help. Grateful acknowledgement is also made to Messrs. Jardine, Matheson & Co. for permission to use some of their privately published material. The Colonial Office official records are essential to any colonial study and have been extensively used, and I acknowledge with gratitude my debt to the assistance provided by the staff of the Public Record Office. Unpublished Crown Copyright material in the Public Record Office has been used with the permission of the Controller of Her Majesty's Stationery Office.

G. B. E.
HONG KONG,
31 October 1961

PART I

EARLY GOVERNORS

1

CAPTAIN CHARLES ELLIOT, R. N.

FOUNDER OF THE COLONY OF HONG KONG

THE FOUNDING of the Colony of Hong Kong was closely bound up with the career of Captain Charles Elliot, R. N. Many others might claim to have shared in this episode, for example, Lord Napier, the British merchants who demanded an island trading station, Palmerston and Aberdeen who were the two Foreign Secretaries during this period, and Sir Henry Pottinger who negotiated the actual cession. Yet Elliot has been regarded as the founder of the Colony, and justifiably so since no account of its origins would be intelligible without some reference to him. It was he who negotiated in January 1841 the so-called Convention of Chuenpi by which the Chinese Commissioner Keshen or Ch'i-Shan (琦善) agreed in principle to the cession of the island, though, it must be admitted, he did so in terms sufficiently vague as to be capable of bearing any interpretation he might later have chosen to put upon them. The Convention did no more than embody the main points of agreement and was not definitely and finally concluded; but in accordance with its terms, Elliot ordered the occupation of the island, which was carried into effect on 26 January 1841. In a proclamation of 2 February he announced that "pending Her Majesty's further pleasure, the government of the said island shall devolve upon, and be exercised by, the person filling the office of the Chief Superintendent of the Trade of British subjects in China, for the time being". In consequence, he became the first responsible official in control of the Colony; not, it will be noticed, the first Governor. Both sides denounced the Convention, and Elliot was recalled and replaced by Sir Henry Pottinger, who secured the cession of Hong Kong in the Treaty of Nanking, 29 August 1942, and who became, on the ratification of the treaty on 26 June 1843, its first Governor. But in spite of apparent failure, Elliot had played a fundamental role in bringing about the birth of the Colony.

He was born in 1801 at Dresden, where his father held a diplomatic appointment at the Court of the King of Saxony. He was of a distinguished Scottish family, his uncle, Gilbert Elliot, being the first Lord Minto and an eminent lawyer. He entered on a naval career, and as a midshipman was present at the attack on the Barbary pirates at Algiers in 1815. He saw service on the East

Indies and West Indies stations, and on the West Coast of Africa; rapid promotion earned him the rank of Captain in 1828, at the early age of twenty-seven. He then retired from active service and followed his father in seeking a career under the Foreign Office. He still retained his connection with the Royal Navy, however, and secured promotion to honorary flag rank on the retired list, as Rear-Admiral in 1855, Vice-Admiral in 1862, and Admiral in 1865.

His first important official appointment was that of "Protector of Slaves" in the Colony of British Guiana, and he was brought home to advise the Government on the various administrative problems connected with the Slave Emancipation Act of 1833. It was in this year that the Honourable East India Company's Charter was renewed on terms by which it lost its monopoly, now almost nominal, of the China trade, and it was decided to replace the Company's control in Canton by an official Commission consisting of a Chief Superintendent of Trade, a Second and Third Superintendent, and a staff of officials to supervise British trading interests there. The aristocratic Lord Napier, former naval officer and sheep farmer, was selected to lead the mission as Chief Superintendent. Charles Elliot was offered the rather minor post of "Master Attendant", with the duty of interviewing and passing instructions to the masters of merchant vessels, which he accepted with some reluctance. In due course he arrived at Macao with Napier in July 1834 and at Canton early in the following month. From his subordinate position Elliot witnessed the failure of Napier's efforts to induce the Chinese to open up trade and treat with the mission on terms of equality. Napier's official instructions contained directives that were partly self-contradictory. On the one hand, he was ordered to be conciliatory towards the Chinese and "cautiously abstain from all unnecessary use of menacing language" and to avoid action "as might unnecessarily irritate the feelings or revolt the opinions or prejudices of the Chinese people", and on the other, he was told to "proceed to Canton and announce his arrival by letter to the Viceroy" which actions were contrary to the Chinese regulations for the control of the Western traders. Napier was forced to retire to Macao, where he died on 11 October 1834, without having gained a single objective. J. F. Davis became Chief Superintendent, and Elliot was promoted to be the Secretary to the Commission. Davis did not remain long. He had served many years in Canton as a Company official, and he retired in January 1835, leaving Sir George Robinson as Chief Superintendent. Elliot now became Third Superintendent. He complained afterwards that "Sir George Robinson has virtually suspended the functions of his colleagues. The Chief Superintendent has only informed me of what he is going to do or not to do"

Evidently Elliot and Robinson did not see eye to eye.

J. F. Davis thought highly of Charles Elliot and recommended him to the Foreign Office as an able man who both desired and deserved a position of greater responsibility. "The talents, information and temper of that gentleman would render him eminently suited to the chief station in this country", reported Davis just before he left Canton. Elliot was asked to present his views privately to an official at the Foreign Office, a Mr. Lennox Conyngham, and Palmerston, the Foreign Secretary, seemed sufficiently impressed to allow him the opportunity of carrying them into effect. A reorganization of the Commission was decided upon; in June 1836 the posts of Second and Third Superintendents were abolished and Elliot was offered the post of Chief Superintendent, able to act alone. This dispatch did not arrive until January 1837 but its action had been anticipated in the previous month, for in December 1836 Robinson had resigned, and Elliot had assumed control.

Elliot had criticized Lord Napier for his attempt to force the Commission on the Chinese by insisting on residing at Canton, and attributed his failure to his pretensions of exalted rank. He criticized Robinson, too, saying "to be perfectly frank, I will not conceal my own feelings of sincere regret that the strong necessity of taking up the cautious and conciliatory instructions of the Government with an earnest spirit to give them effect is less apparent or palatable to my colleague Sir George Robinson than it is to be wished it were". He criticized the British merchants as showing "a very heedless spirit" towards the Chinese at Canton. The failure of 1834 was, he thought, not entirely due to the Chinese, and Elliot's policy was, briefly, to attempt to make a fresh start by adopting conciliatory measures, which had been so strongly insisted upon in the instructions to the Superintendent, and to secure an improvement in the conditions of trade by winning the confidence of the Chinese provincial officials. He had, he said, "a strong persuasion that a conciliatory disposition to respect the usages, and above all to refrain from shocking the prejudices of this government" would prove to be the most advantageous policy. There was no need to force the Commission on Canton if the Chinese did not want it there. The main objective was to maintain the flow of trade, and leave for the time being the question of sending a diplomatic mission and the negotiation of a commercial treaty. Elliot thought that such a treaty might well produce more difficulties than it solved because the Chinese would interpret it to suit themselves. The Home Government rejected the demand of the British merchants to use force and accepted the policy of conciliation, except on two points in which existing Chinese regulations were to be disregarded. Elliot was told that he must correspond with the Chinese officials directly on all important issues and not send his communications through the Co-hong merchants as the regulations demanded, and secondly, he must not use the Chinese character for "petition", when writing to the Viceroy, the form habitually used in China by inferiors when addressing superiors.

The Elliot policy of conciliation and of gaining concessions by winning confidence did have some success, and bore out his view that "it is easier in this country to get on than to get in". He was the first Superintendent to be recognized by the Chinese, he secured the privilege of having his letters forwarded by the Co-hong merchants to the Viceroy with the seals unbroken, and he was allowed to take up his residence in Canton in April 1837. However, he continued to correspond with the Viceroy in the form of a petition. Palmerston insisted that the character for "petition" (禀 "pin") should not be used. As the Viceroy refused to receive any letter unless superscribed with that character, the correspondence between Elliot and the provincial officials came perforce to an end, and Elliot left Canton in December 1837 for Macao, where he continued generally to reside until he left for home four years later.

It was the opium question which finally made Elliot's position untenable. In 1838 he ordered all British to cease opium smuggling within the Bogue on the ground that it was provocative to flaunt the contraband trade before the eyes of the Chinese officials. The Chinese then argued that if he could suppress opium inside the Bogue, he could do the same outside it. Commissioner Lin Tse-hsu (林則徐) came to Canton in March 1839 with the special task of suppressing the opium trade. He decided to confiscate the whole stock of opium and kept the foreign community in confinement until it was handed over; he demanded that some of the worst offenders be surrendered and that all Western merchants should sign a bond promising not to import opium on pain of death. Elliot heard this news at Macao, and fearing the worst, he courageously made the journey to Canton and found himself incarcerated in the factories with the rest. He acted with considerable dignity and showed no little power of leadership over merchants, many of whom made his position unnecessarily difficult by their blatantly illegal activities, their disregard for Chinese feelings, and their opposition to his own conciliatory policy.

Elliot withdrew the whole British community from Canton to Macao after the opium had been surrendered and appealed to the Home Government. When Lin exerted pressure against Macao, the British community had to take refuge on board ship in the harbour of Hong Kong. Hostilities began, though war was not actually

Captain Charles Elliot, R. N.

declared. Lin Tse-hsu seemed quite genuinely surprised that Elliot would not allow the merchant community to return to Canton nor sign the bond agreeing to the full penalty of the law if opium were carried. Elliot had now made up his mind that trade must be carried on under conditions which would give greater security and remove the chance of the sort of pressure that Lin had used in March 1839, but when the hostilities came he acted with great moderation and the minimum of force. His aim was by all means to get the trade flowing again, and to appeal to self-interest on either side to secure a settlement.

Palmerston had now decided that the time for a permanent settlement of commercial relations with China had come. Charles Elliot and his cousin, Rear-Admiral George Elliot, were named joint plenipotentiaries; they were given detailed instructions as to the mode in which the force at their disposal was to be employed, and the terms they were to demand. Briefly, they were to occupy the Chusan Islands, blockade the coast, proceed to the Peiho River to deliver Palmerston's letter to the Chinese Government, and there open negotiations. They were to demand reparation for the value of the opium destroyed, for the expenses of the hostilities, and for the debts of the Hong merchants. They were told to negotiate for the opening of more ports on satisfactory terms to be embodied in a commercial treaty, or, as an alternative, for the cession of an island or islands off the coast to serve as a centre for British trade, under British control.

The expedition set out for the north in June 1840, occupied Chusan, attempted to deliver Palmerston's letter, and at an interview at the mouth of the Peiho River with the Chinese Commissioner, Keshen, agreed to resume negotiations at Canton. The Admiral fell ill on his return and resigned, leaving Charles Elliot once more in sole control. Negotiations were opened with Keshen as arranged and, after some brief hostilities, Elliot announced the main terms of an agreement on 20 January 1841. This Convention of Chuenpi ceded Hong Kong, with the proviso that Chinese customs duties were to be payable there "as if the trade were conducted at Whampoa". The British Government was to be paid an indemnity of £6 million. As proof of his goodwill, Elliot ordered the evacuation of the Chusan Islands before the terms were actually agreed on.

These terms were very lenient, and much less than he had been told to demand; even so they conceded more than Keshen was authorized to give, and he absented himself from what was intended to be the final session of the peace negotiations in February 1841. The war was therefore renewed. Both British and Chinese thought their respective negotiators had yielded too much, and both Keshen and Elliot were recalled, though news of this took some time to reach them.

On 24 February 1841, Elliot announced the renewal of hostilities. The Bogue forts were once more taken on 26 February and the expedition entered the Canton River. Elliot again strictly controlled operations to allow every opportunity to resume negotiations, and the number of occasions on which he granted an armistice exasperated the naval and military officers. On 19 March the Canton factories were re-occupied but the imminent attack on the city was called off and an armistice granted in order to resume trade, so that by 21 May the whole of the season's tea had been shipped. Negotiations were continued with Yik Shan or Yishen (奕湘), Keshen's successor, and Elliot reported favourably on the prospects of a settlement. The last British ships had barely loaded and sailed when the Chinese renewed hostilities by an attack on British warships at Canton in May. An assault on the city was prepared, but was called off on 27 May as Elliot agreed to spare the city the humiliation of a British occupation. Yik Shan agreed to pay $6 million as ransom and withdraw all troops twenty miles from the city except for those raised locally. A few days later, early in June 1841, the British troops left the river for Hong Kong, to prepare to carry hostilities to the north. On 21 July, 1841, while on his way to Hong Kong from Macao to join the expedition, Elliot was shipwrecked in a typhoon but fortunately escaped with his life. News of his recall arrived almost immediately after this and he left for home on 24 August 1841.

In view of the detailed instructions he had sent, Palmerston was justifiably annoyed when the news of the Convention of Chuenpi arrived, and decided on Elliot's recall. "It seems to me that Captain Elliot is disposed to act on an erroneous principle in his dealings with the Chinese and to use too much refinement in submitting to their pretensions", he wrote. He told Elliot, "You have disobeyed and neglected your instructions; you have deliberately abstained from employing, as you might have done, the force placed at your disposal; ...throughout the whole course of your proceedings, you seem to have considered that my instructions were waste paper which you might treat with entire disregard". Palmerston had proposed but Elliot had disposed; and Elliot, not Palmerston, had decided the pattern of events on the China Coast in 1840 and 1841. These events have had to be narrated in an account of Elliot because they reveal the man.

Elliot's policy of conciliation, leniency, and moderate war aims was unpopular all round, and aroused some resentment among the naval and military officers of the expedition. Belcher, Captain of the *Sulphur,* acidly noted that as Canton was about to be attacked, some Chinese appeared on the walls with white flags, shouting "Elliot, Elliot, as if he were their protecting joss".[1] The British merchants disliked him because they were convinced that force was essential in dealing with a people who were incapable of acting on principle. Elliot was to find, as liberal-minded men after him found, that any attempt to treat the Chinese reasonably led to charges of folly and weakness. He was so eager to demonstrate to all his faith that the Chinese would honour their undertakings that he more than once brought his wife to the scene of his activities, and unintentionally exposed her to the hazards of war.[2]

Elliot had no doubt whatever that the Chinese could be defeated as he referred to them as "a helpless and friendly people"; nor was he wanting in personal courage. He came to the Canton factories in March 1839 at no little personal risk, and during the hostilities eyewitness accounts describe him as frequently under fire and embarking on the small steamers in their task of reconnoitring, in disregard of his personal safety. He had definite ideas about negotiation with the Chinese which were shared neither by the British Government nor by the British residents. His main object was to keep trade moving to enlist the commercial self-interest of the Chinese in the cause of ending the conflict, and he thought that if the Chinese could be convinced of the moderation of British intentions, they would themselves, without force, bring about a settlement. He believed that the Canton area would remain the centre of trade, and that the opening of other ports was not therefore very important. The cession of Hong Kong at the Convention of Chuenpi was a fundamental part of his policy, for the Canton trade would thus continue, with the difference that Hong Kong would replace Canton as its centre. He even agreed that Chinese customs dues were to continue payable as if the trade were at Whampoa, so that the Chinese should have no cause to complain of loss of revenue. He was opposed to a commercial treaty because he thought the Chinese would evade it by subtlety of interpretation, and he made no demand for the settlement of the Hong debts because repayment was already being arranged.

There was another side of the problem which the Home Government tended to ignore; the problem of opium, and the unruly character of many of the British opium traders over whom the Superintendent of Trade had so little authority. On 18 July 1839, Elliot wrote to Palmerston, "The true and far more important

---

1 Capt. E. Belcher, *H.M.S. Sulphur in China 1840–1,* London, 1843, Vol. 2, p. 214.
2 Capt. E. Belcher, ibid., Volume 2, p.86.

question to be solved is whether there shall be honourable and extending trade with this Empire; or whether the coasts shall be delivered over to a state of things which will pass rapidly from the worst character of forced trade of plain buccaneering". These were no idle words, for earlier in 1839, he had ordered a notorious opium dealer, James Innes, to leave the China Coast. Innes replied, "Your order to leave China...is waste paper...and I give you distinctly to understand that looking on your order as illegal, I shall land and stay in China whenever I consider it prudent to do so, without any reference to you". Such direct defiance also partly reveals why Elliot, whose whole policy was based on conciliating the Chinese, thought it essential to demand the cession of an island; for only by securing some British soil on which alone a British administration was able to function, could such men as Innes be controlled. Of course, such an island would also make impossible the kind of pressure Lin Tse-hsu exerted in March 1839.

In June 1841, Elliot addressed to the Governor-General of India, Lord Auckland, a long defence of his policy towards the Chinese. He argued that the best treaty with the Chinese, "if treaty be necessary or advisable until the Chinese seek one", "was that which contained the least number of stipulations". Only two articles were essential. One, the cession of Hong Kong, and two, a most-favoured nation clause by which all concessions or privileges granted to a foreign country should also be granted to Great Britain. The essential thing was to obtain "a secure seat for the trade without loss of time, under our own flag". Hong Kong was his solution to the Chinese problem. No open ports were necessary if all Chinese merchants and Chinese ships could have free access to Hong Kong. He envisaged the continuance of much of the old Canton system transferred to Hong Kong, and in the meantime his aim was "temporarily to prop up and use the existing machinery", and keep trade flowing. If more ports were opened under a commercial treaty, "the Emperor's signet would not guarantee life and property" and he stigmatized the Chinese Government as "most perfidious". The cession of Hong Kong would be an act of justice to the native population because "indescribably dreadful instances of the hostility between these people and the government are within our certain knowledge".

Elliot's conduct of the war, his sparing of Canton in March 1841, which appeared to the military and civilians alike as incredibly pusillanimous, was thus the result of deliberate policy and conviction. He was undoubtedly a man of personality and strength of character. When caught in the typhoon in July 1841 on his way to Hong Kong in the *Louisa*, Elliot took command, and with great skill and intrepidity beached the ship.[1] Although there was a price of $10,000 on his head, he induced the inhabitants of the island to take him back to Macao for $3,000 and landed there in "a Manila hat, a jacket, no shirt and a pair of striped trousers and shoes". One of the naval captains remarked of him "...but that he was wanting in natural talent, or principle, or a wish to serve faithfully his Queen, his Government and his country, his most unscrupulous detractors have scarcely ventured to maintain". He appeared to command respect and to impress all by his courage, ability, and character. Except for a few friends he was aloof and dignified, and devoted to the task he had undertaken. He unbent on one occasion, when he sailed round the infant Colony which he had been instrumental in founding, and was reported by one eyewitness to be "vastly pleased by what he saw".

His position was difficult; the Chinese claim to superiority, the restrictions on the trade at Canton, the contraband trade in opium, the lack of discretionary power, all combined to make an intractable problem. Yet there was one fatal defect in his policy. He never sufficiently took into account that his possession of force, in response to his own request, was inconsistent with the continuance of his policy of conciliation, at least along its old lines. Defending himself on his return to England, he said, "It has been popularly objected to me, that I have cared too much for the Chinese. But I submit that it has been caring more for lasting British honour and substantial British interests to protect a helpless and friendly people". He saw that to secure a settlement based on force was not difficult; it is to his credit that he aimed at a settlement which would respect the fundamental interests of the two countries. On his departure on 24 August 1841, an army medical officer[2] summed up the general impression Elliot made: "Captain Elliot certainly had a few friends who regretted his departure, but the majority of the foreign residents in China were delighted to get rid of him. In private life he was much esteemed, and even in public, except when employed diplomatically, he evinced talent of no ordinary description; all gave him credit for zeal and activity, but he wanted the dignity and decision of the diplomatist". Though the cession of the island of Hong Kong was his work, it is not surprising that he is nowhere commemorated there.

The Prime Minister, Peel, said that he "was disposed from his intercourse with him since he returned home, to repose the highest confidence in his integrity and ability". He was accordingly retained

---

1 K. S. Mackenzie, *Narrative of the Second Campaign in China*, London, 1842, p. 185, from an eyewitness account by a naval secretary called Morgan.
2 D. Macpherson, M.D., *The War in China*, London, 1843, p. 201.

in government employ and served as chargé d'affaires in the Republic of Texas, 1842–46, and then under the Colonial Office as Governor of Bermuda, 1846–54, of Trinidad, 1863–69. He received the K.C.B. in 1856 and died at Witteycombe, Exeter, on 9 September 1875.

2

SIR HENRY POTTINGER, BART.

FIRST GOVERNOR OF HONG KONG, SOLDIER AND MAN OF ACTION

SIR HENRY POTTINGER, accompanied by Rear-Admiral Sir William Parker, arrived at Macao on 10 August 1841 on the overland route via Suez in the remarkably short time of sixty-seven days. The *Chinese Repository* thought this a record; it declared, "The rapidity of their travelling is notable, we believe exceeding that of any who ever came from Europe to China". Parker had been appointed the new naval Commander-in-Chief in the Far East. Pottinger had been named British Plenipotentiary and Superintendent of Trade in place of Captain Charles Elliot, who had been recalled for reasons given in the previous chapter.

The fact that the new Plenipotentiary was chosen to succeed a man who had been superseded for pursuing hostilities with what was regarded as insufficient vigour, provides some clue to his personality and character. Pottinger had clearly been selected because he was believed to be the man to conduct the war with the necessary decision and determination. He had already proved himself a man of action.

Pottinger was born in the year of the French Revolution, 1789, at Mount Pottinger in County Down, and acquired in his youth an Irish accent which he never lost. Leaving Belfast Academy when he was twelve, he went to sea. He intended to make seafaring his career, and in 1803 he left for India to join the East India Company's maritime service. There he changed his mind and transferred in the following year to the Honourable Company's military service. He became a cadet, and was commissioned Ensign in 1806. He took up languages at which he showed no little proficiency, and in 1808 was sent to Sind as a member of a British mission.

These were the dark years when the whole European continent was under Napoleonic control or influence. Napoleon's campaign in Egypt and Syria had threatened India, and the British Government was anxious to get more information regarding the border-lands and peoples between Persia and India. However, negotiations for the sending of an official government mission broke down. Henry Pottinger and a friend, John Christie, both officers in the Company's army, volunteered to undertake the hazardous task of an unofficial mission of enquiry and intelligence in the area. Their offer was accepted and in 1810 they set off, disguised as native horse-dealers, on a journey that took Pottinger sixteen hundred miles and cost his companion his life. Pottinger admitted later that they were immediately recognized as Europeans in spite of attempts to maintain the disguise. They probably owed much to the two native servants who accompanied them, but even so, the exploit revealed courage, determination, and enterprise.

On his return, Pottinger was appointed to the staff of the Bombay Presidency. He continued to receive military promotions up to the rank of Colonel, but was employed thereafter on the political side of the Company's administration. In 1836 he became their political agent in Sind, and when the Afghan War came in 1839, he organized the passage of the expedition through that province. He returned home in 1840, after twenty-seven years of continuous service abroad, and his services were rewarded with a baronetcy and promotion to the honorary rank of Major-General in the Company's service.

Such was the man chosen by Palmerston to replace Charles Elliot as Plenipotentiary and Superintendent of Trade in China, to carry on hostilities against the Chinese in the way necessary to secure compliance with the British demands. Palmerston had not mistaken his man. The new Plenipotentiary landed at Macao on 10 August 1841, and delighted the officers of the expedition and the resident merchants by the decision with which he acted. The period of delay and apparent vacillation caused by Elliot's conciliatory policy were at an end. He announced his arrival and his commission, but refused to meet any Chinese officials who were not entrusted by the Emperor with power to negotiate.

On the question of Hong Kong, which had been taken over by Elliot, he was non-committal; the main task was the war. He lost no time in ordering the expedition up the China coast, leaving Macao in the steamer *Nemesis* on 19 August 1841, less than ten days after his arrival. The island of Hong Kong excited his interest, but was allowed to delay him less than twenty-four hours, during which, he later wrote, he was "literally overwhelmed" by work. By 25 August he was at Amoy. Thereafter followed the occupation of the Chusan Islands and the fall of Chinhai and Ningpo.

There was no doubting the energy with which the campaign had been conducted by the new Plenipotentiary who "was never absent when active operations were going on".[1] Indeed, his zeal outstripped his judgement. At the fall of Ningpo, Sir Henry wanted to have the

---

1 Bernard and Hall, *The Voyage of the Nemesis*, Vol. 2, p 213.

city pillaged if the ransom were not paid, as a warning to the Chinese, but the astonished commanders of the naval and land forces refused to agree, and the proposal drew unfavourable comment from the Home Government. The *Chinese Repository* commented, rather charitably, "We are unwilling to believe that it was Sir Henry Pottinger's purpose to raze it". There were very few indeed who could believe it. The expedition made Chusan its main base while preparations were made for a further advance.

It was at Tinghai, on Chusan, that the British were the victims of an amusing subterfuge. The Chinese had asked and received permission to bury their dead outside the city, but the constant funeral processions at length aroused some suspicion. One coffin was opened and was found to contain silks.

In December 1841 Pottinger returned to Macao, and the following February he moved the headquarters of the Superintendent of Trade to Hong Kong. He was keen on retaining the island, and wrote enthusiastically, "Within six months of Hong Kong's being declared to have become a permanent Colony, it will be a vast Emporium of commerce and wealth". He retained this view even after the new Tory Government, which had taken office in September, sent him revised instructions stating definitely that Hong Kong and Chusan were not to be regarded as permanent conquests. Palmerston had demanded either the opening of additional ports with a commercial treaty or the cession of an island or islands. The latter alternative was now to be dropped.

Pottinger did not remain long in Hong Kong. By June 1842 he was back again with the expedition, which was preparing to ascend the Yangtze River. Shanghai and Chinkiang fell, and Pottinger was at Nanking on 5 August. Yik Shan the "rebel-quelling General", had been replaced by Kiying or Ch'i-Ying (耆英) and Eleepoo or Ilipo (伊里布) as Imperial Commissioners. Many attempts were made by the Chinese to open negotiations, but Pottinger stated his terms and would not yield at any point, nor would he agree to treat with any officials who were not specifically given full authority to negotiate. An intercepted letter from one of the negotiators to the Emperor complained bitterly that to all his representations "the barbarian Pottinger only knit his brows and said 'no' ". During the negotiations at Nanking the Chinese were told, "The basis on which alone peace between the two countries can be negotiated has been too repeatedly notified by Her Majesty's Plenipotentiary to be misunderstood, and it remains unchanged". This was vigour in all conscience. The whole tone of Pottinger's dispatches home leave no doubt that he believed his military successes had enabled him to secure acquiescence in almost any British demands.

The Chinese accepted his terms in the Treaty of Nanking, in which he not only was granted the trade conditions he had been authorized to demand, but also secured the cession of the Island of Hong Kong. The Treaty of Nanking was a triumph for Pottinger. In the space of twelve months he had brought hostilities to a successful conclusion and had avoided what the Home Government most feared, the quagmire of a prolonged war on the mainland. The commanders of the forces were publicly thanked by Parliament, and since tradition prevented a similar mark of appreciation being shown to a civilian, Pottinger was given the G.C.B.

When he wrote home announcing the treaty, he said of the Colony, "The retention of Hong Kong is the only single point in which I intentionally exceeded my modified instructions, but every single hour I passed in this superb country convinced me of the necessity and desirability of our possessing such a settlement as an emporium for our trade, and a place from which our subjects in China may be alike protected and controlled".

The Home Government, however, could not recognize the cession until the treaty had actually been ratified by the two Governments concerned. The ratifications of the treaty were duly exchanged at Hong Kong on 26 June 1843. Kiying came to Hong Kong for the ceremony and was entertained with great festivity at Government House. The weekly paper *The Friend of China* described the Chinese Commissioner's visit in the most libellous terms, referring to him as "considerably obese", and "dressed just like one of the nodding figures in the tea-shop windows at home", and likened him to "a large boiled turnip". But Pottinger was anxious that good relations with the Chinese should be encouraged, and Kiying apparently enjoyed the fare provided. One report said that Kiying sang some Manchu songs at the official banquet, and another that Sir Henry Pottinger sang too, making the vocal entertainment reciprocal. On the previous evening, at a more private dinner party at Sir Henry's house, Kiying asked for and received a miniature of Mrs. Pottinger whereat Kiying, we are told, "treated the picture with great reverence, putting it on his head, drinking a glass of wine while holding it in front of him, and ordering his attendant to send it home in his state chair".

It is fairly clear that Pottinger's hospitality had been more lavish than that to which the Chinese Commissioner had been accustomed, and that Pottinger was deliberately acting thus. It was the nature of the man, having waged war against the Chinese with forthrightness and vigour, or, as one of the officers on the expedition termed it, "with a penchant for energetic measures even of somewhat an

SIR HENRY POTTINGER, BART.

indiscriminable nature", that he should turn around and match his former hostility by equally forthright acts of friendship. Pottinger deliberately attempted to mark a new era by setting an example of friendly relationships which he hoped individuals as well as governments would follow.

Pottinger did not remain long in the Colony. Having brought hostilities to a successful conclusion he was anxious to return to India where, it was rumoured, he had been promised the important post of Governor of the Madras Presidency, and in July 1843 he resigned. The Home Government naturally wished him to remain to supervise the execution of the treaty and organize the government of the new colony, but it accepted Pottinger's wishes. In the autumn of 1843 a successor was appointed in the person of Sir J. F. Davis, who in 1834 had succeeded Lord Napier as Chief Superintendeent.

During the period of settlement following the Treaty of Nanking and the establishment of peace, Pottinger became unpopular and was subject to very severe criticism which lost him much of the reputation he had acquired by his conduct of the war. It was widely believed in Hong Kong that the Governor was not temperamentally suited to the task of laying down the foundations of the new régime on the China coast, and that this failure cost him the peerage for which his earlier successes had marked him out. The evidence available does not support this view but rather tends to show that Pottinger revealed constructive ability, and that his unpopularity was due to the fact that he alone upheld the public interest in the face of self-seeking officials and merchants. It must be admitted that Pottinger shone under conditions that required action in the field, decision, and determination, and did not easily submit to the slower tempo that administrative action required, finding the task of organizing the peace less to his liking and less consonant with his normal disposition. It is also true that having secured a treaty, he was anxious to return home and leave administrative duties in other hands.

The task of implementing the treaty proved to be more difficult than was at first realized; the problems of organizing the new dispensation for China and Hong Kong were complicated and onerous. Pottinger very frequently complained of overwork, and in one dispatch spoke of "the great and manifest difficulties with which I am surrounded" and "the hopelessness of being able to extricate myself without help coming from England". Writing home on 22 January 1844 to explain the delay in submitting a financial estimate he asked that the Home Government "will be pleased to bear in mind the complicated and multifarious duties that unceasingly press on me, and that call for a degree of laborious exertion...

which I may truly aver few would be able, however willing, to undergo". There was some delay in sending out higher officials to take over the important administrative posts in the Treaty Ports under the Foreign Office, and in Hong Kong under the Colonial Office, and Pottinger was forced to make such stopgap appointments as he could while the mercantile houses enticed his choices away with the offer of higher salaries. In any case, Pottinger was unable to make permanent appointments. The only men readily available for junior posts were of the adventurer class, many from Australia, and other roving types. Another difficulty was that Pottinger had to serve two masters, being responsible to the Foreign Secretary as Pleni-potentiary, and to the Colonial Office (then part of the War Office), as Governor of Hong Kong. J. R. Morrison, son of Robert Morrison, and Pottinger's right-hand man in dealings with the Chinese, died in Macao in August 1843, and Pottinger's dispatch announcing this clearly revealed him in a state of despondency. He had one windfall when a Bombay lawyer called Burgass, "happening to come to China", was promptly offered the temporary post of Legal Adviser to the Government and Clerk of the Councils at a salary of £800 a year.

Pottinger was too forthright and too decided in his opinions to be easy to work with. He quarrelled with the naval authorities, who having elected to establish the naval depot at Navy Bay at the western end of the island, then changed their minds and decided to keep it near the centre of the growing town, where Admiral Sir Thomas Cochrane had, with A. R. Johnston's consent, landed naval stores and coal during the hostilities. Pottinger properly described this as "a perpetual and irreparable detriment to the Colony", but he was unable to induce the navy to move back to the site originally chosen. He also quarrelled with the military on similar grounds. The War Office sent out a Major Aldrich to prepare a plan for the defence of the Colony and arrange for the necessary military works and barracks. The Aldrich plan, dated 28 June 1843, envisaged a large permanent defended cantonment in the central area to house a large portion of the suggested garrison of 4,500 men. Pottinger criticized the whole plan as grandiose, argued that such a large garrison was not required, and condemned the military locations near the centre of the town as having the effect of arresting development and dividing the town into areas. The proposed naval and military plans would make, he declared, "this face of the island a mere military position...in lieu of...a vast emporium of commerce and wealth", and he gave it as his opinion that Hong Kong could not be held for twenty-four hours against an enemy with naval superiority.

Pottinger also criticized the military administration of the Colony during the severe fever epidemic in 1842, when there were so many deaths among the troops that they were transferred to transports anchored in the harbour. Pottinger was anxious to defend the Colony, "as I have been in some degree, the instrument of its becoming a possession of the crown of England", and wrote, "I am forced to record my total dissent as to the insalubrity of the climate". He went on to say that sickness amongst the troops was due to faulty supervision by the officers; they were allowed to be out at all times regardless of the heat and rain, and to bathe for prolonged periods, and consumed excessive quantities of Chinese spirit, *saam shui*. These serious strictures resulted in a full-scale military enquiry which reported that Pottinger's charges of exposure and lack of control were not substantiated.

There were great difficulties about allotments of land. Elliot had held out to the merchants the hope of allotments of land in perpetuity as freeholds with a nominal annual quit rent; then, because the Home Government would not recognize the Convention of Chuenpei by which Elliot had secured the island, Pottinger was ordered to discontinue all grants of land of any sort. His deputy, A. R. Johnston, who was left behind "charged with the government of Hong Kong", disregarded these instructions and continued to make grants of land to the merchants. Pottinger wrote, "Under an avowed misconception of my orders, I had hardly left the Island, when Mr. Johnston framed rules for fresh grants". The Government refused to recognize any grants made prior to the exchange of ratifications of the treaty, or to receive any rent in respect of allotments made before that date, and so Pottinger was faced with a difficult situation. It was made even more complicated by the lack of a survey, and by allotment holders extending their properties by constructing encroaching verandahs or by a little illicit reclamation from the sea. When the Home Government decided that freehold tenure could not be given, and that the land should be offered on lease for a period just sufficient to induce the merchants to erect permanent buildings, the unpopularity of the decision fell on Pottinger. The merchants felt they had been tricked by him, that he had been responsible for the fact that the tenure held out by Elliot and Johnston was not honoured. He wrote home that he "had been held up not only as the immediate cause of all private dissatisfaction which [apparently] prevails, but as the originator and approver of all the public mistakes and oversight". What was happening was that everybody was staking out claims to land; it was a period of opportunism and greed, and Pottinger had the disagreeable task of upholding the public interest alone; officials such as Johnston and William Caine, and army officers, joined in the land speculation. Hong Kong in 1843 was a land of opportunity.

Pottinger became unpopular, too, because of the robbery, crime, and piracy which became so much a feature of life in and around the Colony. The organization of a police force was a pressing problem, but there was much delay because Pottinger's suggestion of recruiting a trained force from Britain was rejected. Instead, he had to create a stopgap force out of material available on the spot —soldiers and seamen—who proved quite unsatisfactory.

He had the further task of setting up the Legislative and Executive Councils. This was done in the summer of 1843 within a few weeks of the Colony's founding. Because there were so few men available of the right calibre, however, the action was premature, and when J. R. Morrison died and Johnston went on leave, the gaps could not be filled. The Councils did not begin to function until January 1844. Then, in three months, the Legislative Council passed twelve Hong Kong Ordinances and five Consular Ordinances. An Indian newspaper remarked "The gallant Plenipotentiary was a legislative incarnation of the 'go ahead' principle of our transatlantic brethren; he coined laws almost as readily as the mint did rupees. ...Her Majesty's Governor of Hong Kong should be known hereafter as Sir Henry Notification". Much of the legislation was naturally hurried and later disavowed, but Pottinger can hardly be blamed for this in the absence of competent law officers. To his credit, the first Hong Kong Ordinance passed was directed against slavery, though it was subsequently disallowed.

In his negotiations with the Chinese to implement the Treaty of Nanking, Pottinger gained additional unpopularity. He warned the British against smuggling and against trading with China except through the five open Treaty Ports. In December 1842 there was a riot in Canton over quarrels between Chinese and 200 lascars who had been allowed ashore without supervision. Pottinger refused to support the claim of the British merchants for compensation, "or to protect or indemnify persons who by their misconduct or culpable negligence render themselves obnoxious to the Chinese Government or people". His policy was to convince the Chinese of British good faith in abiding by the treaty, and of British trust that China would do the same. "There are no grounds whatever for distrusting the sincere wish of the Government of China to preserve the peace that has been happily established", he wrote. He came into conflict with the navy by demanding that warships should not be moved along the Chinese coast without his sanction, to avoid giving offence to the Chinese. He checked naval interference with piracy on the same ground. When he asked the British merchants to help him in drawing up the new Chinese tariff, they refused to co-operate.

Pottinger negotiated the Supplementary Treaty of the Bogue which was signed in October 1843, by which questions left outstanding by the Treaty of Nanking were settled. This supplementary treaty contained clauses dealing with the relations between Hong Kong and China, laying down methods of control, and imposing tonnage duties on junks going to Canton. These clauses caused great anger among the Hong Kong merchants, because it was felt that they contravened the earlier declaration of the freedom of the port. The merchants of Hong Kong wanted to drive a coach and four through the whole treaty settlement by allowing the Hong Kong junk trade to be carried on outside the five Treaty Ports. Unfortunately for Pottinger, an English version of the treaty appeared without these clauses, and they became known only through the Chinese version. He was violently attacked, and charged with being duped by the wily Kiying. Pottinger replied that he had published only extracts of the treaty, but this was clearly an unsatisfactory answer because it left unexplained why only those clauses of particular moment to Hong Kong happened to be omitted.

Pottinger continually complained of overwork. Wherever he turned there were problems and difficulties, and nobody who could be much help. "His secretary was an assistant surgeon in the Bombay army; his financial secretary, the mate of a ship; his judge, an Indian soldier; his assistant judge, the second mate of a country ship", said one later historian.[1] Pottinger wrote home complaining that he had always to act on his unassisted judgement. "I have stood alone", he wrote. Under these circumstances it is not surprising that he made some errors. The clauses in the Treaty of the Bogue arranging for control of Chinese junks and the provision of official information about them were quietly dropped as contrary to the interests of the new settlement. Pottinger at first agreed that the Chinese in Hong Kong should be subject to Chinese law administered by Chinese judges, and then changed his mind. Piracy became serious because he restrained British naval action in the interest of good relations with the Chinese Government. He argued against the British Government's wish to restrict the opium ships from using Hong Kong. Impetuous man of action though he might have been, it is impossible not to feel that the blame for his unpopularity should not be laid at his own door.

Relief from his arduous duties finally came in the person of Sir J. F. Davis, who arrived in May 1844, and Pottinger left Hong Kong

---

1 J. W. Norton Kyshe, *History of the Laws and Courts of Hong Kong*, Vol. 1, p. 188.

by H.M.S. *Driver* a month later. Even then there was trouble. Unknown to Pottinger, Admiral Sir Thomas Cochrane had granted passage to a Spanish naval officer from Manila. When Pottinger arrived on board and discovered this, he insisted on the Admiral cancelling the passage, which the Admiral refused to do. It was two days before the dispute was settled by the voluntary withdrawal of the Spanish officer, and the ship set sail.

Arriving home, Pottinger was received with great honour, made a member of the Privy Council, given a pension and the freedom of many cities, and presented by the Foreign Secretary, Lord Aberdeen, to the Queen at a levee. He amused the Foreign Secretary by his strong Irish accent and his ignorance of, and lack of interest in politics. Pottinger was keen to continue his career abroad. He was made Governor of the Cape in 1846, and six months later he became Governor of Madras, the post he really wanted, but his record there as an administrator was not particularly successful. He died at Malta on his way home from India in 1856, and was buried there.

The verdict of the Colony, expressed by Eitel, that "the deserved fame of the Plenipotentiary had been seriously tarnished by the acts of the Governor", needs qualification. Perhaps he attempted too much, but he consistently upheld the interests of the Colony, and this was true of very few at that time.

3

Sir John Francis Davis, Bart.

SECOND GOVERNOR OF HONG KONG,
EAST INDIA COMPANY OFFICIAL, SCHOLAR, AND SINOLOGUE

JOHN FRANCIS DAVIS was an outstanding personality of the early years of the Colony. His many years' residence in the Far East had given him much valuable commercial and administrative experience and he had a competent knowledge of the Chinese language. His appointment in 1844 as Governor, Plenipotentiary and Superintendent of Trade was a fitting recognition of his qualifications. Yet he made himself hated by the Europeans in the Colony, and the historian Norton Kyshe wrote of him, "Sir John Davis had gone home branded as a libeller two years before the usual term of office, having been permitted to resign. An unexampled career of oppression had rendered miserable the existence of his subordinates; . . . and he had left these parts without having a single friend".

He was born on 16 July 1795, the son of an East India Company official whose footsteps he followed in the Honourable Company's service. In 1813, at the age of eighteen, he was appointed to their factory at Canton. He at once took up the study of Chinese and within two years published a translation of the *San Yu Low* (三予樓), or the *Three Dedicated Rooms*. He was evidently a promising young man and was chosen to accompany Lord Amherst on his diplomatic mission to Peking in 1816. On the return of the unsuccessful mission, he lived in Macao and Canton, and continued to devote himself to his commercial career and the study of Chinese, making rapid progress in both.

He began to produce a series of literary works. A translation of three Chinese novels appeared in 1822; in 1828 and 1829 came a number of publications, the *Hsien Wun Shu* (賢文書) or *Chinese Moral Maxims*, which was printed in Chinese at the Company's expense, the translation of a Chinese novel under the title *The Fortunate Union*, and a book called *On the Poetry of the Chinese* (漢文詩解) in which the poems were given in the original and in translation. In the preface to a later edition of this last work, Davis recalled that when Lord Palmerston first saw it, with its Chinese characters, he declared he thought it was a book on entomology! He also translated a Chinese play, *The Sorrows of Han* or *Han Koon Tsew* (漢宮秋). This was done for the Oriental Translation Committee, associated with the Royal Asiatic Society which administered the Oriental Translation Fund to encourage the translation of works from the chief Asiatic languages. It paid publication expenses and further encouraged the study of Asiatic languages by offering four prizes a year of £50–£100 each, and four gold medals. Davis was a member of the Committee and apparently an active one; many of his works were dated 1828, the year in which the Fund was instituted, and many appeared in the following year. Davis's keenness led him to deplore the absence of dictionaries and still more the use of pidgin English, which he called "that base and disgusting jargon which still continues to be spoken and understood at Canton". Davis stood out as a linguist, and was one of the few Company officials who took the trouble to study Chinese; the Company had had to employ Robert Morrison, the first Protestant missionary to China, in the absence of interpreters of its own. Chinese was not Davis's only interest; it is impossible to peruse any of his books without being struck by the profusion of Latin, Greek, and French quotations which appear on almost every page, and though that is no evidence of great attainment, it is a fair inference that languages generally interested him.

He must have been an able official as well as a scholar, for in 1832 he reached the highest position in the Company's service in the Far East, the Presidency of the Select Committee in Canton. As it happened he was the last of the line. The next year, the Company lost its monopoly of the Canton trade, and its nominal control of the British activities there. In its place Lord Napier was sent out as Chief Superintendent of Trade at Canton to lead an official British mission, and Davis remained to join it with the position of Second Superintendent. The mission was unsuccessful and was forced to retire to Macao. Davis became Chief Superintendent on the death of Napier in October 1834, but he did not occupy this position long. He disliked the new free-trade régime, and he disliked the rough adventuring class of merchants who were coming to Canton. The Chinese refused to accept or recognize the mission, and Davis made no effort to force himself on them. He reported all the facts home, asked for fresh instructions, and then resigned in January 1835 after holding the office for only some three months. He criticized the Chief Superintendent's powers and later wrote, "The imperfect and impracticable state in which its functions were left by the late government, both in relation to the Chinese and to British subjects, brought me home in despair in 1835". He returned home after serving abroad for twenty-two years.

He devoted himself to writing. His main work, *The Chinese: a general description of the Empire of China, and its Inhabitants* was published in 1836. It was popular and successful and was from time to time revised and re-issued, and became a standard work. In 1841 appeared *Sketches of China,* giving his account of the Amherst Mission to Peking. He also contributed to the *Edinburgh* and *Quarterly Reviews.*

His record had been imposing, his books revealed him as an authority on China, and his selection to succeed Sir Henry Pottinger as Plenipotentiary, Superintendent of Trade, and Governor of Hong Kong was not surprising. He arrived in Hong Kong on 1 May 1844.

He had all the qualifications necessary for success, yet his conduct and policy aroused such strong local opposition—which intensified as time went on—that when he left the Colony just less than four years later, he was regarded with hatred and contempt. He was the most unpopular governor in the Colony's history.

Perhaps it is fair to say that he had the most unpopular task, that of setting up a government in Hong Kong and thus putting an end to the administrative chaos which had existed since the foundation of the settlement. This was unpopular with the merchants because they were subject to taxation for the first time; they demanded the utmost freedom from government interference—except when they got into trouble. Davis complained that it was more difficult to govern the few hundred English than the many thousand Chinese. He was not a free agent. The Home Government demanded the raising of a colonial revenue as part of its general policy to make all colonies self-sufficient. The reason for this was that the powerful group of free traders in Parliament were anti-colonial in outlook and attacked all colonial grants on the ground that colonies were unnecessary. But Hong Kong was unable to defray all its government expenses, and the broad formula accepted was that the Home Government should bear the cost of administration and defence, and the Colony the cost of its public works and other local services.

Davis was in a difficulty because the port had been declared a free port, precluding the levying of customs duties. He had to rely on land rents, and the decision that the leases were to be for no more than 75 years, taken before he arrived, was now put into effect. The merchants were soon up in arms and alleged that Davis had failed to honour the promise of perpetuity of tenure given or implied by Elliot and Johnston. Further revenue was raised by licences for the sale of salt, tobacco, and liquor and for the occupations of auctioneer and billiard-saloon keeper. A 22½ per cent. duty was imposed on the value of all goods sold at auction. Monopolies for quarrying and the retail sale of opium were farmed out to the highest bidder. Davis was accused of interfering with the freedom of the port by these measures. In fact, he had little choice in his financial measures. The most that could be brought against him was that he was the too willing tool of the Home Government in forcing the Colony prematurely along the path of financial independence and solvency. The merchants adopted the uncompromising line that no taxation should be imposed. They argued that Hong Kong was primarily a military post and trading station serving British interests in general, so the Home Government should pay for it. Failing this, merchants in the Treaty Ports should not escape their share if taxation were necessary.

Worse was to follow. In February 1845 the Governor introduced an ordinance taxing all property to provide revenue to pay for a police force. It had been the intention to introduce some form of municipal self-government to control local services such as police and roads, with the right to levy local rates to meet the cost. The amount of these rates was to have been decided by the municipal government. Davis's high-handed action was resented. The merchants appealed to the Secretary of State, who upheld the right of the Governor to levy rates, but Davis found it politic to meet public opposition by reducing the assessments by 40 per cent.

It was the acute problem of law and order arising from the influx of disorderly elements from the mainland that had led Davis to take over direct control of the police. It was this same problem that brought Davis into conflict with merchant opinion at the very outset of his governorship.

In August 1844, only a few weeks after his arrival, Davis introduced a Registration Ordinance which had already been proposed by Pottinger as a police measure. To make it more palatable to the Chinese, it was imposed on all the inhabitants, European and Chinese alike. The former were to pay five dollars annual registration charge and the latter one dollar. It was a statesman-like measure, but was opposed by both sections of the community. The Chinese ceased work and prepared to leave the island *en masse,* and the Europeans presented a memorial phrased so strongly that Davis refused to accept it. Eventually the Registration Ordinance was amended in such a way as to apply only to the Chinese. Davis seems to have been surprised at the uproar he had occasioned and referred to it as "this ill-conducted opposition". He had been absent from the Colony from August, when the ordinance was passed, until October, and it was due to come into force on 1 November. Nothing had been done to warn the community of its impending passage, but since Davis was away it is difficult to know how far he can be blamed for this error in tactics. In any case, he should have suspected that opinion was not ripe for equal treatment of foreigner and Chinese.

SIR JOHN FRANCIS DAVIS, BART.

On the question of opium Davis must share responsibility with Pottinger for the failure of British policy to fulfil the expressed intention of the British Government that the cession of Hong Kong should not result in providing a centre for contraband trade beyond the reach of Chinese officers. In February 1844, just before sailing, Davis wrote that he rejoiced that the British Government did not intend to contenance opium at Hong Kong; yet by June, one month after his arrival, he was acquiescing in the fact that "opium is now tacitly tolerated by the Chinese Government". But the difficulty was that the opium dealers would have circumvented any interference by using other ports and sailing under other flags.

The establishment of the opium monopoly in the Colony led to an open quarrel with Robert Montgomery Martin, the Colonial Treasurer, and the most able of his officials. Martin objected to any revenue from vice, and became an outspoken critic of the Colony, which he thought unsuitable from every angle. He advocated that it should be given up in return for Chusan. He opposed the whole system of taxation imposed by Davis, and eventually threw up his post in Hong Kong and returned to England to carry on a bitter campaign against the Governor and against the Colony. The subsequent growth of Shanghai shows that Martin's views regarding the prospects of Chusan were essentially sound. Davis, during his first tour of the Treaty Ports in 1844, saw, to his credit, that Shanghai was destined to become the greatest of the new ports, but he did not conclude that Hong Kong should on that account be given up. Yet he made the mistake of treating the memorandum of Martin too lightly and sent it home without troubling to answer its accusations.

Davis attempted to establish good relations with the Chinese Government, in spite of the anti-foreign feeling in Canton which caused Europeans to be molested and barred from entering the city. He did not force the Chinese to yield on this question, and in the agreement handing back Chusan to them, he agreed to delay insisting on the right of admission to Canton which he could have demanded as a *quid pro quo*.

In the summer of 1846 there was further rioting in Canton, touched off by trouble between a notoriously truculent English merchant, Compton, and a Chinese hawker. The British Consul regarded Compton as at fault, and with Davis's approval fined him $200. Molestation of Europeans continued, and Kiying delayed redress. In March 1847 Davis collected troops, rendered the Bogue forts useless, descended on Canton, and secured the acceptance of all his demands from Kiying. This surprising piece of "gunboat diplomacy" is to be explained chiefly by the fall of Peel's Conservative Government in 1846 and the appointment of Palmerston as Foreign Secretary in the new Whig ministry of Lord John Russell. Palmerston complained of the "low tone" of previous communications with Kiying, and demanded firmer action than that of Peel and Aberdeen, to whom Davis was attached by political ties. Also, Davis needed Palmerston's support, because he was quarrelling with Hulme, the Chief Justice.

This quarrel which sprang from various sources led to the Governor's undoing. Davis regarded the magistrates as administrative officials under his control, while Hulme regarded them as judicial officials under his own supervision. In making rules for the Supreme Court, the Judge gave himself what seemed to Davis an excessive vacation of five months, and the issue was taken to the Legislative Council. The quarrel between the two men became personal; Davis refused to address Hulme by the usual courtesy title of "Your Lordship" and Hulme denied the title "Your Excellency" to the Governor. The Compton case brought more bitterness, for on appeal to the Supreme Court at Hong Kong, Hulme quashed the sentence on Compton, remitted the fine, and accused the Consular Court of irregularities. This involved a serious matter of principle, and Davis argued that the British in China could not be controlled if strong administrative action could not be taken, free from judicial interference. When Hulme defied the Legislative Council on the question of his vacation, Davis determined to get rid of him and in a strong letter of complaint to the Secretary of State, Earl Grey, asked for the Judge's dismissal. He also wrote privately to Palmerston accusing Hulme of drunkenness. Grey criticized Davis's treatment of the Judge and refused to agree to his dismissal. Davis then resigned. At the same time, Palmerston passed Davis's private letter to himself on to Earl Grey, who insisted on a full enquiry if the charges of drunkenness were not withdrawn. Davis tried desperately hard to avoid an enquiry but Grey was adamant, and the accusations had therefore to come out into the open. An enquiry was held before the Executive Council in November 1847. Hulme was found guilty and suspended. Davis who had already resigned, had little incentive to patch up the affair. Public opinion was overwhelmingly on the Judge's side, and his subsequent exoneration and reinstatement gave great satisfaction to the island's community.

Davis was undoubtedly a man of strong character. He was able, scholarly, an authority on the Chinese, keen in argument, never at a loss to defend himself, urbane, bland, and self-assured. There is no doubt that in outlook and temperament he had nothing in common with the merchant class, for whom he showed only contempt. In December 1842 he sent a memorandum to the Foreign

Office referring to "the ill-conduct of British subjects in China" and urging that any British official in China should be given adequate powers to control them. He irritated people by being invariably able to give excellent reasons for doing what he wanted. His dispatches were models of clarity and succinctness. Local opinion was disregarded, and he came more and more to live in seclusion, aloof from local sentiment.

However, his organization of the government of the Colony secured a baronetcy for him in 1845, and showed that he was appreciated by the authorities at home. He was instrumental in founding the Hong Kong Branch of the Royal Asiatic Society, of which he was the first president. He was also interested in education and took the first steps in creating a public system of education by setting up a committee to administer financial assistance to Chinese schools.

It was a tragedy that his low estimate of the character of the merchants led him to adopt an excessively authoritarian attitude, and to disregard the wishes of these people whom he despised. Small wonder that he was cordially detested. He once presented a cup, the Plenipotentiary's Cup, for a horse race, but so great was the feeling against him that not a single horse was entered for the event. No speeches or banquets marked his departure in March 1848, in marked contrast to the festive send-off given to General D'Aguilar who had left a short time before. All the newspapers were scathing. *The Friend of China* wrote, "Never surely, in the Heavens above, or in the earth beneath, or in the waters under the earth, did there ever exist, embodied or disembodied, such a pleasant little gentleman as Sir John Davis", and another paper remarked that Sir John evidently preferred to walk out rather than wait to be kicked out.

The imperturbable Governor was not in the least put out. At home he continued his studies and founded a scholarship at Oxford for the study of Chinese. He received the K.C.B. in 1854 and the Oxford degree of D.C.L. in 1876. He died in November 1890 at the age of ninety-five.

4

SIR SAMUEL GEORGE BONHAM

THE THIRD GOVERNOR OF HONG KONG

IT WAS said that if Hong Kong had an angel for a governor, it would still be dissatisfied. Sir George Bonham surprised these critics by being popular, the first popular Governor of the Colony. He was no doubt fortunate in succeeding a man who had earned an enduring hostility for himself among the foreign community that would have been difficult to equal. He was fortunate, too, that unpopular decisions had already been taken and could not therefore be laid at his door. But he was himself a considerate, friendly, and affable man, and Government House, which had been cut off from the community, now became a social centre and symbol of a new social harmony in the Colony.

Bonham came with a good reputation. He was born in 1803, the son of a captain in the East India Company's maritime service who was lost at sea in 1810. The orphaned boy was destined for service with the East India Company, too, but before going East he was given a legal training which enabled him to join the Company's service on the administrative side. His first post was that of Writer at Bencoolen, the Company's factory in Sumatra, and three years later he became Assistant to the Resident at Singapore. In 1837, when only thirty-four years old, he was made Governor of the Straits Settlements, Singapore, Malacca, and Penang, which were at that time administered by the Company. Ten years' successful administration brought him to the notice of the Government at home and on Sir John Davis's resignation in 1847 Bonham was appointed to the principal British post in the Far East, that of Superintendent of Trade, Plenipotentiary, and Governor of the Colony of Hong Kong. To speed him on his way, he was given the C.B.

He arrived in the Colony on 20 March 1848, and was welcomed with cheering. Over the next six years, until he laid down his offices in April 1854, he steadily won the goodwill of the Colony, and retained the approval of the Home Government. He was knighted in 1850, and on his visit to England in 1852 on sick leave, was made a Baronet.

Immediately he brought a more personal touch to the governorship. Nine unfortunate Chinese who had been condemned to death for murder and piracy on the unsupported evidence of an informer, had their sentences commuted to transportation. He began to adopt the method of informal discussion with leading members of the community, and published ordinances in draft so that the local community might have an opportunity of making representations upon them before they were passed into law. Fifteen leading merchants, all Justices of the Peace, were more directly and frequently consulted, though there were strong complaints against this creation of an unofficial aristocracy, especially on the part of those who felt themselves to be equally qualified to be members of it.

In one respect, the Governor's task in shaping policy was made easier by the 1847 report of the Select Committee of the House of Commons on the China Trade, which had made recommendations concerning the administration of the island. There had been much trouble under Sir John Davis; the Chief Justice had been dismissed for drunkenness; the Colonial Treasurer had quit his post to lead a crusade against the Colony and against its administration; there were memorials by the inhabitants against the Governor's policy; the trade of the Colony had not developed as expected; and there were complaints in Parliament about the cost of the Colony's administration. The 1847 Select Committee recommended that a share in the government of the island should be given to those residents who were British nationals, and that some form of municipal government should be set up to deal with purely local affairs. It also suggested the publication of ordinances in draft, three to six months before they were enacted, the encouragement of schools for the Chinese, and the provision of opportunities for learning the Chinese language. It criticized the "system of monopolies and farms and petty regulations" and agreed with the merchants' contention that the cost of maintaining the Colony should not be thrown entirely on the residents, but should be a charge on all who were interested in the China trade. It urged a reduction in the civil establishment of the Colony, and thought that the Governor should be subject to only one department at home and not two.

This report was the dominating factor in determining administrative policy. The Colonial Office and the Colonial Governor were clearly on safe ground in implementing the findings of the Committee. The two main points made by the report were the necessity for a measure of constitutional reform and for the reduction of the Colony's cost to residents. The change in the governorship in 1848 caused some delay, and on his arrival Bonham found himself faced with definite demands from an impatient community. So it was directly as a result of the Parliamentary Committee's recommendations that the Legislative Council was enlarged by the addition of two unofficial members. In February 1849 Bonham proposed that two local inhabitants might be nominated to seats in the Executive and Legislative Councils. The Home Government accepted the proposal for the Legislative Council only, and agreed that two members of the community should be nominated by the Governor at his discretion. Characteristically, Bonham called the Justices of the Peace together and suggested that they elect the two unofficial members of the Legislative Council from among their own number. The Justices met on 6 December 1849 and nominated David Jardine and J. F. Edger, and these two men became the first unofficial members of the local legislature.

Bonham was not successful in setting up a local municipal council, yet by close consultation with the Justices he avoided all unpopularity over this failure. He called the fifteen favoured Justices together in 1849 and outlined a scheme to set up a "a Municipal Committee" which would control the police, on condition that it met the difference between the cost of the police and the amount raised by the police rate. The Justices naturally criticized the possibility of increased taxation, and suggested that there should be a municipal council to control police, roads, and those matters normally controlled by municipal corporations in England. They also made the fatal suggestion that land rents, which formed the most important part of the Colony's revenue, should be handed over to the municipal council. Bonham would not accept this. If the local residents wanted a municipality to control local affairs, then additional revenue, quite distinct from the general Colony revenue, must be raised for that purpose. Bonham maintained his offer of a police committee which should also deal with roads and streets, and sewers, provided the requisite funds were provided by additional rates and taxation. The principle was that self-government must be paid for, and on this principle the negotiations broke down. It says much for Bonham's methods of approach that his argument produced no ill-will, but it is probable that the merchants were more satisfied with having representation on the Legislative Council than with the thought of a municipal council which they might not be able to control if its members were to be popularly elected as in England.

The Colony had not been solvent since its foundation. The taxpayer at home bore the cost of its defence, naval and military, and in addition Parliament annually voted a grant to meet the amount by which local expenditure was estimated to exceed revenue. This had been £49,000 in 1845, £36,900 in 1846, and £31,000 in 1847. These votes aroused much opposition, and the 1847 Select Committee reported that the civil establishment was on too lavish a scale. The Home Government decided to reduce expenditure and

Sir Samuel George Bonham, Bart.

Bonham arrived in Hong Kong in the spring of 1848 just in time to implement the new policy of retrenchment.

The Home Government decided to make a flat annual payment of £25,000 commencing with 1848, and Bonham was therefore under the obligation of reducing the gap between income and expenditure to that amount. He justifiably complained of the virtual impossibility of suddenly recasting the Colony's budget, since a greater part of the financial year had already elapsed. He thought increased revenue could be obtained by additional taxation, but refrained from such an unpopular step, which the Parliamentary Committee had itself opposed. Instead, he cut expenditure in every possible way and was eventually able to balance his budget by delaying the drawing of his own salary until the following year. He reduced the estimates for 1849 to £38,986 from an actual expenditure for 1848 of £62,308. Fortunately revenues tended to increase without any new taxation. This fact, and the cuts in expenditure, allowed the Parliamentary grant to be reduced; it was £20,000 in 1850, and in 1854, the year in which Bonham left, he was able to reduce the grant to a suggested £8,500. In the year following his departure, the Colony was self-supporting for the first time, except for military expenditure.

The Home Government went further in its zeal for economy, and ordered Bonham to conduct a special enquiry into every branch of government, including the naval and military, with a view to securing reductions in the establishment. Bonham was able to suggest economies by amalgamating some offices, reducing the salaries of others, and suggesting that certain military officers, those with engineering and medical qualifications for example, should take over appropriate civilian duties on a part-time basis. These changes were to be made only as vacancies arose, and the Colony's finances improved so much that the necessity for many of them vanished before they could take place.

In judging Bonham as Governor it must be remembered that he was the victim of this demand for a complete and thorough-going retrenchment.

Under these circumstances, his administration could not but be barren of great projects. He cannot escape some censure; he knew from his own experience that Hong Kong people were taxed more lightly than those in the Straits, and yet he refused to risk his popularity by taking the appropriate action.

In view of all this retrenchment, it is surprising that anything was done; yet during his governorship the Anglican Cathedral was completed (in 1849), Government House was begun and almost completed, and the first official reclamation scheme was enacted.

A disastrous fire broke out in December 1851 in the Chinese area of Chung Wan, close to what is now the Western Market. Bonham helped by rehousing the homeless and temporarily remitting land rents and rates; the whole district was rebuilt, a creek filled in and a sea wall built, topped by a fine new road, Bonham Strand, perpetuating the Governor's name. Jervois Street, near by, was named after the Lieutenant-Governor. The remorseless financial retrenchment did hold back some improvement, however. For example, the police force was cut down, the plan for a large Botanical Gardens was shelved, and there was a hold-up in road-building, the laying out of building sites, drainage construction, and similar public works.

Bonham delayed the solution of unpopular problems. He put off action on the question of replacing the flogging and branding of criminals by some more humane penal method. He made the Anglican Bishop of Victoria, George Smith, Chairman of the Education Committee, and thus in charge of public education, and the education grants were now used to develop Christian education as much as possible. Bonham was fortunate in that there was economic prosperity during his régime; more shipping used the port, American whalers put in for stores, Japan, California, and Australia were gradually opened up and developed, and the growing Chinese coolie emigration brought greater wealth.

Relations with China deteriorated. A few days before Bonham's arrival the Imperial Commissioner, Kiying, was recalled. He had followed a policy of appeasement towards Pottinger and Davis. His successor, Seu Kwang Tsin (徐廣縉) or Hsu Kuang-chin, was strongly anti-foreign, and Yeh Ming-chen (葉名琛), the Governor of Kwangtung Province, shared his views. The chief difficulties were the right of entry to Canton, China's imposition of a small charge on tea in the Chinese godowns, which was designed to recoup the Hong debts paid by the Chinese Government in accordance with the Treaty of Nanking, and Britain's desire to give up the Treaty Ports of Foochow and Ningpo, at which trade had not developed, in return for two other ports. The British also wanted the right to travel inland to trade at inland centres.

The two year period of grace after which Kiying had promised Davis the right of entry to Canton was due to expire in April 1849. Bonham met Seu, found him an "advocate of antiquated principles", and after much negotiation, failed to secure the fulfilment of Kiying's promise. Seu's excuse was that he could not force the opening of Canton against the will of the populace. Bonham took a moderate line suggesting that there was little to be gained by entering Canton except danger to those who attempted it, and the Home Government agreed that the issue was not of sufficient magnitude to justify war. Palmerston contemplated strong coercive action in defence of treaty rights but when he thought of blockading the grand canal at its junction with the Yangtze, Bonham suggested there might be difficulties. The Emperor's death in 1849 and Seu's absence from Canton, fighting rebels in Kwangsi Province, gave him further opportunities for temporizing. Bonham argued that though the Chinese were guilty of breach of faith and had created obstacles, the trade was valuable enough to be worth the difficulty of maintaining it. He pursued a pacific policy. In May 1850 he sent Palmerston's letter of protest to the Peiho River by the captain of H.M.S. *Reynard*, but he could not get it delivered. Bonham felt that direct communication with the officials at Peking was not possible at that time. After the dismissal of Palmerston in 1851, Earl Granville, the next Foreign Secretary, sent Bonham revised instructions which limited his freedom of action more severely.

Bonham went on leave in 1852, and found on his return that the T'ai P'ing rebels had established themselves at Nanking and threatened British interests at Shanghai. Bonham wished to avoid being drawn into taking sides, and adopted a policy of neutrality. In March 1853 he went to Nanking in H.M.S. *Hermes* to contact the Tien Wang (天王) at first hand. His action, which was deprecated at home but applauded by the merchants in Shanghai and Hong Kong, enabled him to gauge the success of his policy of neutrality, and at the same time to attempt to appraise the standing and achievement of the rebel movement. He reported unfavourably on the T'ai P'ing leaders, though many criticized and condemned his views.

He retired in April 1854, still comparatively young. He had proved to be popular, approachable, affable, and common-sensed. He had rarely got into trouble because he pursued no vigorous policy. A French official in Hong Kong described him as a *bon vivant* who did his job *tranquillement*. He was easy-going, but it must be admitted in his defence that the policy of retrenchment in the Colony, and the unsatisfactory relations with China gave him little scope. He had one curious idea that a study of Chinese warped the intellect and undermined the judgement; he accordingly promoted men who had no knowledge of the language.

Eitel called Bonham "the first model governor of Hong Kong". This flatters him. Without exerting himself or showing much leadership, he showed friendliness, consideration, and a nice sense of what was better left alone.

5

SIR JOHN BOWRING

TRAVELLER, LINGUIST, HYMN-WRITER, AND FOURTH GOVERNOR

BOWRING CAME to the Far East as Consul at Canton in March 1849. In 1853 he went home on leave and a year later returned, with a knighthood, as Plenipotentiary, Superintendent of Trade and Governor of Hong Kong. Sir John arrived in the Colony on 12 April 1854 and left five years later, on 5 May 1859; so altogether his career in the Far East covered a period of ten years. He had accepted the consular post in China fairly late in life, being fifty-seven at the time, and he was sixty-two when he began his governorship, in contrast to his predecessor, Sir George Bonham, who had become governor at forty-five. He had had no intention of taking up a career in China and found himself embarked on it only by the accident of a decline in his personal fortunes which compelled him to seek official employment at an age when he might have been contemplating retirement. His life had been full and varied, as traveller, businessman, writer, linguist, exponent of free-trade ideas, and member of Parliament. The University of Gröningen had honoured him with a doctorate, and as Doctor Bowring, he acquired an almost international reputation. In the Far East, it was his fate, perhaps his misfortune, to hold high position in exceptional times; during the Crimean War, the Second Anglo-Chinese War, and the T'ai P'ing Rebellion. In the Colony there was much tension as well as petty bickering and libellous attacks without parallel in the history of the Colony, fomented by a scurrilous Press. Under these circumstances, it is small wonder that the promise of his earlier career and achievements was not fulfilled. Sir John was a disappointment; his place as Plenipotentiary was taken by Lord Elgin in 1857, and two years later he was allowed to resign. Under him Hong Kong became "the land of libel and the haunt of fever".

John Bowring was born in 1792 near Exeter, of a well-known Devonshire family which had for generations been prominent in the West of England cloth trade. He was educated privately and then apprenticed to a merchant in Exeter. His aptitude for languages was remarkable, and during his apprenticeship he learned French, Italian, Spanish, Portuguese, German, and Dutch, all of which he was said to have spoken with some fluency. In 1811 he obtained a clerkship with a London commercial house, and was sent on business to Spain, Portugal, and the Scandinavian countries. He established himself in commerce on his own account, continued to travel all over Europe, and learned to speak Russian, Polish, Serbian, Czech, Magyar, and later, on visits to the Levant, Arabic. Although nearly sixty when he came to Canton, he took up the study of Chinese, and made sufficient progress to publish a translation of a Chinese novel under the title *The Flowery Scroll*. The poet Hood addressed some amusing lines "To Bowring, man of many tongues", from which the following are quoted:

> All kinds of gab he knows, I wis,
> From Latin down to Scottish
> As fluent as a parrot is
> But far more polly-glottish.

In 1824 he was invited to be co-editor of the *Westminster Review* which had just been founded by a friend, the philosopher Jeremy Bentham, to propagate radical views, and he subsequently had full control of it. Bowring's commercial activities were ceasing to attract him. As he travelled and acquired languages, he began publishing translations of the poets of various countries, and he evolved a grand scheme of making available in English a selection of the poetry of every European country. His editorship allowed him to carry on this literary work, for which he was given an honorary Doctorate of Gröningen University in 1829. Henceforth he was known, and liked to be known, as Doctor Bowring.

To his linguistic, literary, and commercial pursuits Bowring added an interest in economic questions, and more particularly in methods of national accounting, and in the broad issues of free trade. The repeal of the Test and Corporation Acts in 1828 allowed the state service to employ men who were not Anglicans and Bowring, who was a Unitarian, was made a commissioner to reform the public accounts. That appointment was cancelled because of his radicalism in politics, but he was soon employed on various missions of enquiry into trade and methods of accounting. He became a Member of Parliament in 1835 but lost his seat two years later. In 1841 he was elected Member for Bolton, and took considerable interest in the China trade and in conditions in the new Colony, no doubt largely because his son was with Jardine, Matheson & Co.

In 1847 he ventured all his fortune in an ironworks in Glamorgan, and when, unluckily, a prolonged trade recession followed, he was forced to seek an official appointment. Through his friendship with Palmerston, he was offered the consulship at Canton. Although he had undoubtedly established a considerable reputation, some thought him more versatile than scholarly, and regarded him as conceited and a little bombastic. One commentator wrote, "Of all men, high or low, that I ever met in society, this Dr. Bowring is the most presuming and the most conceited...pushing and overbearing in his manner, and like other parvenus, assuming an official importance which is highly ridiculous".

Bowring arrived in Canton in the spring of 1849, at a critical moment. The Cantonese were resisting every effort to allow the British into Canton, and trouble was avoided only by leaving the claim in abeyance. When Bonham went home on leave Bowring came to Hong Kong to deputize for him as Plenipotentiary and Superintendent of Trade, though he did not become Acting Governor of the Colony. He made a good impression generally, being quite popular with the Chinese, and he revived the Hong Kong branch of the Royal Asiatic Society. When Bonham returned in 1853, Bowring was granted leave on medical grounds and went home. In 1854 he secured the appointment he desired, as Plenipotentiary and Superintendent of Trade, and Governor of Hong Kong. The historian Eitel amusingly noted "that it was said of him locally that he had come back big with the fate of China and himself". He had just been knighted too. "To China I went", he wrote, "...accredited not to Peking alone but to Japan, Siam, China, and Corea, I believe to a greater number of human beings, (indeed no less than one-third of the human race) than any individual had been accredited before".

Bonham's retirement was the occasion of an attempt at radically altering the conditions of appointing the Colony's Governors. The 1847 Select Committee had criticized the Governor's responsibility to two separate ministers, the Foreign and Colonial Secretaries. Davis had recommended that consuls in China should cease to be subject to the Colony's authorities, and Bonham had taken the same line. As a result, an order in council, promulgated in 1853, withdrew from the Hong Kong Legislative Council its legislative control over British subjects in China. Then, on Bonham's retirement, it was decided to separate the post of Governor from that of Superintendent of Trade; but this could not be done without special legislation. A compromise plan was adopted, of which Bowring was the unfortunate victim, which separated the positions while leaving them combined in name. Bowring was to be Plenipotentiary and Superintendent of Trade, but he was to be Governor of the Colony in name only. William Caine, the Colonial Secretary, became Lieutenant-Governor, with the clear understanding that he was to have sole control over the local colonial government. To emphasize Bowring's nominal position as Governor, he was given half the salary of his predecessor. At first he made the best of this novel situation; "I have China, Corea, Siam, I have no time for Hong Kong", he said, but seated as he was in Government House, he soon began to interfere with Caine's control of the island's affairs, to the latter's legitimate resentment. The dispute was referred home, and in 1855 Palmerston terminated the arrangement, allowing Bowring to assume the full post of Governor, but without additional salary.

Bowring proved active in the defence of British interests. On the outbreak of the Crimean War in 1854, he accompanied the fleet to the Siberian coast. In April 1855 he secured a commercial treaty with Siam. Unfortunately, his policy towards China led to war. During the period of his consulship at Canton, 1849–52, and during the year that he deputized for Bonham as Plenipotentiary and Superintendent of Trade, he had given ample indication of his attitude.

He attempted to familiarize himself with the Chinese and their way of life in every way. He learned their language, did translations, attended Chinese theatres, and tried to make friends. He felt this personal contact would remove all difficulties, and he was supremely confident that he could succeed in solving the problems of Anglo-Chinese relations where Pottinger, Davis, and Bonham had failed. He owed his appointment to Palmerston, and was encouraged to adopt Palmerstonian methods in China. He had taken a strong line over individual cases of alleged injustice, for example, forcibly rescuing an Englishman imprisoned for debt, but at the same time he was conspicuously fair to Chinese involved in Consular Court cases, winning their confidence to such an extent that many tried to enlist his services.

To Bonham, his restless activity was distasteful. Bowring was eager to secure the right of admission to Canton and though he had been a leader of the Peace Society in England, he believed it was dangerous not to oppose the slightest infraction of the treaties. The instructions of Lord Granville, who succeeded Palmerston as Foreign Secretary in 1851, which directed him to avoid all display of force, and postpone the renewal of negotiations over Canton, restricted his impulsive desire to gain the credit for securing the elusive right of entry to Canton. Soon after he took office in March 1854, he asked to see Imperial Commissioner Yeh, who had now replaced Seu, but Yeh proved to be as anti-Western and obstructive as Seu. Bowring's most constructive effort was in urging the close co-operation of all the foreign envoys in China. In October 1854 he accompanied the French and American envoys to Shanghai, and continued with the French envoy to the Peiho, in a fruitless endeavour to open up direct communication with the Chinese Central Government, and overcome the stonewalling of Yeh at Canton.

In 1856 came the dispute over the lorcha *Arrow*. There had been increased attacks on shipping owing to the disturbances caused by the T'ai P'ing rebels. As a result, Chinese holders of crown leases in Hong Kong were given the right to register their ships on a colonial register of shipping and to sail them under the British flag, that is, under British protection. The *Arrow* had been so registered, but the registration period had expired after she had left port; technically, therefore, she was no longer entitled to the privilege of protection. In October 1856, she was boarded in Canton and her crew removed by order of the Provincial Government on a charge of piracy. The British Consul, Harry Parkes, protested, claiming that the vessel was under British protection, and that the procedure for handing over criminal suspects should be carried out as laid down by treaty. Bowring upheld Parkes and demanded an apology. When none was forthcoming, he called for reinforcements from home, and began hostilities against Canton.

That this man, who had been president of the Peace Society, should have precipitated war against China over a comparatively trivial incident was incongruous but not astonishing. Bowring had wanted treaty revision and a full settlement, but Yeh had proved so obdurate, and had been conspicuously rewarded for his anti-foreign successes, that Bowring had determined to settle the Canton question once for all as the necessary prelude to a full settlement. His action was strongly attacked at home, and led to a general election. Lord Palmerston, who had supported Bowring, emerged victorious, but it was decided to entrust the negotiations to a specially appointed Plenipotentiary, Lord Elgin. As a result Bowring lost what he most wanted, the prestige attaching to a settlement with China. He had made a gross error of judgement and as a result, the governorship of the Colony was separated from the diplomatic representation of Great Britain in China, in order to negotiate the very settlement he wanted to achieve. He had succumbed to the temptation to make events serve his sense of self-importance. He made his bid to be an influential figure, and he lost. The result was that he had to remain a spectator in impotent silence at Hong Kong. Lord Elgin studiously disregarded him.

The irony was that with his authority now circumscribed and confined to the island of Hong Kong, Bowring had the mortification of seeing the situation there get quite out of control. Petty bickering, personal abuse, libel actions, lawsuits, and official enquiries in which government officers were involved, reduced the

SIR JOHN BOWRING

administration of Hong Kong to its nadir. Masses of reports and accusations reached home. *The Times* said, "Every official man's hand in Hong Kong was against his neighbour...the hostilities are more difficult to remember than the intestine wars of the Seleucidae", and went on to say that "any attempt to deal judicially with this congeries of intrigues, accusations and animosities here in England must signally fail". The Colonial Secretary of State, Bulwer Lytton, was asked in the Commons to lay the papers on the table of the House, and replied that "he shrank from the responsibility of laying such a mass of papers on the table. He would rather lay the table on them".

A new Attorney-General, T. Chisholm Anstey, arrived in the Colony in 1856. He was a man of upright character but peculiar temperament, and was soon involved in bitter disputes with a number of its residents, including the Police Magistrates, D. R. Caldwell, the Registrar-General and W. T. Bridges, the Acting Colonial Secretary. Bowring appeared anxious to shield the latter two, yet he took no action to check the invective of the mutual accusations. The main scandal was the charge Anstey brought against Caldwell, whom he accused of associating with pirates, particularly a police informer, Ma Chow Wong, who had been found guilty of piratical activities. Bridges, the Acting Colonial Secretary, was suspected of shielding Caldwell by burning incriminating papers, and the head of the police, Charles May, was accused of giving private information to the Press. Eventually, after an official enquiry, Caldwell was exonerated and Anstey was suspended for bringing false accusations against him.

The Governor was approaching seventy years of age, and was not at his best. Bishop George Smith said charitably that "he looks very ill, and is involved in a great deal of trouble". Bowring was genuinely liberal in politics and outlook, and was constitutionally incapable of taking a despotic stand against this mass of miserable intrigue. The Home Government concluded that a stronger man was necessary to control the subordinate officials and enforce a more disciplined sense of responsibility. He seemed to be incapable of making a decision, annoying Colonial Office officials by his habit of expecting them to take his decisions for him, and his dispatches were long and wordy. In the spring of 1859 he was allowed to resign. It was decided that Bruce, the new Minister to Peking, should also be Superintendent of Trade, and it was felt that Bowring should be spared the humiliation of having all his former Foreign Office responsibilities taken from him.

Bowring had been critical of the state of the Colony and had embarked on a programme of reform which would have established his name as an enlightened colonial administrator if he had been able to carry it out completely. If he had been able to control his officials, his liberalism would have made an outstanding contribution to Hong Kong's development. As it was, however, his liberalism could find only limited application. He was radical in politics and Unitarian in religion, and neither of these beliefs were popular with the foreign community at Hong Kong. He was a follower of Jeremy Bentham, and thought that the ideal of "the greatest happiness of the greatest number" applied to Hong Kong as elsewhere. It was sound Benthamite practice to use the legislature as the agent of reform, and Bowring suggested a thorough reconstruction of the Legislative Council which would increase the unofficial members to five, of whom two would be elected by all holders of crown leases. It was not difficult to find objections to this compromise scheme, and it was rejected by the Secretary of State; but the proposal was significant as the first recognition of the Chinese community's importance. Another of Bowring's proposals, that Chinese should be eligible for important positions, such as Legislative Council member, or magistrate, was accepted at home, though he was warned to be cautious in recommending any such appointments. It stands to his credit that such a principle was advocated and accepted.

He gave the Registrar-General the additional title of "Protector of Chinese" with powers making him the channel of communication between the Chinese community and the Government. He was shocked at the cost to the Chinese of lawsuits and at some lawyers' habit of employing touts to obtain cases on a commission basis. He secured a reduction of legal fees by a system of official cost-fixing and by temporarily amalgamating the two sides of the legal profession. He tried to deal with the corruption among officials by setting up a Commission of Enquiry, but little was done because it was difficult to get sufficient evidence. His solution was to work for a new type of honest official, capable of dealing directly with the people, to bridge the chasm which he so much deplored between the foreign and Chinese communities. He was able to introduce the cadet scheme by which senior officials should be trained in the Chinese language for the consular service but its extension to the Colony had to be left to his successor. He forced officials to give up objectionable brothel property. He urged the abolition of the privilege of private practice for officials with professional qualifications because it restricted their independence from the great commercial houses who were usually their best clients. When an attempt was made in January 1857 to poison the foreign community by putting arsenic in their bread, Bowring resisted all demands—the product of temporary indignation—that the bakery's employees should be hanged forthwith, and insisted that the normal processes of law should be observed.

He was concerned about the education of Chinese and Eurasian children, complained of the small proportion of the revenue devoted to education compared with the police force, and argued that child neglect bred crime. He wanted more secular control of education, and less teaching of Christianity, but he found that there was so little interest in education except on the part of the religious bodies that he could not do without them. There were five government schools in 1854; when he retired in 1859 the number had increased to nineteen, mainly because of his own encouragement and enthusiasm. He secured the appointment in 1856 of a Chinese-speaking Inspector of Schools, The Rev. W. Lobscheid.

Bowring was also interested in the project of a Botanical Garden to increase knowledge of Chinese plants for commercial purposes and as an embellishment to the Colony. He proposed an important central reclamation scheme, which included a new *praya* and public wharves. The project was conceived as a public amenity, but he came up against the interests of the merchants, who were in fact doing a little illegal reclamation on their own, and they were strong enough to get his scheme voted down in the Legislative Council. The Chinese lot-holders supported him, however, and he was able to begin the scheme on a voluntary basis. The area between Happy Valley and the harbour was reclaimed and called Bowrington.

His claim to be a liberal, humane, and public-spirited man cannot be seriously questioned; in happier times and amongst more co-operative colleagues, Bowring might have made a more substantial beginning in the necessary humanizing of the administration towards the Chinese. But he was only partly the victim of circumstance; the war he brought on himself. In the Colony, however, he was the victim of unco-operative officials. Caine became a Lieutenant-Governor with nothing to do after Bowring assumed full control, and he kept himself aloof. Bowring was distinctly unfortunate in having as his Attorney-General, Anstey, who was an extremely peculiar person. D. R. Caldwell, the Registrar-General and Protector of Chinese, was also unsatisfactory, and was later proved guilty of collusion with pirates. For much of the time Bowring had to rely on the services of a prominent barrister, W. T. Bridges, who had acted as Attorney-General before Anstey arrived, and then served as Colonial Secretary during the absence on leave of W. T. Mercer. Bridges was an unscrupulous lawyer who made a fortune in the Colony. In 1858 he was reprimanded after an official enquiry for accepting a retaining fee from an opium farmer in connection with tne passing of the Opium Monopoly Ordinance, though he was at the time Acting Colonial Secretary. Bowring erred in continuing to use Bridges's services and his only excuse must be that he was at his wits' end to find suitable stopgap officials. His Colonial Treasurer was Rienaecker, a promoted clerk, who served efficiently until his health failed. It was not until 1859, at the close of his governorship, that two officials arrived to serve as Colonial Treasurer and Auditor-General and relieved the shortage of senior officials. Bowring must be regarded as distinctly unfortunate in his colleagues, and his very liberalism and respect for law militated against his taking a firm line with them.

As it was, his period of office is associated with "the worst period of the Colony's history". "Hong Kong is always connected with some fatal pestilence, some doubtful war, or some discreditable internal squabble, so much so, that in popular language, the name of this noisy, bustling, quarrelsome, discontented little island may not inaptly be used as a euphonious synonym for a place not mentionable to ears polite", wrote *The Times*.

Bowring was a complex character; he had self-confidence to the point of conceit, and could not disguise it. He had ability, as his ease in languages proved, he had energy, he had a clear idea of what he wanted to do based on a radical political philosophy and he had the humane outlook of a sound administrator. His administration should have been a brilliant success. Instead, it must be judged a failure. He lacked the judgement and character necessary for high office. In too many of his dispatches, a brilliant marshalling of fact and argument is followed by a pathetic request for advice or instructions. He was too ready with ideas and a welter of schemes, and lacking in steady application. His excessive fondness for putting his ideas on paper in private letters to Palmerston and Sir George Grey show him to be egotistical, however enlightened. Granted this criticism, his contribution to Hong Kong remains considerable.

He left the Colony on 5 May 1859. The foreign community showed their hatred and contempt by ignoring him, but the Chinese said farewell with presents and other indications of their high opinion of him. On his way home he survived the wreck of his ship in the Red Sea. He was given a pension, and continued an active life, lecturing and writing. He even married again, and lived to see his eightieth birthday.

6

SIR HERCULES ROBINSON

THE YOUNGEST OF THE GOVERNORS OF HONG KONG

HERCULES ROBINSON, the second son of Admiral Hercules Robinson of Rosmead, Westmeath, in Ireland, was born in 1824. He entered the army but retired after three years and accepted government appointments under the Irish Commissioners of Public Works and the Poor Law Board, and was employed on emergency relief measures during the Irish famine of 1846. In 1854 he secured a colonial appointment as President of Montserrat in the West Indies, became Lieutenant-Governor of St. Christopher the following year, and in 1859 was chosen to succeed Bowring as Governor of Hong Kong at the early age of thirty-five, the youngest of the Colony's line of Governors. He arrived in September with his wife and infant daughter.

The appointment of a British Minister to Peking had naturally diminished the status of the governorship, yet this post was an important one still, and a promotion for this carefully-selected young man.

The chief consideration in making Robinson's appointment was that a man of strong character was required to restore Hong Kong's confidence in its public service, after the scandals that had brought it into disrepute under Sir John Bowring. The new Governor was hurried out without the usual leave in England, and was left in no doubt that his main task was the reform of this service.

By a series of fortunate accidents, sweeping changes in personnel were in process, or had already taken place, which made his task easier. Caine retired in 1859, and Chief Justice Hulme in the spring of 1860. The quixotic Anstey had been dismissed following his suspension in 1858, and W. H. Mitchell, a magistrate, also resigned. W. T. Mercer, the Colonial Secretary, remained, but he had managed to keep aloof from scandal. The two officials still under suspicion were Charles May, of the police, and D. R. Caldwell, the Registrar-General.

The Caldwell case had become a *cause célèbre*. He had been accused by Anstey of associating with pirates and had been acquitted. The acquittal had aroused dissatisfaction, and one newspaper editor, Tarrant, openly alleged that incriminating papers had been burnt by the order of W. T. Bridges with the object of saving

Caldwell, who was his close friend. Bridges prosecuted Tarrant for libel, one of a long series of such actions that marred Bowring's régime, but the latter was acquitted. This brought Caldwell and Bridges under suspicion, and there was a demand both locally and at home that the Caldwell case be re-opened.

The new Governor was ordered to make a public enquiry into the conduct of May and Caldwell before the Executive Council, which, with the exception of Mercer, was now composed of new men. In August 1860, the Civil Service Abuses Enquiry was begun; its hearings lasted thirteen months and provided a great test for the new Governor. The enquiry faced every kind of difficulty: equivocation, proved unreliability of witnesses, problems of interpretation and translation, and failure to produce evidence. At one point Caldwell refused to co-operate, but Robinson would not be discouraged. Finally, Caldwell was found guilty and suspended; May was completely exonerated.

Robinson was clearly faced with the need of a broader civil service reform. In the 1859 Annual Report, he complained of the lack of a well-organized civil service in the Colony. In 1862 he put forward a cadet scheme, similar to that set up by Bowring for the consular service, by which young men, recruited by examination, were to be trained in the Chinese language, with a view to taking over the highest posts in the Colony's public service. Robinson's plan was not original, for examinations were introduced into the civil service in England in 1855 and the service was made competitive in 1860, but he saw that it was a necessary reform in Hong Kong at that juncture. He next took steps to improve the standing of officials by raising their salaries. The increased salaries were placed in a Civil List so that they would not need to be voted each year and thus become the possible target of repeated criticism. Robinson introduced a reform which curtailed the freedom of official members of the Legislative Council to vote against measures proposed by the Governor; another forbade officials to communicate with the Press on matters relating to official business. He continued to allow officials to enjoy private practice, a privilege which Bowring had so strongly complained of, and introduced a pensions scheme at the instance of the Secretary of State in England, which was modelled on that recently introduced in Ceylon.

These reforms have provided the basis upon which the Colony's public service has been built. Sir Hercules Robinson's contribution was an important one. He had seen that reform of abuses among government servants was not sufficient without an improvement in their salary and status.

The new Governor was anxious that the interests of the Chinese community should not be overlooked pending the arrival and training of the new cadets. The Chinese were quite unaccustomed to a free Press, and the scurrilous newspapers in the Colony, which readily attacked the Government, its officials, and the British officials in China, were the subject of much criticism. Murrow, editor of the *Daily Press,* began to issue a Chinese edition, which appeared three times a week. Robinson thought the licence of the English-owned Press would create unrest, especially since the papers had played a large part in the recent scandals. Therefore, although he maintained the freedom of the Press, he made it necessary for editors to put up much bigger sums as sureties for their good faith. In 1862, he brought out an edition of the *Government Gazette* in Chinese. which published ordinances and official notifications in accurate translation.

He met opposition from the Chinese when he introduced an ordinance in 1860 to set up closer control over pawnbrokers, who went on strike and closed their shops. There were similar strikes when ordinances were passed ordering the compulsory registration of cargo-coolies (1861) and chair-coolies (1863). In each case the Governor took a firm line and refused to make any concession to the pressure. He was, however, aware that misunderstanding was largely due to the language barrier, that essentially the problem was one of accurate translation and interpretation, and he took great care to obtain the Chinese point of view and to see that his was also understood. He estimated that out of 120,000 Chinese in the Colony, less than 500 knew anything about the British laws or institutions under which they lived. He found that although the salt monopoly had been abolished in 1858, gangs were still collecting salt revenue from the Chinese, taking advantage of their ignorance. His Chinese edition of the *Gazette* was designed to stop this. The experiment of governing the Chinese through their own *tepos* was dropped, and the Registrar-General was made the channel for all communications with and from the Chinese.

Another problem from which he emerged with credit was that of the administration of Kowloon. This small peninsula commanding the harbour from the north was leased from China largely for military reasons in March 1860. The Convention of Peking, 24 October 1860, ceded the area, cancelling the lease. Unlike Bowring, Robinson was not at first eager to extend control over Kowloon as part of the Colony of Hong Kong. However, he soon adopted the stock arguments then prevalent, that the area was of no use to the Chinese and that because it shielded a lawless element, it was a menace to the peace and security of the island. His main problem was not the cession of Kowloon, but the organization and disposal of the new area, which was to be a dependency of Hong Kong, and governed as a part of the Colony. The naval and military authorities, when asked to state their requirements for land in Kowloon, wanted almost all of it. The Admiralty demanded the whole of the coastline except some four hundred yards, and the inland area would have been virtually a military cantonment.

Robinson protested vigorously, and claimed the new acquisition for commercial and residential purposes to safeguard the future interests of the Colony. A commission representing naval, military and civil authorities failed to agree on land allocation and the question had to be referred to the Government at home. Robinson suggested that the Colony might decline to assume responsibility for administering Kowloon, but it is doubtful if the Duke of Newcastle, the Secretary of State, would have allowed this. He ruled that the first object must be the needs of the naval and military services who were there on duty; the merchants were there for their own profit. Robinson had agreed that the services should have first claim, but he was not prepared to give up Kowloon entirely to the armed services. There ensued three years of squabbling which ended in 1864 when the services secured the best areas with the right to earmark further sites for possible further fortification. At one point, when the army began building hutments on some high ground overlooking the Chinese border (now called Boundary Street), Robinson demanded that they be taken down or he would send men to demolish them. The Colonial Office later supported Robinson in resisting the excessive claims of the services, and in a dispatch dated 10 November 1863, the Duke of Newcastle paid tribute to the Governor, saying that the Colony was much indebted to him for "the warm and intelligent advocacy of its interests". It was due to Robinson that much of Kowloon peninsula was saved for public development.

His whole administration was marked by vigour, and under him many of the schemes which Bowring had talked about were carried out. Bowring had wanted to free the government schools from church influence; Robinson took up Dr. James Legge's reforms and brought about sweeping changes. In 1861 the old Education Committee was replaced by a Board of Education, and Legge's plan of having a Central School, efficiently run under a European headmaster who should also act as Inspector of Schools, was adopted. This was the starting point of a new attitude to the problem of education. The policy of bringing the Bible into the schools was gradually given up and replaced by a greater emphasis on a purely Chinese vernacular education, with some teaching of English. The Central School had a chequered history; at one point under Governor Sir George Bowen, 1883–5, the intention was to develop it into a

Sir Hercules Robinson

collegiate institution which would ripen into a university. In actual fact it remained for many decades a very elementary type of school, but that was hardly Robinson's fault.

Bowring had taken up the currency question, but again, it was left to Robinson to carry out his solution. British policy regarding colonial currencies was to attempt some uniformity by introducing British coins based on a gold standard. The Chinese, however, refused to be weaned from their attachment to silver, which circulated, whether coined or not, by weight and fineness, though clean coined Mexican dollars did command a high premium. The result was that earlier currency proclamations making British coins legal tender, became a dead letter. Silver dollars were used, and, for small amounts, Chinese copper coins called cash. Many of the European merchant houses had adopted the Chinese system, since they employed compradores to make cash settlements. Bowring advised adoption of the silver dollar as the currency unit and its division into cents, but he never clearly separated the case for a silver standard from his proposal to coin a British silver dollar in a Hong Kong mint. He further complicated the issue by linking the question with that of civil service pay.

The development of trade, population, and commercial activity in the Colony following the new Treaty Settlements of 1858 and 1860, forced Robinson to act. He secured the acceptance of the principle of a silver standard based on the Mexican dollar, and obtained from the Royal Mint supplies of subsidiary coins, silver ten-cent pieces, bronze one-cent pieces, and copper cash. He then induced a reluctant Home Government to agree to the establishment of a Hong Kong Mint to coin a Hong Kong silver dollar; but this part of Robinson's plan proved a disastrous failure. In 1862 he effected one further valuable reform, that of keeping the Colony's accounts in dollars and cents.

Robinson pushed forward some of the public works projects that had been planned or begun. He was anxious to introduce a good water supply, and rejected as useless various existing schemes for tapping the streams. He wanted much bolder action and organized a competition which resulted in the Pokfulam Reservoir scheme. He built a new jail on Stonecutters Island, and continued the *praya* and central reclamation scheme which Bowring had begun as far as he could against the opposition of the European lot-holders. The city was lit by gas in 1864. The Colony took over the Post Office and issued its own stamps for the first time in 1862. He was the first Governor to be interested in the Peak, and had a path cut up to it and a house built there. Changes such as these helped to give a modern character to the Colony. It reached it twenty-first birthday in 1862, and seemed suddenly to have grown up.

In one respect, that of sanitation, Robinson was unsuccessful. The Colonial Surgeon, Dr. Murray, in his annual report for the year 1861, scathingly castigated the Colony's insanitary condition. Robinson refused to receive the report on the ground that an annual report was not the proper place to make such criticism, which should have been put forward and dealt with in the course of the year. A sanitary commission was set up, but nothing came of it.

Robinson had come to Hong Kong in 1859 expecting the worst. He had described the Colony as "publicly and socially ill at ease with itself". In his first annual report he referred to it as "so totally unlike any other British dependency, and its position is in so many respects so grotesquely anomalous". In his second annual report he expressed the view that Hong Kong was not destined to become a great Chinese settlement and would never reach a fourth of the size of Canton. Nevertheless he succumbed, as others have, to the spell of Hong Kong, and when he went on leave in 1862, he was presented with an address from the foreign community paying tribute to his "indefatigable zeal and efficiency" in promoting the public welfare, and to his "kindness and urbanity of private intercourse". When he left in 1865, there was genuine mutual regret at the parting.

The historian Eitel, who came to China in 1862 and must have known Robinson, wrote that the Colony was critical of the Governor, and that he was considered lucky to be there at a time of great commercial prosperity and general development, the result of greater trade and cultural facilities granted by China in the Treaty of Tientsin in 1858 and the Convention of Peking in 1860, at the conclusion of the Second Anglo-Chinese War. Eitel wrote that "his duties carried him to the extreme verge of his abilities", and that he would have been "infinitely less successful" if he had not enjoyed the assistance of W. T. Mercer, the experienced Colonial Secretary. There is no doubt that he enjoyed a period of prosperity and had the services of more loyal and reasonable officials than had previous governors. He was strong-willed, and certainly kept his subordinates in order, being ready, when necessary, to use drastic methods. Eitel described him as "affable and possessed of pleasing social manners" and attributed some of his success to "the extensive and beneficial social influence" exercised by Lady Robinson. His verdict was that Robinson was "the most fortunate and successful Governor" up to that time, implying that he was successful, in part at least, because he was fortunate. Eitel was in touch with local opinion, and this judgement may well contain an element of truth but there seems little reason to deny Robinson credit for his contribution to Hong

Kong. He himself evidently thought highly of his own work, for in November 1862 he wrote to the Duke of Newcastle complaining that he had been overlooked in the honours list. The comment in the Colonial Office was that he had been given a knighthood, and that he was fortunate that after only eight years he had risen to one of the highest posts in the service. "These self-seeking and jealous remonstrances greatly detract from the merit of the writers", the Duke of Newcastle commented.

Robinson was not original. Indeed, he was cautious in approaching new ideas. He has been described as genial, kind, not pompous, dignified, a good speaker, and a sportsman, and as one of the greatest of the nineteenth-century colonial governors. He came to the Colony to restore order in the public service, and whatever may have been his good fortune, did so successfully without any major disturbance in the service or in public confidence. This was one of many achievements.

His distinguished later career bears out the impression that his success cannot be entirely identified with fortune. In 1865 he was made Governor of Ceylon, in 1872 of New South Wales, and in 1879 of New Zealand. The following year he was sent to the Cape of Good Hope as Governor and High Commissioner for South Africa to handle the Boers' demand for independence following the Zulu War. He remained nine years in South Africa and played a notable part in saving Rhodesia. In 1895 he was recalled from retirement and sent to South Africa to meet the tense situation in the Transvaal, and his personal prestige may have prevented war after the débâcle of the Jameson Raid. In 1896 he was raised to the peerage as Lord Rosmead, but soon had to retire owing to ill-health, and died in 1897.

PART II

EARLY HONG KONG
GOVERNMENT OFFICIALS

7

ALEXANDER ROBERT JOHNSTON

FIRST ADMINISTRATOR OF HONG KONG

A **LEXANDER** JOHNSTON was not among the most important officials in the Hong Kong Government during its early years, in either length of service or the value of his contribution. Yet his name heads this select list of officials, because he was the first administrator of the island. In June 1841, Elliot appointed him as his deputy so that he himself should be free to carry hostilities once more to the north, following the breakdown of negotiations at Canton. Johnston's name might with some justification have even been included in the list of governors. He held no appointment under the Colonial Office, for his administration coincided with that anomalous period when Hong Kong was occupied but not recognized as a colony. His active control lasted only a short time—from June to December 1841, and again from June to December 1842, not much more than twelve months. But he is part of the Hong Kong story, and though he earned no great reputation and made no great contribution, his name figures prominently in the records of the Colony's earliest days.

Johnston was born into a family of colonial officials. His father, Sir Alexander Johnston, was Chief Justice of Ceylon before becoming a Judge of Appeals before the Privy Council in 1831, and his brother held a diplomatic appointment in Spain. A. R. Johnston began his career in 1828, in Mauritus, as a Writer under the Colonial Office, and shortly after became a clerk in the Colonial Secretary's Department. Economies in the civil establishment of that Colony forced him to give up his post, and he returned to England. In 1833 he was appointed Private Secretary to Lord Napier, who, on the abolition in 1833 of the Honourable East India Company's monopoly of the China Trade, was sent to Canton to assume the post of Chief Superintendent of Trade. When Napier died in October 1834 he was succeeded by J. F. Davis, and Johnston became Secretary and Treasurer of the Commission. Davis remained only a short time, and soon after his retirement in January 1835, Johnston was promoted to be Third Superintendent of Trade. In November the following year he rose to the post of Second Superintendent. On the reorganization of the Commission in 1837, which abolished the offices of Second and Third Superintendents, he became Deputy

Superintendent of Trade, Captain Charles Elliot's right-hand man. When Commissioner Lin incarcerated the foreign community in the factories at Canton in March 1839 with the object of forcing them to deliver up all stocks of opium, Johnston accompanied Elliot on the dangerous journey from Macao to Canton which Elliot made in an attempt to protect the interest of the foreigners. Three days later, when Elliot determined to assume responsibility for surrendering the opium in accordance with Lin's demands, it was Johnston who was deputed to leave the factory area and visit all British ships to convey Elliot's instructions and arrange for the actual handing-over to the Chinese officials. His report that the last-named carefully examined, classified, and repacked the surrendered stock led Elliot and others to the mistaken belief that the Chinese did not intend to destroy the opium. In the hostilities that followed, Johnston accompanied the expedition to assist in the negotiations, and one of his tasks was to attempt to negotiate with the Chinese officials for the release of The Reverend Vincent Stanton, who had been captured near Macao in August 1840.

In January 1841 Hong Kong was occupied in virtue of the Convention of Chuenpi. Though it was never ratified, Elliot determined to retain the island and began to make arrangements to sell land there for building, and create a skeleton government to attract merchants. On 22 June 1841, he placed Johnston in charge of the government of Hong Kong as his deputy, with the assistance of J. R. Morrison, while he himself prepared to campaign in the north. A few weeks later, on 10 August, Sir Henry Pottinger arrived to take control of Britain's relations with China in place of Elliot, who had been recalled. In the absence of any definitive treaty ceding the island, the Home Government would not recognize Hong Kong as a colony, and it ordered that all public works, and particularly those concerned with the disposal of land, should be halted except those consistent with the needs of effective military occupation.

Pottinger retained Johnston in his post in charge of the government of Hong Kong, as his deputy. He visited the island on 22 August, on his way to join the expedition in the north, but spent only one day there, and his instructions to Johnston had to be given in that brief time, which was primarily occupied with the pressing questions of the war.

Johnston's administration of the island earned Pottinger's censure when he returned the following December, for failing to carry out his instructions. Johnston had been told to make no changes until the future of the island had been decided at home, but he began to dispose of additional land for development. On 15 October 1841 he issued a notification saying, "it is now found desirable that persons applying for lots of land for the purpose of building upon, should be at once accommodated". He divided the lots into three classes—marine, town, and suburban—and laid down the rate of annual rents to be paid for each. These rents were later found to be much below their proper level, judged by the standard of what people were willing to pay. Johnston not only continued to sell land, he evolved quite an elaborate plan for doing so. This drew from Pottinger the rebuke, "You have entirely exceeded the authority vested in you and you have likewise acted in direct opposition to the views and sentiments recorded in my notification to H.M. subjects on assuming charge... [that] all was to remain precisely as I found it until H.M. pleasure should be made known". Johnston explained that he had not been specifically instructed not to grant further lots of land, and Pottinger replied, "I am well aware of the difficulties you had to contend with and also satisfied with your motive for acting as you did". Possibly Pottinger had not made the position clear. The more likely explanation is that Johnston was unable to stand up to the pressure from merchants who were eager to get land cheap, knowing that it would appreciate in value if the island remained under British control.

Johnston earned Pottinger's displeasure on other grounds. He had carried on an independent correspondence with the Governor-General of India, for which Pottinger reprimanded him, and he failed to carry out instructions to demolish a small British fort, Victoria Fort, on the Kowloon peninsula, whose evacuation had been agreed on.

When Pottinger left in June 1842 to rejoin the expedition, Johnston was again left in charge, but he was much more strictly limited in his freedom of action, and was left in no doubt that he was not free to pursue his own policy. He was told that "no further grants of land are to be made on any pretence" except for barracks for the troops and their families who were now beginning to arrive from Britain.

But there is something to be said for Johnston's administration. In November 1841 he sent Pottinger a long account of the progress that the settlement was making; part of Queen's Road had been improved, the prison had been completed, the Magistracy almost so, and rapid progress was being made with the Record Office, a building designed to house the land records. He reported that many people were making application for land, and some were building houses. A bridle path was being cut up the hill, to be continued to Aberdeen (Chek Pai Wan), and wooden barracks had been constructed at Stanley. He had made regulations for the bazaar, or the Chinese area; the streets there were to be straight, and twenty feet broad, side verandahs being allowed. There were to be three commissioners, or headmen, to be elected by the Chinese occupiers, to make "minor regulations" for the bazaar's good conduct. One of the three commissioners, to be elected among themselves, was to be responsible to the Government and receive a monthly salary. A meeting of all occupiers was being called immediately, to raise sums to buy one or more fire-engines, as the bazaar area's flimsy structures had been the scene of many fires.

This letter is clearly written by a man who felt himself in charge, and who did not understand that the recall of Elliot had created a new situation. Johnston was acting on Elliot's policy of encouraging and arranging for a growing settlement. He was also clearly carrying out Elliot's promise that Chinese law and custom should be respected, and thus two systems of administration, British and Chinese, should be set up side by side to enable the Chinese to continue their own mode of government. Johnston evidently did not realize that the British Government had not decided either for or against the retention of the island, and that it was not for him to lay down policy. After Pottinger had made the position clear, the interesting arrangements for a Chinese administration of the bazaar were dropped. It must also be pointed out in defence of Johnston, that Pottinger himself found that during his stay on the island in 1842, he was obliged to make some allocations of land, to religious bodies for example, and to officials, including Johnston, who had to be given some accommodation. Johnston was allowed to choose two plots of land, on one of which, close to the parade ground, he built a large house which was subsequently taken over by Pottinger as Government House. In 1842 Johnston also raised a subscription to build an Anglican Church to replace the mat-shed structure on the parade ground.

In October 1842 he reported to Pottinger on the prevalence of crime and disorder in the settlement, and said he lacked "the means of visiting adequate punishment". Isolated houses were attacked, often by gangs who landed from boats, and there was much piracy. He said that the jail was full, but that he had no authority to award sentences severe enough to deal with many of the inmates awaiting trial. Such conditions helped to convince the Colonial Office of the need to retain full control of the arrangements for law and order in Hong Kong, and the danger of allowing the Chinese to share this responsibility.

In December 1842 Pottinger returned and assumed control of Hong Kong, and Johnston remained Deputy Superintendent of Trade, a post whose name was changed the next year to Assistant and Registrar to the Superintendent of Trade.

In June 1843, on the proclamation of Hong Kong as a Colony, Johnston, Caine, and Hillier were sworn in as Justices of the Peace, the first J. P.s to be created. One authority says that Johnston also acted as the first postmaster at the Colony's Post Office, but this does not appear to have been reported to the Colonial Office in London.

In August 1843, following on the proclamation of the Colony, Pottinger set up the Executive and Legislative Councils, and Johnston was nominated a member of both. The Legislative Council, however, did not function. It consisted of Pottinger as Chairman, A. R. Johnston, W. Caine, and J. R. Morrison; but the last-named died in the same month, and Johnston went home on sick leave in October 1843, having been out in the Far East for ten eventful years.

He returned in September 1845 and resumed his position as Secretary and Registrar to the Superintendent of Trade. In June 1846 he was made a member of the Executive Council in place of the Colonial Secretary, F. W. Bruce, who went on leave prior to taking the post of Lieutenant-Governor of Newfoundland. Johnston retained his seat on the Executive Council until he retired to England in March 1853 with a pension of £600 per year.

He played little further part in the affairs of the Colony, and he never again occupied any post in the local administration on the colonial side. He remained a well-known local figure, but was not directly concerned with the island's affairs, except as a Foreign Office official dealing with commercial questions.

In August 1856 he wrote to Labouchère, the Secretary of State for the Colonies, asking that he should be given some recognition for his services. He gave an account of his official career, and claimed that he founded the Colony of Hong Kong, having been left in charge of the island by Elliot and Pottinger. When Pottinger returned from Nanking, Johnston said, he found a thriving colony, clearly implying that it was thriving because of him. This claim is very doubtful. His administration of the Colony's affairs was, rather, a source of embarrassment. It seems safer to conclude that he found himself placed in control of the island by accident; he built himself no great reputation, and the most generous thing that can be said is that he was a not incompetent official. At least the Colonial Office must have thought so as it did not accede to his request.

8

WILLIAM CAINE

FIRST MAGISTRATE OF THE COLONY

WILLIAM CAINE was an outstanding figure in the early history of the Colony. For nineteen years, 1841–59, he held a series of important posts in the Government and served under six administrations from Charles Elliot's to that of Sir Hercules Robinson. On two occasions he acted as the officer administering the Government, and for a year, 1854–5, he was the Lieutenant-Governor in full control. Throughout the whole of this time he was an influential official; he impressed his personality on the administration of law and order in the Colony, and the local Chinese view of British rule was largely coloured by his character and outlook.

In April 1841 Caine was selected by Elliot as Magistrate of the infant Colony of Hong Kong. He had been an army man, a Captain in the 26th Regiment of Infantry (the Cameronians). He was born in 1798, was taken to India as an infant and followed the army as a boy. It was said of him that "he had been a soldier since he was strong enough to carry a drum" and as a boy he took part in the campaign of 1804 against Holkar, one of the Mahratta leaders in central India. He was commissioned in 1814 and held a distinguished record, both as a leader of men in the field and as a staff officer. He filled positions of responsibility in various military campaigns in India. For example, he acted as Brigade-Major, and occasionally as Regimental Judge-Advocate dealing with disciplinary questions, and he gained a reputation for efficiency and devotion to duty.

When hostilities against China came in 1839, the 26th Regiment was ordered to embark for China as part of the expeditionary force being prepared in India. Caine, though only a Captain, was selected as Adjutant-General to the expedition, but the Home Government decided that such an important post should be held by an officer of field rank. He was then offered the post of Deputy Judge-Advocate-General but he elected to remain with his regiment. He took part in the occupation of Chusan and was appointed a member of the Military Commission of Control of the island, and Chief Magistrate.

In January 1841 Charles Elliot negotiated the Convention of Chuenpi by which Hong Kong was ceded as a place of residence for British merchants, and arrangements were made at the same time for Chusan to be handed back to China and its British garrison and military government withdrawn. In April, Caine accepted Elliot's offer of the position of Magistrate in Hong Kong. Since he had held this position in Chusan, he was an obvious choice, but he was not altogether happy about this civilian appointment. During the operations against Canton which took place that summer he more than once asked leave to rejoin his regiment, which was taking part. Charles Elliot's answer was, "It necessarily becomes your duty to forego (however painfully) the privilege of being with your corps on any military operations in which it may be engaged"; so Caine remained in Hong Kong, and, indeed, stayed another eighteen years. His active military career was at an end, though he continued to hold honorary rank and was promoted to the rank of Brevet-Major in December 1841.

In many ways his career epitomized the early Hong Kong. The Colony administration had perforce to be manned by army officers, who generally had had experience in India, and so imported into the Colony something of the East India Company's traditions. Caine's task was to organize an ordered social life in the Colony.

When he assumed office there was an administrative void, and he had to create and begin to operate the machinery of law and order. Until a house could be built, his only shelter was a mat-shed hut, and he had to rely on the military for the supply of police personnel. His warrant of appointment, dated 30 April 1841, advised him to exercise his authority "according to the laws, customs and usages of China, as nearly as may be, (every description of torture excepted) for the preservation of peace, and the protection of life and property, over all the inhabitants of the said Island". Other sections of the community were to be dealt with according to the customs and usages of British police law. There was as yet no Legislative Council and consequently no code of local statute law, and much had to be left to his discretion. The only limitation was that penalties imposed on the Chinese were not to exceed three months' imprisonment or a fine of $400 or, in the case of corporal punishment, one hundred lashes with the rattan. Those guilty of crimes, whose gravity was judged to merit heavier sentences had to be referred to the head of the government. Even allowing for this limitation of his authority, Caine's task was arduous and responsible.

Elliot was anxious to encourage the growth of the settlement and appointed additional officials in the summer of 1841, but Caine remained single-handed in the administration of justice. Elliot was recalled by the Home Government which repudiated his Convention of Chuenpi and wondered whether to retain the island at all, and he left in August 1841. His successor, Sir Henry Pottinger, ordered a cessation of all public works except those required by the military. Whatever doubts existed about the future of the Colony, there were none about the necessity of ensuring law and order for the duration of the military occupation, and Caine was kept fully occupied. He set about his duties with great energy. He assumed charge of a small, granite jail, erected on the site of the present Central Police Court, the road to which was appropriately named "Old Bailey".

He interpreted his duties broadly. In India it was customary for the Magistrate to control the allocation of land. Caine began to do so in Hong Kong, but the Land Officer took legitimate exception, and appealed to Pottinger, who upheld him.

Following the establishment of the Colony in June 1843, Caine was placed on the colonial establishment as Chief Magistrate, and when the Supreme Court was established the following year, he assumed the additional titles of Sheriff and Provost Marshal; he was also one of the first to be appointed an official Justice of the Peace.

Crime was rife in the island and the most audacious burglaries, robberies, and criminal assaults occurred. Caine met this lawlessness by a ruthless application of flogging with the rattan, with or without imprisonment; indeed, flogging was so prevalent that questions were asked in the House of Commons. His methods were arbitrary, and he was accused of applying the discipline of the barrack-room. Yet his approach was not without effect. Confronted by an exceptional incidence of crime, he resolutely attempted to combat it. In the first years of the Colony he could be found at all hours of the night attempting to do himself work for which adequate police assistance should have been provided. He remained dignified, and his efficiency was always gentlemanly; he was severe, but impartial. The result was that though he was feared, he was respected; he was never actively disliked. There was some criticism, and one newspaper acidly commented on the magistrates in these terms: "They mete out justice according to the judgement which God has been pleased to grant them; equitably in their own opinion no doubt...law, there is none".

It was easy to criticize Major Caine. He was no doubt as ignorant of British law as he was of Chinese laws, customs, and usages. The Home Government refused to recruit police from England except for three officers and it would be fair to say that Caine never at any time had an efficient police force; he had to rely on the troops.

His efficiency and devotion were recognized by his eventual promotion to the highest offices. In August 1843 he was nominated by Sir Henry Pottinger to a seat on the Executive and Legislative Councils. However, because of lack of personnel they could not function, and early in 1844 they were reconstituted with a very limited membership—Pottinger, D'Aguilar, the Major-General Commanding, and Caine. Sir John Davis arrived in May 1844 with many new officials; he expanded the size of each Council beyond the number allowed by his instructions, and when this was disallowed, he dropped Caine from the Legislative Council in May 1845, but retained him on the Executive Council. In September the following year he was again a member of both Councils, but temporarily resigned from the legislative body in December to make room for an acting Attorney-General.

After deputizing for the Colonial Secretary in the summer of 1845, and again in June 1846, Caine was appointed to that important post in November. He was Colonial Secretary for the next eight years, as well as Auditor-General. When Davis conducted his expedition to Canton in April 1847, Caine was left in charge of the Government and the garrison.

At the enquiry conducted by the 1847 Select Committee of the House of Commons, the Major was described by one of the witnesses, Captain Balfour, as "a very efficient officer of great distinction". Caine, when asked by the Colonial Office for his comments on the report, described the difficulties of the Colony's early days and contrasted "the unpleasantness of my duties" with his life as a soldier, observing that "nine-tenths of our Chinese subjects and about half of our low European inhabitants have been in the most depraved condition". He referred to the fact that he often patrolled the town three nights a week, and his assistant another three.

In December 1848 following the full enquiry that Bonham was ordered to make into the Hong Kong establishment, he noted in a home dispatch that Caine had served thirty-five years without intermission and that he had every confidence in him and was perfectly satisfied.

It has already been mentioned that when Bonham retired in 1854 the Home Government decided to separate the post of Governor of the Colony from that of Plenipotentiary and Superintendent of Trade; Caine was chosen to be Lieutenant-Governor of the island and Bowring was to have the two Foreign Office posts. It was found impossible to effect this separation without special legislation, and Bowring retained the nominal position of Governor on the understanding that Caine should be the *de facto* Governor. The plan broke down because Bowring refused to accept a merely nominal role in Hong Kong; but from April 1854 to June 1855 Caine, as Lieutenant-Governor, acted as head of the Government and promulgated ordinances over his own name. In respect of this short period, his name could properly be included in the list of Governors of the Colony.

The arrangement was terminated by Palmerston after Bowring

created trouble, and from June 1855, the latter assumed full control. Caine retained his title of Lieutenant-Governor and was made the "senior member of the Legislative Council"; in fact, he generally found himself with nothing to do. He was disappointed at the outcome and in July 1855 applied to be given the position of Commanding Officer of the garrison with the rank of Colonel, but the War Office refused its sanction. In 1858 he applied for the governorship of the Straits and was again disappointed. The following year he was permitted to retire on a pension of £600, subsequently increased to £1,050.

Caine had managed to maintain a dignified aloofness toward the personal animosities which marked the governorship of Sir John Bowring. His friends Bridges, Caldwell, and Hillier were all attacked and charged with corruption or inefficiency by the quixotic Chisholm Anstey, who arrived in 1856 as Attorney-General. Caine was very loyal to them and attempted to defend them in private, but in public, he refused to take any part in the sordid proceedings on the ground that his friendship with the accused men did not allow him to judge the issues with the necessary impartiality.

Caine was, however, involved in one case, against William Tarrant, later editor of a rather spiteful paper, *The Friend of China*. Tarrant had been an official in the Surveyor-General's Department, and in 1847 in the course of his duties he reported that Caine's compradore had extorted sums of money from market stall-holders and others, on the ground that he was able to bring some influence to bear on the Major, for or against them. The Governor, Sir John Davis, appointed a Committee of Enquiry which not only exonerated Caine, but recommended that Tarrant be prosecuted for libel. The unfortunate Tarrant lost his post, and was duly brought to court, but the prosecution eventually had to be dropped, because it could not be proved that Caine was libelled by the charge against his compradore.

Tarrant became editor of *The Friend of China,* and his success in the trial emboldened him to carry on a vendetta against Caine which continued for twelve years, with growing innuendoes that Caine had been implicated. Caine ignored these attacks until 1859, when he was about to leave the Colony on retirement. He postponed his departure, and prosecuted Tarrant for libel. Having decided to act, he went about it with his customary efficiency and decision. He retained every member of the local Bar, and forced Tarrant to defend himself in court without professional assistance. The Chief Justice commented unfavourably on this proceeding but Tarrant was convicted and sentenced to twelve months' imprisonment.

Caine finally left the Colony on retirement on 28 September 1859 after eighteen years' unbroken service there, and died twelve years later at the age of seventy-three. The Colony's Caine Road is named after him.

Caine was popular with the mercantile community for his zeal and efficiency in the performance of his public duty and because he was hospitable and friendly. He won the respect of the Chinese too, for though he had a commanding personality which instilled respect, it was combined with dignity and impartiality. The soldier had been successfully converted into the civil servant. He was, however, criticized because he was known to have speculated in land in the early days of the Colony, and after he left some articles appeared in the Press reflecting on his personal character.

Bowring described him as "of the old—the very old—school" and "uninformed of what is passing and has passed in England".

In spite of refusing to allow Caine to assume full government of the Colony as had been intended, Bowring thought well of him, agreed that he had many excellent qualities, and said, "I have not exchanged an unkind word, for though he shakes his head and perceives infinite difficulties...it is always with good humour". It was quite true that he had hardly seen England. In 1859, at the time of his retirement, he had had forty-five years' continuous service under the Crown in India and the Far East, without home leave. He was very dissatisfied with his pension of £600, and his protest led to its increase to £1,050. Even that left him dissatisfied, and in June 1860 he wrote to the Secretary of State, the Duke of Newcastle, in a fruitless request for a knighthood. He made another attempt the following year, and in 1864 even addressed a petition to the Queen, again without avail, in which he complained of "disgrace and neglect".

To the Colony's Chinese, Caine was the most prominent government official. The manner in which he was regarded in Hong Kong may perhaps best be illustrated by a story in H. C. Sirr's book *China and the Chinese,* published in 1849. A man who had just arrived in Hong Kong asked a Chinese the name of the Governor; this not being understood, he asked who was "the great man". "Major Caine", came the immediate reply.

9

JOHN WALTER HULME

FIRST CHIEF JUSTICE

IN 1844 John Walter Hulme was appointed Chief Justice of the Hong Kong Supreme Court. He was the first to hold this post, which he occupied for sixteen years, eventually retiring from the Colony in April 1860. His name is familiar to many as the judge who was suspended from office on a charge of drunkenness, and who was the central figure in one of the most extraordinary episodes of British colonial history. He was subsequently cleared of the charge and reinstated, and went on to gain the esteem of all sections of the community.

Hulme was called to the Bar from the Middle Temple, and went into partnership with Joseph Chitty, whose daughter he married. Chitty was one of the leading lawyers of his day and a prolific author of legal treatises. Hulme himself published *A Practical Treatise on Bills of Exchange,* and appeared set for a distinguished career at the Bar. But as will be seen, he was a man of convivial habits and of a generous disposition, and he probably spent money lavishly. In addition, he had a large family to support. These circumstances compelled him to accept a lucrative appointment as Judge of the Supreme Court of Hong Kong. The Colonial Office had had some difficulty in making the appointment and Hulme had to be offered £3,000 a year before he would consent to undertake the office. He did, however, give up all claim to a pension.

Hulme arrived in the Colony in the early summer of 1844. As the Attorney-General had not yet arrived however, there was some delay in opening the Supreme Court. A local wit aptly quoted, "He could not stir, but like a comet, he was wondered at", and suggested that the British Government sent out the officers of the Supreme Court piecemeal because they were afraid that "neighbour would have assaulted neighbour from sheer desire of being tried by his peers, and favoured with a bumper of English justice". Eventually, the first sessions of the Supreme Court were held, on 1 October 1844. Judge Hulme also became a member of the Hong Kong Legislative Council, contrary to the principle that the judiciary should be independent of the legislature. There is no doubt, however, that it was desirable that a competent lawyer should assist in the framing of ordinances.

Hulme proved to be a popular and respected judge. He gained a reputation for severity, but none doubted his impartiality and strict adherence to the forms of justice. The problem of correct interpreting and the securing of efficient interpreters occupied him continually, aand he spent much time evolving the procedure for the swearing of oaths by Chinese in giving evidence in court.

Unfortunately, there were immediate differences between the Chief Justice and the Governor, Sir John Davis, which ripened into an open and bitter quarrel. The two men were very different in temperament. The Governor was urbane, witty, able, reserved, and aloof, yet masterful and dominating, while the Judge was sociable, friendly, intelligent, and efficient, with a complete independence of outlook.

Hulme was one of a group of senior government officials whom Davis brought out with him on his appointment. At Bombay it had been arranged for them to continue to Hong Kong in H.M.S. *Spiteful* but the ship was unable to accommodate the whole party. As the Hulme family would have needed half the available room, and as Mrs. Hulme was the only lady in the party, Davis decided the Hulmes should be left behind, to come on by a later passenger ship. This was much to Hulme's annoyance, especially as the change cost him £250.

The two men quarrelled over the making of rules governing the Supreme Court procedure. The Judge claimed to be quite independent in his control of the court, whose rules had to be passed by the Legislative Council to have legal sanction as part of the Supreme Court Ordinance. This gave Sir John an opportunity of reviewing them and suggesting amendments. In particular he objected to the long vacation of six months which the Judge had given himself; there were to be no criminal sessions between June and December, and Davis felt this was an injustice to witnesses and accused persons awaiting trial. Hulme answered that the six months applied only to criminal cases and not to civil cases, and that he personally had only four months' vacation which was not excessive. He firmly resisted all amendments and Davis retaliated by having new rules passed by the Legislative Council which almost abolished the Judge's vacation altogether.

They quarrelled over the control of the Magistrates' Courts. The Magistrates, Caine and Hillier, regarded themselves as part of the administration and subject to the Governor's control. Hulme regarded the lower courts as courts of law for which he was ultimately responsible. On one occasion, for example, three Portuguese fled to Hong Kong from Macao where they had been accused of crimes. Their extradition was applied for by the Governor of Macao, and Sir John Davis instructed the Magistrates to send them back to the

Portugese colony. Hulme, who was very properly jealous of the Courts' independence, a cardinal principle of English constitutional practice, regarded this as an unwarrantable interference by the executive, believing that such cases should be decided by law, and not by the orders of the Governor.

In November 1846 came the Compton case. Compton was an English merchant in Canton who caused a riot by kicking over a Chinese stall and beating its owner with his stick. Compton was a hectoring sort of man, noted for his repeated acts of violence towards the Chinese, and in this case he admitted that his action had very probably caused the riot in which $46,000 worth of damage was done. Compton was fined $200 by the British Consul at Canton and Davis confirmed this decision. Compton appealed to the Hong Kong Supreme Court, as he was entitled to do, and Hulme reversed the verdict, remitted the fine, and commented severely on the irregularities of the hearing before the Consul. In effect he criticized the whole administration of British consular authorities in the Treaty Ports. Sir John was highly indignant. "It will never do", he wrote home, "to have two plenipotentiaries in China, one doing justice to our ally, and the other immediately undoing it". In a further letter to the Secretary of State, Earl Grey, he added that since Hulme's judgement in the Compton case, the feeling in Canton was that as long as Hulme was there "they can shoot the Chinese with impunity". Behind this particular quarrel lay an important issue of principle. Davis thought that the control of British subjects in China should be under the administrative officials to assure conformity with British policy, to secure speed, ease, and simplicity of procedure, to avoid the expense and delay of remitting a case to the Supreme Court at Hong Kong and to bolster up the authority of the Consuls. Hulme believed in the full application of the law and in the citizen's right to court protection against arbitrary action by administrative agents of the Crown, and held that all judicial actions should be capable of review through appeal to the Supreme Court.

Davis now determined to have Hulme dismissed. In November 1846 he wrote a strong letter of complaint to Grey on the question of the Supreme Court vacation and Hulme's opposition to any revision of court rules by the Legislative Council. At the same time he wrote a private letter to Lord Palmerston charging Hulme with being an habitual drunkard. Davis's object was to strengthen his official complaints by these private aspersions on Hulme's character, and so reinforce the case for his dismissal.

Palmerston sent this private letter to the Colonial Office where Earl Grey took a serious view of the contents. He at once wrote to Davis and demanded that an enquiry should be instituted into the truth of the charges, which were too serious not to be made openly, and he insisted that Hulme should be given a chance to defend himself. The Governor had never had any intention of publicly and openly accusing Hulme of drunkenness. He accordingly evaded Grey's demand, fearing the scandal and harm to the public service of such an enquiry, and pointed out that his remarks had been contained in a private and confidential letter. Grey was adamant that a public investigation of Hulme's character was necessary unless Davis unequivocally withdrew all accusations. He argued that the fact that these had been made in a private letter added to their impropriety, because Hulme had no knowledge of them and was therefore unable to defend himself.

Meanwhile the relations between Governor and Judge had further deteriorated. The sessions of the Vice-Admiralty Court were fixed in April 1847 without consulting Hulme, though the latter was expected to preside. Personal animosity was behind the two men's petty bickering as to whether Hulme was entitled to be called the "Lord Chief Justice". Davis had confidently expected that Hulme would be recalled as a result of his complaints to the Colonial Secretary of State, but when the latter's reply was received in August 1847 it was found to contain a magisterial rebuke of Davis's own conduct. Hulme did not escape censure, however, as Grey thought all parties had "failed in self-command". But as a result of the letter, the Governor resigned. He had tried to get rid of the Judge, but had contrived his own downfall instead. So when Grey's letter insisting on the enquiry into Hulme's conduct arrived in November 1847 Davis had ceased to have much interest in the issues; he had already resigned and events were allowed to take their course.

Three charges were brought against Hulme, two of specific cases of drunkenness and one of habitual drunkenness. They were: (1) that Hon. J. W. Hulme, Esq. on 22nd November 1845 at a public entertainment given by Rear Admiral Sir Thomas Cockrane to the Chinese Commissioner and suite on board the flagship *Agincourt* in Hong Kong harbour, was in such a state of intoxication as to attract public attention; (2) that Hon. J. W. Hulme, Esq. on Thursday 23rd July 1846 at the residence of the Hon. Major-General George D'Aguilar, C.B., at Victoria was deeply intoxicated and unable to take care of himself; (3) and that the said Hon. J. W. Hulme, Esq. had been addicted to the habits of intoxication whilst at Hong Kong.

The Major-General was indignant that an incident which occurred in the privacy of his house should be the subject of an official enquiry, and gave evidence with extreme reluctance and only after an assurance from Davis that his duty to the Queen as a military officer required him to do so. "No man was ever more thunderstruck than I was", wrote Hulme to Grey when he received notice of the charges, and his action is not surprising, since the incidents referred to had taken place over a two-year period. He naturally asked why the charges had not been made at the time.

Since Davis was forced into the proceedings, they were perfunctorily carried out before the Executive Council in November 1847. Many witnesses had left the Colony, and A. R. Johnston and Major Caine had to be called upon to give evidence against Hulme though they were members of the Executive Council, and so his judges and his accusers. Judge Hulme denied the truth of the accusations and explained that his occasional unsteady gait was due to varicose veins.

The Executive Council pronounced no formal verdict. Davis asked each member to declare his opinion, and then summed up. Hulme was adjudged guilty on the first charge; the second charge was considered not proved, and the third disproved. As a result Hulme was suspended, and he left for home on 30 December 1847. All sections of the Colony showed their sympathy. Testimonials were presented to him, and leading residents saw him to his ship amid the sound of crackers, and, inappropriately perhaps, the drinking of champagne!

The proceedings had been so irregular that it was no surprise when they were not upheld by the Secretary of State. Hulme was held to be completely innocent of the charges and was reinstated and returned to the Colony in 1848, with his character completely vindicated. He wanted to take proceedings against Davis and asked Earl Grey for "some mark of the Queen's favour". Grey advised him against taking such action and would not even grant an interview while Hulme was in London.

Hulme remained jealous of the independence of the Courts to the last. On one occasion in 1852 he refused to pass the death sentence on two Malay sailors found guilty of murder on the ground that on a previous occasion the Governor, Sir George Bonham, had commuted a death sentence contrary to Hulme's advice, and he felt it would be unfair to pass the death sentences in this case. This action incurred the censure of the home authorities.

He was not in good health during this period, and had to be given several periods of home leave. He had a narrow escape one day riding to Stanley on horseback when a bridge collapsed under him and he fell thirty feet into the stream below.

The Chief Justice continued to enjoy a great reputation in the Colony. He was regarded as severe but scrupulously impartial. In private life he was undoubtedly sociable and convivial. "Mr. Hulme, like many other good men, was of a gay and mirthful disposition, frank, gentlemanly and social", was one contemporary opinion of him. Anstey, the Attorney-General who created such a stir in the Colony, accused Hulme of being "blind drunk" at Bowring's table on one occasion in May 1856. Hulme and Anstey both appealed to the Secretary of State, Laboucheve, who demanded that Anstey either apologize or bring his charge before the Executive Council, and Anstey withdrew. But Labouchère said of Hulme that no doubt, "from an excitable temperament he may be led on convivial occasions to transgress the limits of that decorum...". Perhaps nearer the mark was one commentator who said, with admirable delicacy, that Hulme was "esteemed for the virtues which sweeten existence", and on occasion Hulme undoubtedly consumed more than was judicious. In September 1851 he applied for a transfer to another colony on medical grounds. In sending this application home, Sir George Bonham commented that Hulme was faced with heavy liabilities, having come to Hong Kong in embarrassed circumstances and becoming further involved by acting as surety for a man who had deceived him. This referred to Hulme's friendship with Shelley, the Auditor-General, whom Davis had accused of being negligent, dissipated, in debt, given to falsehood, and generally quite unfit for high office. Shelley's influence on Hulme was not beneficial.

In 1858 he asked to retire, and was granted eighteen months' leave. He retired in April 1860 and though not entitled to a pension, he was given £1,500 a year. He did not live long to enjoy it, however for he died less than twelve months later on 1 March 1861, at Brighton.

10

ROBERT MONTGOMERY MARTIN

COLONIAL TREASURER AND HISTORIAN
OF THE BRITISH EMPIRE

ROBERT MONTGOMERY MARTIN was born in County Tyrone, probably in the year 1803, of parents who were well-connected but not affluent, and blessed with a large family. He studied medicine without securing any qualification and in 1820 he went to Ceylon to join the establishment of an influential resident who was a friend of his father. In 1823 he went to the Cape of Good Hope, joined the naval expedition to Delagoa Bay as an assistant surgeon and naturalist, and was able to explore the East African Coast, Madagascar, and neighbouring islands. He left the expedition and returned to the Cape by way of Mauritius, and then went to Australia and lived for a time in New South Wales. In 1828 he arrived in India and in 1830, ten years after setting out, he returned to England, having experienced the life of a great many British colonies.

He now devoted himself to writing on colonial questions and to their further study. He produced a *History of the British Colonies,* and though quite unknown, he induced William IV to allow it to be dedicated to him. He undertook a life of Lord Wellesley, from the latter's private papers. He wrote a *History of Taxation within the British Empire,* and published a *History of the Antiquities of Eastern India* using the India House papers. In 1837 he reissued his *History of the British Colonies* in ten volumes and the next year produced a book, *Statistics of the Colonies,* compiled from official reports which he was allowed to consult in the Colonial Office, and which has been described as "the first account of the British Empire with any pretence to statistical accuracy".[1] In 1840 he founded and edited the *Colonial Magazine.* He appears to have been impelled by a genuine interest in colonial questions, and he worked without assistance from government or official recognition.[2]

In January 1844 he was rewarded for his keenness by being made Colonial Treasurer of Hong Kong and Treasurer of the consular establishments in China, and he travelled out with the newly-appointed Governor, Sir John Davis. It was his first and only appointment as a colonial official, and it was not a success.

---

1 C. E. Carrington, *The British Overseas,* p. 506.
2 Biographical details taken from the *Dictionary of National Biography.*

He already had a considerable literary output and showed every intention of adding to it—to the detriment of his official duties. He had also been a free-lance, and found it difficult to accommodate himself to the restrictions imposed by official routine and the need of co-operation with his colleagues.

He arrived in Hong Kong on 7 May 1844, and in less than two months he produced two long reports, one on the Colony's finances, and the other on the whole question of retaining Hong Kong as a colony; they revealed that he had rapidly made up his mind that Hong Kong was useless as a centre of British trade. His financial memorandum, of June 1844, referred to the Colony as a "small barren unhealthy valueless island". He estimated the annual expenditure at £50,000, excluding public works, and the revenue at £5,880, leaving an annual deficit of £42,870. He suggested that additional revenue might be raised from a licence fee of five dollars on all shops and trades, a registration fee of one dollar on all Chinese, stamp duties, and duties on wines and spirits. He also expressed the view that Hong Kong was unlikely to develop into an emporium because it attracted few respectable Chinese, because in the absence of perpetuity of land tenure there would be little investment of capital, and because its growth would be hindered by the opening of the five Treaty Ports. He urged that if further sickness occurred, a move to Chusan would be necessary. He estimated the total annual expenditure, civil and military, including establishments at five Treaty Ports, at £450,000.

Davis was critical of this report. He thought that an opium farm might be set up, as in Singapore, where it provided half the revenue, and he suggested a salt farm and the imposition of additional licences. Martin was made a member of the Legislative Council, and there opposed the Governor's financial proposals, particularly the opium farm, on the principle that public revenue should not be derived from vice.

The second memorandum which Martin presented to the Governor was dated 29 July 1844, and dealt with all aspects of Hong Kong—topography, geology, climate, population, progress, disease, commerce, and religious and social characteristics. It was a vigorous polemic against Hong Kong, well argued and supported by facts, or by what he considered were the facts.

The report's profusion of criticism of Hong Kong may be briefly summarized as follows: the precipices and rocky ravines would always prevent the growth of a large town; the decomposing granite and disintegrating sandstone emitted a foetid odour productive of disease, and the harbour was being filled up by silt; the climate was injurious to health; the mandarins tried to stop respectable Chinese from settling in Hong Kong, and those who came were the worst types, worthless, roving, and with no sense of morality; only a few ships called for orders, but very few "broke bulk", and the conditions that contributed to the commercial prosperity of Singapore were entirely absent in Hong Kong. The report may be summed up in Martin's own words: "I have in vain sought for one valuable quality in Hong Kong", and "I can see no justification for the British Government spending one shilling on Hong Kong". His conclusion was that Chusan's claims to be the seat of British influence on the China Coast were infinitely preferable to those of Hong Kong.

Davis did not treat this memorandum seriously and kept it a month before sending it to the Secretary of State. He did not trouble to make any criticism except to point out that Martin had resided in the Colony for a few weeks only, during part of which time he had been ill, that his account contained many "errors of fact and conclusion" and that in any case, much of the report was a reflection on Pottinger, the preceding governor. Sir James Stephen, the Permanent Under-Secretary of State, agreed that Martin had spent too short a time in Hong Kong to be convincing, but observed that if it were correct that all the China trade would pass through the five Treaty Ports, then Martin was justified in saying that Hong Kong was worthless, and that Davis ought to have given his views in detail and corrected the errors of the report. Lord Stanley, the Secretary of State, agreed that Martin's views, unless incorrect, formed ample ground for a reconsideration of Hong Kong's position, and asked for a full comment from Davis.

Martin was acquainted with Sir James Stephen and wrote to him privately asking to be allowed to resign, with the object of taking a more responsible post. He also privately sent Stephen an even stronger condemnation of Hong Kong, on which Davis was in turn asked for his full comment. Stanley was naturally critical of this private correspondence and Davis was told that if Martin resigned the resignation was to be accepted, and that Martin was in future to send all communications to the Colonial Office in the proper way through the Governor.

In April 1845 Davis sent his observations on Martin's memorandum. He thought that Martin's main objections to Hong Kong were three: (a) unsuitable climate, (b) insufficient public revenue, and (c) no expectation of commercial prosperity. On the first, he pointed out that Hong Kong had the same climate as Macao, where the English had lived for years; on the second, he said Martin had estimated the revenue at about £5,000, yet in 1844 the land rents alone had amounted to £13,000. With regard to commerce, Davis thought that the restrictive clauses of the Treaty of the Bogue had done great injury, and that piracy also hindered trade, but that Hong Kong had one of the finest harbours in the world and possessed great advantages apart from its function as a trading centre.

The Governor and the Colonial Treasurer clearly had such different ideas on Hong Kong that it was impossible for them to work harmoniously, and Davis began a series of complaints to the Secretary of State about Martin. In a private letter to Lord Stanley dated 12 February 1845, he complained that Martin was late with his accounts and said, "Whether from want of method or from attending to other matters (as bookmaking) he is a most inefficient and troublesome person, and I should be very glad to get rid of him". A month later Davis complained again; this time Martin had employed three clerks without Davis's consent. Stanley agreed to their employment but warned Martin against repeating this irregular procedure.

Again in April, Davis made a very strong complaint against the Colonial Treasurer, who had submitted two long memoranda regarding the auditing of accounts, particularly those of other departments. The Governor accused Martin of trying to stir up the same disharmony in other departments as existed in his own.

In June 1845 Davis had another opportunity of attacking Martin when he was asked to comment on the private letter the latter had sent to Sir James Stephen. He again denied that the climate was bad, asked General D'Aguilar for his opinion, and reported him as saying, "Mr. Martin must be mad or something worse... His assertion meets only my contempt, I hope you will send this to Lord Stanley". Davis complained that Martin "goes up and down the coast" and the only result was arrears of work; he reported that Martin had asked for sick leave but could not get a doctor to give him a sick certificate.

In a letter to Davis on 18 June 1845, Martin asked to be allowed to return home, not on sick leave, but because he felt that the defects in "our Chinese policy" were serious and he wished to place them before the Home Government. He considered he had been especially selected as Treasurer because it was thought he would gather useful information, and he said he had made a careful and detailed investigation and was convinced that an immediate enquiry into the British position in China was of the highest importance. He offered to forego six months' salary and pay his own expenses if he were granted the six months' leave. Davis answered that the regulations did not permit this, that in any case the consular officers were stationed in China for the purpose of supplying information, and that he had received no intimation from the Home Government that Martin should be employed on the enquiry he had been making.

Martin maintained that leave for private affairs was allowed, and that he was convinced that "our affairs in China require immediate and special re-consideration". He insisted on returning to England to place his views before the authorities there and on 8 July 1845 he resigned and wrote to Lord Stanley asking for a Court of Enquiry into the circumstances of his resignation.

Earlier, in April 1845, Martin had written privately to Trevelyan, Under-Secretary at the Treasury, urging the evacuation of Hong Kong, at the same time sending him a gift of a chest of the best China tea.

He was particularly anxious to arrive in England before Chusan was due to be evacuated and when he missed the mail at Bombay he wrote to say that he would travel by the quickest way, if necessary, via Persia. He repeated his attack on the Colony, and said that there were hardly 150 resident English there, exclusive of government servants, and only sixteen merchant firms. He implied that the Governor was grossly overpaid because he did not "even spend the interest which he derived from the deposit of his salary in one of the large opium firms". He thought the Legislative Council should be abolished and replaced by a municipal council, and he alleged that the duties of the Colonial Secretary could be performed by an ordinary clerk. He also said the officials "have houses or land there or they have money lent on mortgage, or they traffic in building land".

His reports were printed by the Home Government, and Martin continued his campaign against the Colony, and against the arrangements for conducting British interests in China. In 1846 he published his *Reports, Minutes and Dispatches on the British Position and Prospects in China*, in which he collected his writings on that subject and included the circumstances leading to his resignation. He published *China; Political, Commercial and Social* in two volumes in 1847 and called it "an official report to Her Majesty's Government", dedicating it to the Queen. It contained yet another attack on British policy in China and on the Colony of Hong Kong, and he accused Davis of converting the island into an opium depot. He gave evidence before the 1847 Select Committee of the House of Commons on the China trade which ensured wide publicity and official notice of his views, and the Committee's report echoed some of the criticisms he had made. Martin did not carry much conviction in Downing Street where his action in quitting his Hong Kong post was considered unjustified. Martin claimed to have resigned because to him there seemed to be no other way of getting home to place before the government views which he regarded as so important that any delay would be fatal. He claimed that his resignation was prompted by a sense of devotion to public duty, and was therefore deserving of reward. The Colonial Office was not convinced; his resignation was regarded as final and he was not again offered public employment. Sir James Stephen left the Colonial Office in 1847, but there is no reason to think that the outcome would have been different had he remained.

Martin continued his literary work and his keen interest in Far Eastern affairs, and was one of the founder-members of the East India Association in 1866. Eitel suggested[1] that Martin's hostility to the Colony continued, and that he was responsible for an article appearing in *The Times* in December 1858 commenting on the Treaty of Tientsin of that year. This article stated that opinion in Hong Kong was against the further opening of Treaty Ports, which were so much to the advantage of British trade, on the ground that the Colony's own economic interests were adversely affected.

Robert Montgomery Martin served in the Colony only for the short period of fourteen months, yet his career there was significant because he made himself the mouthpiece of a feeling of *malaise* and disappointment which pervaded the Colony at the time of his arrival. The Colony had failed to develop as anticipated, and instead of becoming a great emporium, commerce had stagnated. The big building constructed by Dent & Co. as an exchange had not been used, and the firm was lucky to sell it to the Government to serve as the Supreme Court. The restrictive clauses of the Treaty of the Bogue were blamed, and it was soon realized that the five Treaty Ports would compete with the Colony as centres of commerce. The result of this new appraisal of the Colony's prospects, prevalent just at the time of Martin's arrival, was a strong opposition to Davis's policy of making the Colony financially self-supporting, a lowering of land values, and a general mood of despondency.

Martin, an experienced writer and publicist, made himself the spokesman of this discontent. His frequent visits to the Treaty Ports brought him in touch with merchant opinion, and the task of collecting data and writing was congenial to him. He saw in the situation a chance to exercise his talent and an opportunity for advancement.

It happened that at this time there was much anti-colonial feeling at home particularly on the part of ardent free-traders who objected when colonies cost money. Parliamentary grants of money to the colonies came in for close scrutiny, and the Hong Kong vote was particularly attacked. The result was that criticism of Hong Kong was sure of an attentive hearing in England. It was therefore to some

---

1 E. J. Eitel, *Europe in China*, London, 1895, p. 346.

extent fortuitous that Martin secured as much publicity as he did.

He was genuinely convinced that Hong Kong possessed such serious disadvantages that it should be given up in favour of Chusan. The weakness of his argument was that he failed to show that Chusan would be any less expensive, or that a colony was necessary at all. Giving evidence before the 1847 Select Committee, he repeated all the old arguments; the most valid criticism he made was that the failure of Hong Kong to grow in economic importance should be openly recognized, that the administrative expenditure should be reduced, and that the effort to make the Colony pay its way by taxation should be modified.

There is reason to believe that Martin was right in this respect and that Davis was moving too fast in forcing the new Colony to shoulder an excessive share of the cost of its public services. Concessions in fact had to be made. There was some substance too in Martin's contention that Chusan was to be preferred to Hong Kong, for the former was excellently placed at the mouth of the Yangtse River, and the phenomenal growth of Shanghai served to demonstrate the advantages of geography in that respect. The fact remains that Martin did not convince those who were able to judge impartially, and when the mood of despondency passed, his views ceased to appeal to the merchants.

He died at Sutton in Surrey on 6 September 1868.

11

WILLIAM THOMAS MERCER

WILLIAM THOMAS MERCER was born in 1822, took his B.A. degree at Exeter College, Oxford, and then studied law at the Inner Temple but did not take the Bar examination. He was the nephew of Sir John Davis, and on Sir John's appointment as Governor of Hong Kong in 1844, he came along as his uncle's private secretary. With such influential backing he did not have long to wait for promotion, and on the resignation of R. M. Martin in July 1845, he was given the responsible post of Colonial Treasurer, at first only in an acting capacity. Thus began an official career in Hong Kong which over the next twenty years took him to the highest positions in the public service of the Colony. Nepotism gave him his chance, but he owed his subsequent success to his own abilities.

The next opportunity came in 1847 when Chief Justice Hulme was suspended for drunkenness. Mercer took his place temporarily as a member of the Legislative Council, holding the seat until Hulme returned. In March 1849 on the expansion of the membership of the Legislative Council proposed by the next governor, Bonham, Mercer was appointed to an official seat as Treasurer, and three years later was appointed a member of the Executive Council. The departure of his uncle, therefore, did not affect his career adversely, or delay his advancement. In 1848, Bonham was ordered to make a full enquiry into the colonial establishment with the object of suggesting large economies. As part of this task, he reported on the chief officials in 27 December 1848, and his comment on Mercer was that he had "capacity far above the office he holds", that he was most eligible to succeed to the Colonial Secretary's office, and that generally he thought highly of his qualifications and attainment. This was high praise for a young man of twenty-six from a governor who had no reason to favour him.

He came to the front over the currency question, which became acute in Bonham's administration because of the fluctuation in the exchange and the high rate of exchange for silver dollars. A currency proclamation in 1845 had made various British and Indian coins legal tender and had laid down parities between them and the silver dollar. In January 1854 the Chief Justice ruled that where a contract had been made in dollars payment must be made in dollars, the currency proclamation notwithstanding. Mercer, with the Governor's approval, then brought a test case before the Supreme Court and secured a judgement that the land rents were to be payable in dollars as provided for in the lease. The Treasurer was criticized for this action by the land-holders, since dollars were standing at a considerable premium. In a memorandum, Mercer gave a résumé of the currency position and pointed out that by accepting sterling coins, the Colony was losing up to 15 per cent. of its revenue.

By 1854 he had become an important official. Bonham retired that year and Caine was made Lieutenant-Governor as part of the policy of economizing by reducing the scale of the Colony's establishment. Bonham's successor, Bowring, was made nominal Governor without salary. At the same time, the Secretary of State nominated Hillier as Colonial Secretary, and Mercer as Chief Magistrate in Hillier's place. This arrangement was altered by Caine, who wrote to the Duke of Newcastle on 15 April 1854 to say that Bowring, with the full agreement of Sir George Bonham and himself, had appointed Mercer to be Colonial Secretary and Auditor-General, at a lower salary, and Hillier was to remain as Chief Magistrate. Mercer was only thirty-two when he gained this promotion to the highest executive office under the Governor.

Bowring was impressed by him also, and referred to him in a private letter (10 March 1855) to Sir George Grey, Secretary of State, as "one of the most accomplished men in the Colony but an unwilling reformer". Mercer had little sympathy with Bowring's reforming zeal and was one of the officials on the Legislative Council who threw out Bowring's bill to construct a *praya* as part of a central reclamation scheme. In fact, Mercer added very largely to Bowring's troubles, though not perhaps deliberately. He was granted home leave of eighteen months, subsequently extended, so that he was away from February 1857 to November 1859. He was fortunate to be out of the Colony during the period of the scandals which marred Sir John Bowring's governorship. But his absence and that of the Attorney-General created difficulties for Bowring, who needed loyal senior officials to carry out his programme of reform.

Mercer recommended his college friend, W. T. Bridges, a prominent local barrister, for appointment as Acting Attorney-General and then as Acting Colonial Secretary deputizing for himself. Bridges, who became Dr. Bridges after receiving an honorary D.C.L. in 1856, was an unscrupulous lawyer, and a strong character who had made a fortune out of the Colony by dubious means. Bowring had hesitated to agree to Bridges's acting appointments, but he was driven to it by shortage of senior officials. Later, when Bridges got into trouble over the Caldwell case and the opium monopoly case, Bowring wrote home admitting his weakness in appointing Bridges to high acting positions when he knew that the lawyer had acquired his money by doubtful expedients. He added that he had been persuaded because Bridges had been strongly recommended by Mercer, who had argued that Bridges's conduct of his own affairs was a private matter, of no concern to the Government unless it became the subject of a criminal prosecution. By good fortune Mercer was able to remain aloof from the scandal, but since Bridges had been employed on his recommendation, he was not held blameless in the public mind. Mercer felt it necessary to dissociate himself from Bridges, and writing to the Duke of Newcastle on 23 August 1862, he disingenuously averred, "I have had a long and friendly but never an intimate acquaintance with Dr. Bridges".

In September 1859 Sir Hercules Robinson assumed the governorship, with the task of reforming the civil service and enquiring into abuses. Bridges retired to England before the enquiry was held. Mercer tried unsuccessfully to leave the Colony at this time, though it cannot be assumed that he did so from any sense of guilt. Indeed, throughout the whole enquiry he was above suspicion. In May 1859 he applied to be moved to a healthier colony and stated that both Lord Carnarvon and Lord Stanley had held out to him some hope of this change while he had been on leave. In May 1860 he applied for a retirement pension, though he was only thirty-eight years of age. He pointed out that Caine and Hulme had just been granted pensions and that he had more service than Hulme and almost as much as Caine. Robinson considered him too young to be pensioned, and paid tribute to him for his most cordial co-operation.

Next year Mercer applied without success for the governorship of the Straits Settlements, and, in supporting this application, Robinson wrote to say that all in the Colony gave him good testimony. In 1863 he again applied for this governorship with a like result.

In the summer of 1861 Mercer became the Officer Administering the Government while the Governor went on a brief vacation trip to Japan, and in October of that year he went home on leave, returning in July 1862. He assumed the government of Hong Kong almost immediately while Robinson went on leave, and acted in that capacity from July 1862 to February 1864, and again in the interval between the departure of Robinson in March 1865 and the arrival of the next governor, Sir Richard Graves MacDonnell, in March 1866. Thus for nearly three years he was in charge of the administration of the Colony.

In December 1862, Mercer, emulating Caine and Johnston, applied for a C.B. as a reward for his services, but there is no record in the Colonial Office archives of any reply. Robinson, who was at home at the time, defended Mercer's request "since we now have the continental system of profuse decorations" and pointed out that

Mercer could easily have made his application indirectly through friends.

When Robinson was moved to Ceylon as Governor, Mercer naturally hoped to be his successor. In sending in his application, Robinson wrote that he had already recommended Mercer and thought such an appointment would be a fitting recognition of long and faithful service, but the reply came that Sir Richard MacDonnell had already accepted the post.

Mercer's administration was competent, without being marked by any outstanding success or failure. Eitel says that he followed faithfully the policy laid down by Robinson[1], yet he admits[2] that the general feeling in the island was that Robinson was fortunate in having such a competent official as Mercer upon whom to rely. Mercer was an eager supporter of the new Pokfulam water-works scheme and organized the extension of the hospital, and Eitel states that it was he who composed the difficulties that had arisen when gas was introduced into the Colony in 1864. He strongly advocated the retention of flogging of criminals in face of the demand from home for more humane penal methods, and it fell to Mercer to organize the hulk for the reception of prisoners pending the erection of a new prison on Stonecutters Island. He wrote a strong condemnation of the proposal to impose on the Colony an annual military contribution of £20,000. The larger issues of this period—the quarrel with the military over Kowloon and the new currency and mint projects—Robinson appears from the records to have kept firmly in his own hands.

Mercer's dispatches were well-written documents and he showed a capacity to marshal his facts and present a well-argued case. Piracy was rapidly becoming serious and the navy accused the Colony of harbouring and supplying pirates, who used Hong Kong junks for their piratical activities. Mercer demanded proof, asking how Hong Kong junks were recognized as such on the open seas. He demanded to know why they had not been brought in, and said that if they were not Hong Kong junks he was not concerned with their doings, "real or supposed". He had difficulty with the Chinese authorities over the rendition of Chinese criminals. He had been ordered to pass an ordinance on this subject, and one clause provided that as a condition of handing over a criminal, a guarantee against the use of torture was to be given. The Viceroy at Canton refused to give this guarantee on the ground that the 1858 Treaty of Tientsin had provided for the rendition of Chinese criminals unconditionally. In the end, Mercer was able to arrange for a

1 E. J. Eitel, *Europe in China*, London, 1895, p. 354.
2 ibid., p. 406.

satisfactory assurance. Mercer panicked badly over the possible danger from American warships during the American Civil War, and urged the need of an increased garrison to protect the Colony. This invited the comment from the Colonial Office that Mercer had earlier opposed the island's military contribution on the ground that it was not necessary to defend the Colony. As Acting Governor his function was of course to administer and not to initiate.

His failure to secure a governorship left him an embittered and disappointed man. He allowed Robinson's successor, Sir Richard MacDonnell, and his family to arrive and find Government House unprovided with the commonest household necessities. MacDonnell wrote privately to the Permanent Under-Secretary of State, Sir Frederick Rogers, in May 1867 that Mercer was going on leave and probably would not return, and that "he seems discontented and used up"; he added, "He is a gentlemanly, scholarly person", and wished him a good appointment. MacDonnell was a strong character, energetic and self-willed, and soon embarked on far-reaching schemes of reform aimed at the elimination of piracy and the removal of police abuses. Mercer could not easily work with such a man and MacDonnell wrote home on one occasion to say that he just went ahead without Mercer and acted as his own Colonial Secretary by handling the correspondence himself. Mercer applied for leave on medical grounds and left the Colony on 13 May 1867. After some demur he was allowed to retire on pension, being then only forty-five years of age. He lived only twelve years longer, dying at Reading on 23 May 1879.

The view in Hong Kong was that he was an able man, but that his association with Bridges and Caldwell was the cause of his failure to reach a higher position in the colonial service. He was a competent official, but whether he would have made a good governor is doubtful. Eitel summed him up with the remark that everybody agreed that he deliberately "let well enough alone".

12

CHARLES BATTEN HILLIER

HILLIER WAS not a man of colourful personality. Over a period of thirteen years from 1843 to 1856, he played an important role in the history of Hong Kong as Assistant Magistrate and then as Chief Magistrate. He was a public figure of some influence and was closely concerned with the early life of the Colony. In those years the most pressing problem was the creation of an ordered society in which the law should be respected by a largely lawless vagabond population, both European and Chinese. The magistrates came in for continuous criticism in performing this thankless task, which was made all the more arduous by the lack of an efficient police force.

C. B. Hillier was appointed an Assistant Magistrate on 26 June 1843 at a salary of £500 a year, and with Johnston and Caine was one of the first men in the Colony to be appointed a J.P. He had had some experience of court work as a junior clerk but his chief qualification for the post was his friendship with Major William Caine, who had been Magistrate since the beginning of the Colony, and had become Chief Magistrate. This sort of appointment was not unusual in the early days of Hong Kong, for men with suitable qualifications were almost impossible to get, and the few who were available were attracted to the better paid commercial posts.

Hillier had followed the sea as a career, and had come to the Far East as the Second Mate of a merchant ship. He was still under twenty years of age when he left the ship in Hong Kong and joined a merchant firm, Fergusson Leighton & Co., and when it failed in 1842, he secured the post of clerk in the Magistrate's Court under Caine. He showed willingness and competence, and Caine took a great liking to the young man, treating him almost as a son. As soon as an opportunity arose, he recommended Hillier to Sir Henry Pottinger for the post of Assistant Magistrate, at first in Stanley on the south side of the island, and later at Victoria, and so Hillier found himself embarked on an important official career on the island.

When the Admiralty Court was established in 1844, he was appointed its Recording Officer, and in the year following was appointed as Coroner in place of Edward Farncomb. Farncomb was the first solicitor to practise in Hong Kong being admitted at the opening session of the Supreme Court in October 1844. He arrived in Hong Kong during the war with China and described himself as "of London" and "an attorney at law and conveyancer". He was appointed Coroner in September 1842 but the emoluments attached to the post were left open pending the advice of the Attorney-General who did not arrive until 1844. He was then offered $5 per inquest subject to the submission of a full report of each case, and to find his own office and clerical assistance. He threw up the post in disgust in April 1845 claiming that the sum offered did not cover the cost of the paper required.

Hillier served temporarily as Chief Magistrate on two brief occasions when Caine was Colonial Secretary. In May 1846 he married the daughter of The Rev. W. H. Medhurst, of the London Missionary Society, a prominent missionary in the Far East. His chance of permanent promotion came in 1847 when Bruce, the Colonial Secretary, was promoted to a governorship. Caine became Colonial Secretary in his place, and after some delay Hillier was given the position of Chief Magistrate. In four years, and while still a comparatively young man, he secured one of the most responsible posts in the government. He had been trained by Caine and he carried on the Caine tradition of severity linked with a complete impartiality. Reading the records, there is no doubt that what was administered in the Magistrates' Courts was not so much the law as a species of rough justice, but lawlessness in the Colony was appalling, and the problem of controlling a Chinese population was quite novel.

Hillier was criticized frequently for his mistakes and for his complete lack of legal training. Decisions were given contrary to the evidence, there were irregularities over the taking of evidence, and there must frequently have been miscarriages of justice. In 1846, by Hillier's order, thirteen men were flogged and imprisoned who were subsequently proved to be innocent and were freed by a writ of habeas corpus. Yet he gained the respect of the Chinese in the same way that Caine had done, because he showed himself to be no respecter of persons. He was criticized in Parliament by Sir John Bowring, later to become Governor the Colony, on the severity of the floggings which were ordered. The particular incident which gave rise to this protest occurred in April 1846. A policeman had arrested a Chinese carrying timber which he suspected was stolen. As they passed some Chinese houses, the constable and his prisoner were stoned, and the latter escaped. Police were later sent into the area, and since they were unable to identify those who had committed the offence, they arrested all Chinese discovered to be without tickets of registration. They were all fined five dollars, or in default, were to receive twenty strokes with the rattan and to have their queues cut. Fifty-four men were unable to find five dollars and they were flogged. There was a great deal of protest from Chinese and others against this sort of wholesale flogging, which was always administered in public.

The Magistrates defended their attitude by arguing that many criminals from the neighbouring province had made their way to Hong Kong, that triad societies encouraged the worst elements, that crime was so prevalent as to make severe measures essential, and finally, that ordinary imprisonment was not regarded by the Chinese as punishment, since jail conditions were probably an improvement upon their normal standards of living.

It is difficult to judge Hillier fairly on these issues; undoubtedly he closely followed Caine's methods, and if it is true that many Chinese suffered severely, it must be admitted that the Magistrates' determination to suppress disorder commanded respect. Both Caine and Hillier frequently patrolled the town to supervise personally the general policing arrangements.

Hillier came in for criticism on the ground that he too often carried out the orders of the Executive Government, and was not sufficiently jealous of the independence of his court. On one occasion in 1846, for example, he had three Portuguese, suspected of being fugitives from justice, arrested and sent back to Macao. This was done on the instructions of Sir John Davis, Governor of Hong Kong, acting on a request made by Macao's Governor, Amaral. This case brought Hillier a great deal of trouble. The Portuguese were acquitted in Macao, and two of them then took legal action against Hillier, claiming $25,000 damages. He was forced to brief counsel for his defence. The proceedings were eventually abandoned, but he had great difficulty in getting the Home Government to defray the expenses for the legal fees he had been obliged to incur, despite the whole case arising out of his public duties as a magistrate, because the Secretary of State ruled that he should have been defended by the Attorney-General.

In spite of much criticism, Hillier's promotion to Chief Magistrate in October 1847 showed that he had the confidence of the authorities. The 1847 Parliamentary Committee of Enquiry into the China Trade was a help to him, for Captain Balfour, Consul at Shanghai, referred in his evidence to the great improvement in law and order in Hong Kong between 1843 and 1847 and praised Hillier, saying he was "a zealous officer and has well qualified himself for the performance of his police duties by acquiring the Chinese language". But Caine was his great ally and patron. "Mr. Hillier was almost like a child of my own", he admitted, many years later. In 1847 at the request of the Governor, Hillier presented a report on the working of the opium monopoly and as a result of his recommendations the monopoly was abolished and replaced by a system of licences.

Hillier went home on leave in July 1852, after fifteen years of continuous service in the Far East. While at home he became embroiled with the Prince of Armenia, and there is a letter in the Colonial Office records in which the Prince threatened legal action against Hillier for calumny. Nothing seems to have come of this, however.

Hillier returned to the Colony in February 1853. The next year he became a member of the Legislative Council, and shortly afterwards, a provisional member of the Executive Council. He was appointed chairman of a Commission of Enquiry into the abuses of coolie emigration, and in 1854 was appointed to the special post of Emigration Agent to supervise Chinese coolie emigration and to see that the provisions of the Chinese Passengers Act were carried out.

In 1854 Governor Sir George Bonham retired. Sir John Bowring was made nominal Governor, without salary, and Major Caine became Lieutenant-Governor in charge of the government of the Colony. Caine now made Hillier Acting Colonial Secretary in his footsteps and the natural expectation was that Hillier would secure the permanency. There was some delay due to the reorganization of the governorship, and in the end Mercer became Colonial Secretary, and Hillier had to be content to stay where he was. When the home authorities reversed the decision to entrust the government of the Colony to a Lieutenant-Governor and Bowring assumed full charge in 1855, the change was a blow to Hillier's hopes.

Conditions further changed for Hillier on the arrival in 1856 of T. Chisholm Anstey as Attorney-General. Almost immediately, Anstey criticized Hillier in his conduct of the Magistrate's Court. When serious cases were remitted from that court to the Supreme Court for trial, Anstey complained that the depositions were "slovenly and careless" and that even evidence of identification was omitted. In one particularly glaring case, Hillier was sent for by the Chief Justice at the instance of the Attorney-General and placed in the witness box to explain why full evidence was not written out when the case was sent forward. Hillier was questioned, and expressed ideas on the nature of evidence which caused the judge to raise his eyebrows in surprise. The incident clearly showed that there must have been considerable irregularity in his court. The disclosures were disturbing, though it did not necessarily follow that there had been a corresponding amount of injustice. Hillier was clearly upset at the disclosures, and a few days later he appeared in court and asked the judge for protection against Anstey's attacks. He is reported to have said, "My Lord, I think it very unfair that a public servant in my position should be maligned behind his back, and I should feel much obliged if you would restrain Mr. Anstey from using the uncalled-for censure which he unsparingly uses against every person". Hillier also said he had appealed to the Colonial Secretary in London, a fact which obviously made it difficult for the judge to intervene in the dispute, and the upshot was that the Attorney-General was asked to draw up a memorandum for the guidance of the Magistrate. Hillier, in a fit of pique, then gave his view that if the Government found him unsatisfactory, it could find someone else for the job of Chief Magistrate, a proposition to which Anstey gave his cordial assent!

The incident left Hillier estranged and embittered. In February 1854 he unsuccessfully applied for a police appointment in England giving as his reasons for wishing to leave the Colony ill-health and the education of his children. A fortunate way out soon came. Bowring, who had recently visited Siam and secured a trade treaty with that country, recommended Hillier for the post of Consul at Bangkok. News came that his appointment was confirmed, and on 10 May 1856, only a few weeks after his quarrel with Anstey, he left the Colony for Bangkok. After a short interval he was succeeded as Chief Magistrate in Hong Kong by a fully qualified barrister, Henry Tudor Davies. At his departure there were many demonstrations of goodwill towards him. "An independent, painstaking and conscientious official", one newspaper called him. The Chinese showed their respect and esteem by a great procession to his house to present gifts and an address. A contemporary account described the procession as "accompanied by music and bearing two splendid sedan chairs containing a basin of water, and the other a looking-glass, implying that his character was as pure as water and as unstained as glass".

The move to Siam proved to be tragic. Quite soon after he had arrived in Bangkok he contracted dysentery, and he died on 14 October 1856 still a comparatively young man, not yet forty years of age. In that short time he had made himself popular amongst Siamese and foreigners, and the mile-long funeral procession was attended by two members of the Siamese royal family.

Hillier cannot be called a great character, but like many of his contemporaries he was a self-made man who by his personal abilities had risen in the public service. Energy, conscientiousness in the performance of his duties, and integrity were his chief virtues, and they were not possessed by all officials then in the Colony. He was criticized for being untrained in law, but he performed his thankless task in Hong Kong with honesty and impartiality. At his death, the Press commented that a fully trained lawyer might have dispensed more law to the Chinese, but it was improbable that he would have dispensed more justice. Hillier Street perpetuates his name in the Colony.

13

THOMAS CHISHOLM ANSTEY

THOMAS CHISHOLM ANSTEY had a short but remarkably stormy career in Hong Kong. He was appointed Attorney-General in 1855 and arrived in the Colony on 30 January 1856; two and a half years later, on 7 August 1858, he was suspended by the Governor, Sir John Bowring, and he left the Colony on 30 January 1859, three years to the day after his arrival. Anstey was a most unusual man, fearless, energetic and upright, but rather unbalanced, and he took upon himself the burden of combating all the abuses, imagined or real, with which he thought the local government was riddled. Since he was not the sort of man to be easily deflected from a task that appealed to him as a kind of crusade, it can be readily imagined that these years were years of turbulence. The public life of Hong Kong reached its nadir.

No wonder *The Times* referred to the Colony as "this noisy, bustling, quarrelsome, discontented and insalubrious little island" and said, "The sound of the name [of Hong Kong] in our Parliamentary proceedings never bodes good to our national interests. It is always connected with some fatal pestilence, some doubtful war or some discreditable internal squabble". Anstey's career in Hong Kong may have been short, but it was certainly exciting.

Anstey was the son of one of the early settlers in Van Dieman's Land, but was born and educated in England. He became a student at the newly-founded University of London, and was called to the Bar at the Middle Temple in 1839, at the age of twenty-three. He was attracted by the Oxford Movement and was among those who followed Newman into the Roman Catholic Church and he continued an ardent Catholic all his life. He secured a judicial appointment in Van Dieman's Land, but soon quarrelled with the authorities, returned to England, and held a legal appointment in the north for a brief period, but resigned for similar reasons. Eventually, he settled down as Professor of Law and Jurisprudence at a Roman Catholic College near Bath, and produced a number of works on the legal position of Roman Catholics in England with particular reference to the weaknesses, from their point of view, of the Catholic Emancipation Act of 1829. He was thus led to take an increasing interest in politics and particularly in Irish questions, and in 1847 he gave up his professorship to become Member of Parliament for Youghal, a small borough in County Cork.

In Parliament he gained notoriety as one of the more recalcitrant and argumentative members, who possessed not only strong views on diverse subjects but an equally strong determination to make them heard. He attacked Lord Palmerston, though he was nominally a member of Palmerston's party, on every subject from foreign policy to home rule for Ireland and Scotland, and currency reform. There was no department of the national policy upon which he was not prepared to be authoritative. He showed in Parliament the same qualities he was later to show in Hong Kong: energy, ability, and tenacity, combined with a tragic lack of balance and moderation. His excessive faith in his own ability to put other people right led him never to miss a chance of addressing the House, and though he was a good speaker he rarely gained a sympathetic audience.

Such was the man who was made Attorney-General of the Colony by Sir William Molesworth in 1856. He had been defeated in the General Election of 1852 and was looking to the Government he had so continuously attacked for an appointment. It was said by some political commentators that Palmerston had done well in sending so awkward a supporter to one of the most remote colonies.

Anstey arrived in the Colony on 30 January 1856. From what has already been said of the man, it must come as no surprise that within six months he had created a furore by charges of corruption and oppression, and had initiated a series of inter-departmental quarrels, personal animosities, and libel actions unparalleled in the Colony's history. It is small wonder that the rather elderly Governor, Sir John Bowring, who was himself quite a liberal reformer, found Anstey's crusade so devastating that he decided calm could be restored only at the price of Anstey's suspension.

Less than a month after his arrival he addressed the Bar on etiquette, indirectly attacking Dr. W. T. Bridges, a leading barrister, and later the Acting Colonial Secretary. The two men became bitter enemies. In March, he criticized the way in which Hillier, the Chief Magistrate, conducted his cases, saying that witnesses were not even properly identified, and evidence was not properly taken; Anstey thought this was discreditable and said so in open court. This brought Hillier to the Supreme Court to complain to the Chief Justice, and the ensuing altercation between the Chief Magistrate and Attorney-General showed clearly the former's ignorance of legal procedure.

In May, Anstey accused the Chief Justice, John Walter Hulme, of exceeding the bounds of temperance; this was extremely serious because the Judge had been suspended eight years earlier on a charge of drunkenness, though, on appeal to the home authorities, the verdict had not been upheld, and the sentence had been quashed.

THOMAS CHISHOLM ANSTEY

Anstey could not have trodden on more dangerous ground. When he was asked to withdraw, he merely repeated the charge in the Legislative Council, and Bowring had no option but to report the matter to the Secretary of State for the Colonies at home. The reply came that Anstey was to be reprimanded and threatened with suspension unless he proved his accusation or withdrew it. Anstey then withdrew, but his recklessness had unnecessarily made another enemy. In the same month, Anstey's reforming zeal led him to induce the Governor to sanction an enquiry into court procedure, legal fees, and costs, as a result of which an ordinance was passed controlling fees and costs, much to the annoyance of the legal profession, which had not been consulted.

Then Anstey attacked W. H. Mitchell, the Assistant Magistrate, who was also Sheriff and Coroner. This was over the supply of special food to some condemned prisoners who were subsequently reprieved. Anstey made an enquiry, considered Mitchell had been guilty of extortion and instituted proceedings against him. The Sheriff appealed to the Secretary of State, and also brought a legal action against Anstey for malicious slander. Bowring wanted the proceedings stopped pending the reference home, but Anstey insisted on maintaining the charge, and Mitchell pressed his charge too. At this same time Anstey criticized the police whom he accused of extortion, alleging that when off duty they roamed about plundering people, and produced their crown as badges of their authority only to assist in their exactions. In June 1856 the case against Mitchell was heard, and amid the applause of the Europeans in court, he was acquitted. Anstey was also acquitted and so nothing was gained by these actions except that much scandal and ill-will was generated. Speaking in the action against Mitchell, the Attorney-General declared his view that Hong Kong "was a petty colony, cram full of abuses and oppression, but no man would speak out"; and in a private letter home, which was published in a London newspaper, he referred to the Colony as "the noisome scandal of the East". He left no doubt that he was out to wage war against these conditions.

In November 1856 Anstey's activities created a riot amongst the Chinese. This concerned a recently enacted Buildings and Nuisances Ordinance which was much disliked both by the Chinese and by the Magistrates, who, in a test case, gave an interpretation contrary to the intention of those who framed the ordinance. Anstey personally patrolled the Chinese quarter with police, and from direct observation picked out offenders, forcing the police to issue a summons in each case. When the cases came on he sat on the bench with the Chief Magistrate, in virtue of being himself a J.P., and heavy fines were imposed. The Chinese replied by closing their shops, pressure being applied to those unwilling to do so; the Government called out military patrols, and issued a proclamation against the closing of shops and markets. The Chinese presented their grievances, and the affair passed off without further incident. It led to the appointment of Caldwell as Registrar-General and Protector of Chinese the following month.

In the spring of 1857, Mercer, the Colonial Secretary, went on leave, and Dr. W. T. Bridges was appointed to act in his place, much to the disgust of Anstey. The latter had now openly quarrelled with the Governor, and the two men rarely spoke to each other. All communication was by letter. But scenes between Anstey and Bowring at a meeting of the Royal Asiatic Society, and between Anstey and Bridges in the law court, left people in no doubt about the personal animosities which had now developed. There was, however, to be a short lull before the storm broke. Anstey secured six months' leave on medical grounds, and from July to December visited India. He left the Colony a not unpopular figure; his undoubted honesty and fearlessness were regarded as admirable qualities which the Colony needed, and there was a disposition to excuse him if his energy in exposing abuse occasionally outran his discretion.

For some time there had been a suspicion that both Bridges and Caldwell, who were close personal friends, were using their positions as high government officers for their own financial advantage, and were engaging in shady transactions. Soon after returning to the Colony, Anstey had opportunities of concerning himself with these scandals, opportunities which he was constitutionally incapable of neglecting. In connection with the Opium Ordinance of 17 March 1858, Bridges was accused in the Press of favouring the holder of the opium monopoly from whom he received a retaining fee as legal adviser. Bridges naturally resented the imputations and demanded an enquiry. A Committee of Enquiry was set up consisting of the Chief Magistrate, Davies, and a local merchant, J. M. Dent, and it eventually reported that while Bridges had not been guilty of any breach of honour or of honesty, he had been at fault in accepting a retaining fee from the opium monopoly-holder at the time he was dealing with the Opium Ordinance in his official capacity as Acting Colonial Secretary. Anstey came out strongly against Bridges during the enquiry and the Governor reported in a dispatch to London that the Attorney-General "has been most actively engaged in the present attempt to discredit and condemn Dr. Bridges".

It was now Caldwell's turn. Caldwell was a brilliant linguist employed as an interpreter and Assistant Superintendent of Police, and had recently been appointed Registrar-General and Protector of Chinese. He had married a Chinese and was suspected of shady transactions regarding brothels, and also of a suspicious liaison with local pirates through his friendship with Ma Chow Wong, who had been convicted of piracy in spite of all Caldwell could do to save him.

Anstey brought to the Governor information against the character and conduct of Caldwell. Since Bowring took no notice, Anstey resorted to the drastic step of bringing this information before the Legislative Council in May 1858; at the same time he resigned his position as Justice of the Peace saying that he refused to serve with Caldwell on the same bench of magistrates. Bowring was now forced to take action, and a Commission of Enquiry under the chairmanship of C. St. G. Cleverly, the Surveyor-General, was deputed to examine nineteen charges against the unfortunate Registrar-General. Anstey protested that these nineteen charges were not his charges, and it is true that he had refused to supply them in writing, but they were based on the information he had supplied.

It is impossible to enter into the details of this cause *célèbre*, but the outcome was that the commission found only four of the charges proved, and concluded that though Caldwell's appointment as Justice of the Peace had been injudicious, yet there was not sufficient reason to remove him from office. Bowring regarded this verdict as clearing Caldwell and as condemning Anstey for causing unnecessary scandal. He sent a copy of the findings to Anstey and at the same time warned him that unless he could justify his conduct he would be suspended. Anstey's reply did not satisfy the Governor, and the question of suspending him was brought before the Executive Council. The Council passed several resolutions stating that Anstey had been engaged in a "long series of officialized quarrels and contentions" characterized by "violent and vituperative language"; that he had been threatened with suspension for slandering the Chief Justice; that repeated warnings had had no effect on him; that his official advice had frequently been injudicious and intemperate; and finally, that his suspension would be considered at the next meeting after Anstey had been advised of these resolutions and given an opportunity of defending himself. Anstey in reply repeated his charges against Bridges and Caldwell, and asked for a fair trial. On 7 August 1858 the Council suspended him, and Bowring sent home a dispatch of prodigious length giving a full review and defence of his proceedings.

Anstey remained in the Colony as a practising barrister for a few more equally stormy months, during which the spate of libel suits continued. He defended William Tarrant, editor of *The Friend of China*, who was prosecuted by the Government for libel in connection with his comment on the Caldwell enquiry. It was brought out at that enquiry that certain books which belonged to the pirate Ma Chow Wong, and which would have provided evidence against Caldwell, had been burnt. Tarrant implied that this had been deliberate, and that Caldwell had escaped more severe censure by this mean and contemptible trick. Tarrant was acquitted, and the verdict was regarded as a triumph for Anstey.

On 30 January 1859, exactly three years after his arrival, Anstey left the Colony, and on arrival in England he learnt that his suspension had been confirmed. He continued for some time to appeal to public opinion and to successive Colonial Secretaries to get the decision reversed, particularly when it was announced in Parliament that a new governor would be sent out to make a full enquiry into the subject of malpractices in the Hong Kong public service. That enquiry was held in 1861 by Sir Hercules Robinson, and as a result Caldwell was proved to have had criminal associations with pirates, and was dismissed. Anstey was thus partially vindicated. He had gone to Bombay to join the local Bar, and when the dismissal of Caldwell was announced he hurried home to make a final attempt to secure a decision in his favour. The Colonial Office did not, however, change its mind, and Anstey returned to Bombay where he died in August 1873 at the early age of fifty-seven.

That he was an extraordinary man, none will deny. He was zealous, but erratic; energetic but impetuous; fearless yet not very practical. A newspaper comment was that "he has clean hands and a keen sense of public duty, and had we had a Governor who could have restrained his impetuosity instead of rousing his indignation, he would have been a great blessing to this colony". *The Times* referred to him as a man of "imperfectly-regulated energies".

It was a tragedy that Anstey, who could have done so much good, did so much harm. On his departure from Hong Kong he received no thanks from the community on whose behalf he had battled so unsparingly, and was dependent on the hospitality of an American gentleman during the few days between selling his house and embarking.

14

DANIEL RICHARD CALDWELL

DANIEL RICHARD CALDWELL gained a lasting local reputation as a linguist. His knowledge of Cantonese, Malay, Hindustani, and Portuguese made him almost indispensable to the Government of the Colony, most particularly in the administration of justice. In spite of his brilliance as a linguist, and of the crying need for such an accomplished man, he became a very controversial figure and he resigned twice, and was dismissed once from the government service. He failed to attain an assured official position. He was never quite trusted and was suspected of being concerned in too many questionable transactions; and as a man of mixed blood and married to a Chinese, he possibly was not completely accepted socially. Yet there is plenty of evidence to show that he was regarded as a European and that positions of trust and responsibility were open to him. His failure is more probably due to personal failings: there was always something slightly shady about him. His contacts with the underground world of early Hong Kong were too close to enable him to remain uncompromised. Scandal and intrigue seemed to shadow him.

The details of Caldwell's early life are obscure. Sir John Bowring, who in 1858 was forced to institute an enquiry into Caldwell's fitness to hold a position in the Hong Kong Government, described him, in a dispatch to the Colonial Office in London dated 9 August 1858, as "a man of mixed blood, born at Singapore; he is married to a Chinese woman converted to Christianity, by whom he has a large family, some of whom are now being educated in England". Norton Kyshe[1] says that Caldwell was born in St. Helena, and quotes as his authority a pamphlet said to have been written by Caldwell himself in defence of his character and official actions at the time of the Bowring enquiry. This pamphlet goes on to say that he "was employed in various mercantile firms in Singapore, Hong Kong, and Canton. Subsequently he returned to Singapore, where he joined the Commissariat Department, coming afterwards with Major Caine in June 1840 in the same fleet, from Singapore to Chusan". But he could not have been employed in Hong Kong, as he says, because Hong Kong had not then been founded; neither was Caine a Major at that date. So Caldwell's account of himself must be

---

1 J. W. Norton Kyshe, *History of the Laws and Courts of Hong Kong*, 2 vols., London, 1898, Vol. 1, p. 82.

suspected of some inaccuracy. Apparently, he was born in 1816, three years before Singapore was placed under the control of the English East India Company; Bowring may therefore have been quite wrong in supposing Caldwell to have been born in Singapore. But it is fairly clear that Caldwell must have lived there for a considerable period before coming to the China coast with the 1840 British expedition. That would be consistent with his expert knowledge of Malay, Portuguese, and Hindustani, and he could have acquired a knowledge of Cantonese there which he was subsequently able to improve. He secured what must have been a temporary appointment with the Commissariat Department of the British Expedition to China, and when the war was over and the expedition withdrawn, he accepted an appointment with the Hong Kong Government.

In January 1843 he became an interpreter on Caine's recommendation, for duty primarily in the Magistrate's Court at a salary of $50 a month. In July this was increased to $125 a month. Then in September 1844, with the arrival of Chief Justice Hulme and the establishment of the Supreme Court, Caldwell was made Interpreter at that court, at a salary of £400 per year, making a total for the two posts he held, of £712 per year. In due course, the Audit Department at home caught up on the circumstance that Caldwell was occupying and receiving salary for two posts, and an explanation was demanded. The Governor, Sir John Davis, urged that the irregularity be overlooked, particularly since the Chief Justice had declared that it would be quite impossible to proceed with the business of the court without his services, and Caldwell had himself been paying a substitute to act in the Police Court.

Shortly thereafter he had to give up the Supreme Court post, and without warning he found his salary reduced by more than half. Later in this same year, 1846, he was made Assistant Superintendent of Police at an additional £125 per annum. Then in October 1847, he was suddenly arrested for debt and had to resign his appointments; he managed to make an agreement with his creditors, emerged from jail, and was re-appointed in December 1847. He explained quite reasonably, that his salary had been abruptly cut and that he had got into difficulties because he had begun to build himself a house. He was re-appointed on condition that he lived at the Central Police Station. May, the Superintendent of Police, said he considered Caldwell's explanation reasonable, that residence at the Central Police Station would provide an economical and regular life for him, and that he was attentive, zealous, and willing. Hillier, the Chief Magistrate, reported that Caldwell possessed latent qualities which, if exerted and accompanied by good conduct *"may* [author's italics] make him a most useful and respectable government servant". Clearly Hillier was not too sure!

The next six years up to 1855 were, for Caldwell, years of triumph, and yet of continuing disappointment. He played a leading part in the attack on piracy, accompanied the naval expeditions in 1849, and supplied the intelligence upon which they were entirely dependent and to which they owed their success in clearing the surrounding waters of pirates. He became Acting Superintendent of Police and, in addition to his police duties, he was virtually indispensable as an interpreter in the courts. Yet various changes in the interpretation arrangements were suggested from time to time with inevitable fluctuations in his emoluments. It is small wonder that he became dissatisfied. In 1855 he applied for an increase in salary, and somewhat bitterly remarked that he was then getting less than he got twelve years earlier, despite his increased responsibilities, and his assistance in the fight against piracy. Caine, then Lieutenant-Governor, reported that he showed undoubted zeal and general usefulness, but that he was unable to do any translation work since he was quite unfamiliar with the written language; and the Home Government refused the request. Caldwell resigned, and went into partnership with a Chinese, Ma Chow Wong, in the management of a small coastal steamer. This venture failed, and within a year he was back again in the government service as Registrar-General and Protector of Chinese, and as General Interpreter to the Government. He was made an official Justice of the Peace in virtue of the office he held, and given wide powers in dealing with the Chinese.

Just prior to Caldwell's re-appointment, a new Attorney-General, T. Chisholm Anstey, arrived in the Colony. Anstey proved to be an extraordinary sort of man who made himself a thorough nuisance by undertaking the self-imposed task of removing all the abuses and exposing all the corruption in Hong Kong. It was not long before Caldwell attracted his attention. In September 1857, Ma Chow Wong was found guilty of being in league with pirates and was condemned to fifteen years' transportation. Caldwell unfortunately was very closely associated with Ma Chow Wong, for the latter had supplied Caldwell with much of his information leading to the capture and punishment of pirates, and convictions had not infrequently been secured by Caldwell on the sole unsupported testimony of that informer. Caldwell did his utmost to save Ma; he petitioned against the verdict, and induced his friend Dr. Bridges, the Acting Colonial Secretary, to conduct an enquiry with a view to re-opening the case. The implication of course was that if Ma was in league with pirates, Caldwell was too. The suspicion was deepened by the fact that an earlier Chinese informant whom Caldwell had used had been found guilty of extortion in connection with piracy charges.

Anstey soon brought charges of complicity against Caldwell, and resigned his commission as a Justice of the Peace because he alleged that Caldwell was unfit to be a J.P., and he would not occupy a seat on the same bench with him. Anstey alleged that Caldwell had passed much of his life among Chinese outlaws and pirates, and that through his wife, who was a Chinese girl from a brothel, he had associated with some of the lowest Chinese in the Colony. Anstey then brought information against Caldwell before the Legislative Council, the chief charges being that he was unfit to be a Justice of the Peace, that he had had a scandalous connection with a brothel "namely brothel No. 3", that he was a speculator in brothels and brothel licences, and that he had had association with pirates.

A Commission of Enquiry was appointed under Cleverly, the Surveyor-General, which found that eight charges had no grounds, seven were unproved though there were some grounds for bringing them forward, and four were proved. The verdict was that though Caldwell's appointment as a Justice of the Peace was injudicious, there was no sufficient reason for revoking it. Anstey had denied that the charges brought against Caldwell were his charges; his argument was that they were points to be enquired into with a view to framing charges. Anstey had brought accusations against other officials, and he was accused of creating dissension and making unjustified accusations, with the result that he was suspended and returned to England. The Superintendent of Police, May, who had searched Ma Chow Wong's home at the time of his arrest, had discovered papers there in Caldwell's handwriting, with records of financial transactions between the two men. It transpired that these papers were taken to the Colonial Secretariat and burned on the instructions of Dr. Bridges. The implication was, of course, that there was a deliberate attempt to remove incriminating evidence, a circumstance which Tarrant, editor of the scurrilous *The Friend of China* called "a contemptible damnable trick...". For this, Tarrant was prosecuted for libel, but cleared himself, and secured damages against the Government. Much suspicion therefore still attached to Caldwell; the whole question came up in Parliament, and a further investigation was demanded.

Bowring earned the Home Government's displeasure by being unable to control the personal animosities, petty bickering, and scandal that marred his administration, and was virtually invited to resign. His successor as Governor, Sir Hercules Robinson, who arrived in the Colony in 1859, was instructed to make a fresh enquiry into the Caldwell case, and a Civil Service Abuses Enquiry was held. During the course of the enquiry, Caldwell had to make good some defalcations in his department by reduction of salary. He then stated he could not live on his income and asked to resign, but permission was refused. He absented himself from his office and refused to attend the enquiry any further, and presented his defence in writing extending to 329 foolscap pages! He was found to be unfit to continue in the public service by reason of his long association with the pirate Ma Chow Wong, and was dismissed from office.

Amusingly enough he was still indispensable to the Government. When Sir Richard Graves MacDonnell, Governor from 1866–72, attempted to control gambling by establishing licensed gaming houses, it was Caldwell who was called in by the Chinese keepers to make the scheme work by acting as their adviser in their relations with the Government. It was reported to the Home Government that he was getting "the monstrous salary" of $25,000 a year for this job. The termination of his official career did not prevent him from gaining the affluence he wanted.

Later he organized a body of Chinese watchmen, or "runners", through whom he was instrumental in detecting crime in the Colony and apprehending criminals, a task which the police force appeared quite unable to perform. In 1870 the Chief Justice, Judge Smale, frankly stated that Caldwell appeared to be the one person on whom the authorities were dependent in this matter. Indeed this extraordinarily versatile man retained the ability to make himself indispensable up to the time of his death on 2 October 1875, at the age of fifty-nine. Often his services were requested if he happened to be in court as a spectator. He also became a sort of counsellor to the leading members of the Chinese community by whom he was trusted and held in high esteem. In August 1866 at two successive meetings of the Legislative Council, tribute was paid to his abilities and services, particularly in the matter of the suppression of piracy, and Pauncefote, the Attorney-General, declared that the high opinion he held of Caldwell's abilities as an interpreter was shared by the whole Bar.

Undoubtedly he had ability and energy, and it may well be that the refusal to grant him a fixed and adequate financial position in the Government drove him to supplement his income by methods which created suspicion; he had risen from obscurity, and his effort to live well and educate his children in England may have had a similar effect. There may or may not have been a weakness of character or want of stability that unfitted him for high office, but one feels he had a legitimate grievance over his treatment. Eitel, who must have known him well, summed him up as "the best colloquial linguist Hong Kong ever possessed".

15

CHARLES MAY

AND THE EARLY HONG KONG POLICE FORCE

CHARLES MAY had the longest career of all the early Hong Kong officials; for thirty-four years following his arrival on 28 February 1845, he occupied important positions in the public service connected with the police and the Magistracy. These two departments evoked much criticism in the early turbulent days of the Colony, and it says much for his character and personality that he was able not only to survive into a more placid era, but also to gain for himself an honoured place in the community.

Sir Henry Pottinger, on his return to Hong Kong from the north at the conclusion of hostilities in 1842, was faced with innumerable problems involving the organization of the island and its relations with the mainland. The problem of policing, of enforcing a minimum of security of life and property, proved to be one of the most difficult. One reason was that the Colony attracted lawless elements, both European and Chinese, the type to be found perhaps in every seaport. On one occasion the Governor himself was jostled and insulted, to his extreme annoyance, by a crowd of Europeans as he was landing after a visit to Macao. Respectable Chinese kept away from the Colony, few Chinese brought their families or showed any intention of settling permanently in Hong Kong, and it was frequently alleged that only the scum of Canton came there. For many years the population was predominantly male, and constantly shifting. Under these circumstances burglaries, armed robberies, and assaults were frequent. The proximity of Chinese territory just across the harbour made escape all too easy. The Chief Magistrate, Caine, and his assistant, Hillier, wrestled valiantly with the problem by imposing harsh sentences, including flogging with the rattan. Hong Kong, as a community able to inspire its members with a sense of loyalty, was very much in the future.

What was needed at that time was an efficient police force, and that unfortunately was denied by the Home Government on the ground of expense. Pottinger recruited a temporary force from soldiers of good conduct as an emergency measure, and recommended that a police force should be recruited in England and sent out. He thought this would cost £6,000 a year, and that rates on property could provide half this sum. This proposal was regarded as much too costly, and it was decided to send out a superintendent and two inspectors from England as officers, but that the body of the force must be recruited locally. It was on this basis that the Police Ordinance was passed in May 1844 setting up the local police force and providing for its payment from a rate levied on property. Police forces were quite new, and criticism of the Hong Kong Force must be tempered by this fact. Sir Robert Peel set up the Metropolitan Police Force for London at Scotland Yard following legislation in 1829, but it was not until 1839 that an act was passed allowing the county police forces to be organized, and this process was to take some twenty years to complete, so that the Colony was actually ahead of some English counties in this respect.

In February 1844, Pottinger wrote home that he intended to make police appointments "to clear the drains"; a perusal of the dispatches on the subject leads to the conclusion that the officials of the Colony were not too clear about the functions and organization of the police. It was something of a new-fangled notion. Caine had been in charge of the police as Magistrate, but now a Captain Haly of the Madras Native Infantry was appointed Superintendent. He resigned, or was recalled to his regiment, after only a few days, and was replaced by Captain Bruce.

Such was the situation when the police officers from England arrived early in 1845. Charles May was appointed Superintendent, and he was accompanied by Thomas Smithers and Hugh MacGregor, who were to be Police Inspectors. MacGregor did not last long; he resigned in December 1846 and his place was taken by D. R. Caldwell, who later became the centre of considerable scandal. Smithers proved to be an efficient officer, but unfortunately he was drowned when a police boat was lost during a typhoon in August 1848.

May's father had been the first Superintendent of the Metropolitan Police Force set up for the London area by Sir Robert Peel in 1829; he had built up a great reputation and many wondered if the son would prove to be as good a policeman as the father. The younger May lost no time in pointing out the weaknesses of the police arrangements in Hong Kong and in suggesting the remedy. First of all there was continual change of personnel which led to inefficiency. For example, of the original ninety men who had joined from the army, only forty-seven remained by the time he had arrived. The rest had been dismissed or had died or left. Some of the former soldiers had volunteered for the police only as a means of securing freedom from the army and courted dismissal by deliberate acts of indiscipline. The army was unable to make good this perpetual turnover of men, and the experiment of using seamen was tried, but they proved even more unreliable than the troops. May recommended a police force of 168 men, 71 Europeans, 46 Indians, and 51 Chinese. He thought the Indians would do better if they were provided with barrack accommodation, while the Europeans were to be given food and quarters in the police stations, and encouraged to remain in the force by the offer of a pension amounting to half pay, after ten years' service. After some demur these conditions were agreed to, and at last the basis of police organization was laid.

The next great problem was to stop police extortion and collusion. Pay was low; a constable, or "private", as he was then called, received $14 a month, and he was naturally tempted to supplement it in any way that offered. Squeeze, extortion, collusion with prisoners to permit them to escape, all appear in the court proceedings which May was forced from time to time to take against his men. In 1847 four policemen were sentenced to twelve months' imprisonment for larceny, and hardly a year passed without some prosecution against members of the police. In August 1856 a constable named Randolph was sentenced to twelve months' imprisonment for demanding money with menaces from persons who were discovered gambling. He is reported as saying during his trial that "it was the usual practice for Chinese to pay $10 or $5 for their release whenever arrested by the police for gambling". In other words it was part of his defence that police extortion had almost the sanction of custom behind it. Chief Magistrate Caine considered that he had the right to exercise broad supervision over the police, and May was often subject to his interference, but there was little improvement. The abler constables sought the higher rewards that were readily obtainable in the employ of the merchant houses, and those who remained were too often of very poor material. Deaths from alcoholism were frequent.

May's attitude was one of dogged persistence in face of these difficulties. He administered his force competently, carried out his duties efficiently, and showed a strong sense of responsibility towards the community as well as towards his men. In 1853 when Hillier, then Chief Magistrate, went on leave, May was made Sheriff and Coroner, and also Assistant Magistrate to act when required, and he again acted as Assistant Magistrate in 1856. In 1857, owing to the war against China and to the fear of insecurity in the Colony, he was asked to resume his duties as Superintendent of Police.

In this year he was made the object of a personal attack for possessing brothel property. This charge arose from the circumstance that Anstey, the Attorney-General, who was ever waging a crusade against graft and malpractice in high places, accused W. H. Mitchell, the Assistant Magistrate, of giving decisions favourable to the interests of tenants of his own property in cases concerning the Buildings and Nuisances Ordinance. This charge led to a libel action by Mitchell against him, and Anstey was proved to have been quite wrong. Bowring issued a warning that government officers ought not to hold property, and since speculation in property was quite common among the officials, this led to trouble. May apparently resisted the pressure to sell out and incurred the Governor's censure. Bowring, writing home in August 1858 in connection with another incident, described May in these terms: "With one or two exceptions, I have been generally satisfied with Mr. May's service until within a very recent period. One of those exceptions was his ownership of a very notorious nest of brothels very near the Police Station, and which he very unwillingly got rid of after very considerable pressure from the Government. Mr. May's salary is £575 per annum with quarters; but by speculations in land and buildings, or from other sources, he has, I am told, realized a large sum of money here, and is therefore in independent circumstances". In defence of May it can only be said that most of the officials were adding to their incomes by outside speculation, and he was no exception. Anstey was right in finding much that was discreditable in the Colony.

May was dragged into the Caldwell affair in 1858. Caldwell was the brilliant linguist and Assistant-Superintendent of Police, who was accused by Anstey of association with piracy and brothels to such an extent as to make him unfit to hold high public office or to be a Justice of the Peace. Bowring held an official enquiry at which Caldwell was in large measure, though not completely, exonerated. A scandal arose, in that certain papers which incriminated Caldwell, and which were discovered by May when he searched the house of a pirate named Ma Chow Wong, were burnt at the Colonial Secretariat by the orders of Dr. Bridges, the Acting Colonial Secretary. William Tarrant, editor of *The Friend of China* accused Bridges of deliberate destruction of the evidence to save Caldwell. Tarrant was accused of libel and at the ensuing trial, at which Tarrant was acquitted, the facts came to light. May, however, put himself in the wrong by divulging confidential government information to the Press. Dr. Bridges, the Acting Colonial Secretary since February 1857, was a great friend of Caldwell and the two men became bitter opponents of May, who had provided the information regarding the paper found in Ma Chow Wong's house. Bridges did everything possible to damage May and have him replaced by Caldwell. Sir John Bowring who took the side of Bridges and Caldwell against Anstey and May, admitted in a dispatch home "...the fact undoubtedly existed, and I had more than once, on Mr. Bridges' representations, to reprimand Mr. May for neglect of or disobedience to, the directions of the acting Colonial Secretary; whereas no complaint was ever laid by Mr. Bridges against Mr. Caldwell".

The whole Caldwell affair caused great scandal. Anstey was suspended, and Sir John Bowring virtually recalled, and a new Governor, Sir Hercules Robinson, was sent out to make an enquiry and clear up the whole affair. Bridges, who had resigned the Acting Colonial Secretaryship and gone back to his full-time practice at the Bar, discreetly left the Colony soon after. Robinson set up the Civil Service Abuses Enquiry in 1860, and it reported on May and Caldwell in the following year. Caldwell was condemned, and forced to resign from the Government. May was completely cleared of the charge of making a false accusation. The Executive Council accepted the report and referred to "the great value of Mr. May's long and meritorious public services, and expressed their unanimous opinion, that his removal from government employment would be a great loss to the Colony".

In January 1861 he had been made the first Commissioner in Kowloon, on the cession of the Peninsula by the Convention of Peking in 1860, but he had to resign pending the outcome of the 1861 enquiry into his earlier conduct with Caldwell. In October 1861 he became Acting Chief Magistrate.

In 1862 there was an overhaul of the Colony's courts. A Summary Court was set up with a puisne judge, and the offices of Chief and Assistant Magistrate were abolished and replaced by two Police Magistrates. May was appointed first Police Magistrate. He held this post for the next seventeen years. The complete vindication of his character, his long experience, and his own qualities gave him an honoured position in the Government, and his services were increasingly used outside the courts. He served on various commissions of enquiry, the Opium Commission of 1872, the Crown Rents Commission of 1875, the *Praya* Commission of the same year, the Gambling Commission, and others. He became Acting Treasurer of the Colony in 1874, and Acting Colonial Secretary in 1878 while J. Gardiner Austin was on leave.

He was allowed sick leave in 1879 and left the Colony in April, but died on board three days out and was buried at sea. The Governor of that time, Sir John Pope Hennessy, referred to "his friendship, his great experience, his natural ability, his straightforward and honest disposition and his thorough loyalty to the government". To emerge from the thankless task of organizing the early Hong Kong Police, to run the gauntlet of public scandal, and to receive such encomiums was indeed high testimony.

16

CHARLES GUTZLAFF

WRITER, SINOLOGUE, OFFICIAL,
AND
FIRST LUTHERAN MISSIONARY TO CHINA

KARL FRIEDRICH AUGUST GUTZLAFF was born in 1803 at Pyritz in the province of Pomerania, then part of the Kingdom of Prussia. He had an unhappy upbringing under an unsympathetic step-mother. He showed great promise at school but poverty forced him to leave early and become apprenticed to a saddle-maker in Stettin, where he continued to study all he could. Then, by addressing an extremely immature poem to the Prussian King, who was on a visit to Stettin, and gaining the royal favour, he won for himself the opportunity of further education. Having expressed a desire for missionary work, he was sent to a mission school, and in 1823 went to Rotterdam to learn Malay. The Greek revolt against Turkey at this time excited great sympathy, and Gutzlaff went to Paris to learn Arabic and Turkish with a view to missionary effort in the Balkans, and with the idea of volunteering to fight for the Greeks.

The Dutch, however, wanted him for Indonesia, and sent him to London for further study. There he met Robert Morrison, first Protestant Missionary to China and founder of Malacca College, where Gutzlaff was to go to gain the experience needed to help the Dutch establish a similar institution in the Dutch East Indies.

In 1827 Gutzlaff arrived in Java, but instead of going to Malacca he was sent to the mission field in Sumatra. He became interested in the Chinese, and in 1828 got permission to go to Singapore. He travelled there by Chinese junk and then went on to Siam, where the London Missionary Society was just beginning its mission. There he married an English lady, Miss Newell, of the London Missionary Society and there he seems to have parted company with the Dutch. He and his wife settled for a time in Bangkok, but in 1831 he lost "this beloved partner", and an infant daughter died the same year.

He was a brilliant linguist and soon acquired Mandarin, Cantonese, and Fukienese, and mastered the Chinese script. He tells us he became naturalized a Chinese subject while in Siam by "adoption into the clan family of Kwo. I also took the name of Shik-Lee". He decided to go to China.

He embarked in a Chinese junk in 1831, got as far north as the

Liaotung peninsula, and finally landed at Macao. It was an exciting and even perilous journey. The pilot "was little versed in navigation", Gutzlaff reported. Also, "All the principal persons on whom depended the management of this vessel partook freely of this intoxicating luxury [opium]". Occasionally no one appeared to be in charge of the ship, and there were attempts to murder him for the sake of his baggage. He distributed tracts and portions of Holy Scripture at the various ports of call, used what little medical knowledge he had, and delivered addresses. He intended to leave the ship at Tientsin and go to Peking but eventually he decided to stay in the ship and make Macao his headquarters. His mind was made up. "I have weighed the arguments for and against the course I am endeavouring to pursue and have the resolution to publish the Gospel to the inhabitants of China proper in all the ways and by all the means which the Lord our God appoints in His Word".

In Macao he worked on a translation of the Bible into Chinese, but his invaluable knowledge of the language led to attractive offers of employment. In 1832 he made a second voyage up the China coast in the *Lord Amherst,* serving as interpreter. This was an East India Company ship which had been sent up the coast by Lindsay, chairman of the Select Committee in Canton, to explore the possibilities of opening the northern ports to British trade. The voyage was undertaken without permission of the Directors in London, and it incurred their displeasure.

Gutzlaff was then offered employment by William Jardine in the *Sylph,* an armed, opium clipper, and after some hesitation, accepted. He has been criticized for his part in these proceedings, and the acceptance of the financial rewards held out to him. He was himself uneasy about it, for he wrote, "After much consultation with others, and a conflict in my own mind, I embarked in the *Sylph*". There is no doubt he was strongly against opium smoking, but he probably argued that nothing much could be done about it until the work of conversion to Christianity had made some progress. He was anxious to see something of China away from the atmosphere of Macao and Canton and to secure funds to carry out his lone mission, for there was no society to back him.

During the years 1834 to 1839 he was at Macao, and they were busy years of preparation. He accepted a post as Interpreter and Assistant Secretary to the British Superintendent of Trade. He published his *Journal of Three Voyages* in 1834, and a report entitled "Remarks on a Voyage to North-eastern ports", was sent to the East India Company. This was followed by a *Sketch of the History of China* in two volumes and then by his *China Opened.* He produced a monthly magazine in Chinese, called *East and West* as well as numbers of religious tracts in the same language. What spare time was left he used to assist his wife (he had since married again) in running a school in Macao. This school was started in 1835, and was conducted in the Gutzlaffs' own house, with the help of a grant of $15 a month from the Morrison Education Society. The pupils were taught, fed, and clothed by the Gutzlaffs, yet even so they did not stay for more than a short time, being withdrawn for economic reasons as soon as they had acquired a smattering of English.

During the war, 1840-2, he was employed as Chief Interpreter in Elliot's conduct of negotiations with the Chinese. He went north with Sir Henry Pottinger as Interpreter, and the task of dealing with the Chinese on Chusan Island fell largely on his shoulders. But he still found time to carry on his missionary activities.

He was nominated by Sir Henry Pottinger as British Consul at Foochow, but the Foreign Secretary considered it essential to appoint a British national. He returned to Hong Kong as Assistant Chinese Secretary to the Superintendent of Trade, and then, on the death of J. R. Morrison in August 1843, became the Chief Secretary. He retained this responsible and well paid post until his death. He was never employed in the local Colony administration, for the staff of the Superintendent of Trade was kept quite distinct from that of the Governor of the Colony.

In Hong Kong, he was now able to begin his grand scheme of converting China. In 1844 he formed the Chinese Christian Union, through which groups of suitable Chinese were to be trained and sent in successive waves into the mission field in China. He showed enormous energy, for he could devote only his spare time to this great ambition. Besides building up his Union, he continued to preach, distribute tracts, and make translations. It was a bold project for one man to dare to undertake the task of making all China Christian, and though he got some financial help, he had to find most of the money himself. The training given in his Union was short and inadequate, and there was no attempt to establish a church organization, for he thought the corporate side of Christian life and worship in China could come later. In 1847 the Basel and Rhenish Missions sent money and men to help him, but there was much criticism of Gutzlaff's methods, and the weaknesses of his plan came to light. Some of the trainees of his Union never proceeded to China at all, but sold their stock of tracts and books to the printer, who sold them back to Gutzlaff. Gutzlaff became aware of this but still persevered in his aim of setting up branches of his Union in every Chinese province.

In 1848 he returned to Europe after twenty-two years absence, to plead for assistance. But the various missionary bodies in the

Colony had sent reports of the unsatisfactory nature of his Union, and this made his appeal more difficult. He returned to the Colony in January 1851, still quite convinced that his methods were sound, and threw himself into the task of rebuilding his Union. He was not spared to effect this, for years of overwork brought a premature death on 9 August 1851, at the early age of forty-eight.

The Colonial Chaplain, The Rev. E. T. K. Moncrieff, preaching in the Cathedral, paid a striking tribute to this extraordinary man: "The details of his system may admit of debate, but the general principle cannot. . . . His chief error seems to have been hoping too well, believing too much of his people. The attempt which he made and carried out till his death was the most gigantic ever to evangelize *en masse* a great nation. No one should say a word of this kind man till he himself has laboured as much and to the same extent, at his own cost, and done better".

He impressed by his enormous energy and determination and by the scope of his activities, as much as by his brilliant linguistic attainment. Some of the men who were to make names for themselves in China, like Sir Thomas Wade, had their linguistic training under him. He was the first to advocate the value of forming botanical gardens in Hong Kong. Yet with all this work, he never omitted to go out and preach in the street himself. Writer, traveller, linguist, teacher, and full-time official, this many-sided man was foremost a missionary. The Rev. George Smith, afterwards Bishop Smith, said of him: "Though he doubtless saw many things through the medium of a sanguine mind, and his opinions are consequently received with caution by the Missionaries; yet his past missionary labours for the benefit of the Chinese were conducted in a spirit of boldness and courage worthy of an apostolic age".[1]

He was much criticized, but he seemed to regard the conversion of China as a matter of urgency. His errors were those of a man in a hurry; his methods may excite a smile, but his devotion can only command respect.

---

[1] The Rev. George Smith. *A Narrative of an Exploratory Visit to Each of the Consular Cities of China,* 2nd edition, London, 1847, p. 72.

17

Some Other Officials

THE EARLIEST Hong Kong officials were those appointed by Elliot (or by A. R. Johnston in pursuance of Elliot's policy) during the summer of 1841, in ignorance of the fact that his own recall was imminent, and that the cession of the island was not to be recognized by the Government at home for another two years. Some of these appointments were disallowed and others were restricted in the scope of their activities. The next appointments were made by Sir Henry Pottinger in June and July 1843 when the island was declared a British Colony. It was not until early in 1844 that the first permanent officials were recruited from England.

Elliot appointed an experienced official, A. R. Johnston, as administrator, but for the rest he had to rely upon the officers of the expedition to meet his needs; the most important of them, Captain William Caine of the 26th Regiment, who became a magistrate, has already been mentioned. Lt. Pedder, R.N., Lieutenant of H.M. Steamer *Nemesis*, who had served with distinction in the Canton River in 1841, became Harbour Master and Marine Magistrate. He was reappointed by Pottinger in June 1843, and confirmed when the first permanent appointments were made early in 1844, and he proved an efficient officer until his death at Ryde in the Isle of Wight in March 1854, while on home leave. The Assistant Harbour Master was an Italian, Lena, who had also served in the expedition, and who won the commendation of the Commodore. He retired due to ill-health in December 1851. In August 1841 Captain G. F. Mylius became Land Officer, assisted first by Lt. Sargent, and then in April 1842 by Edward Reynolds who was made Land and Roads Inspector in June 1842 with the power to prevent encroachments. Reynolds resigned in November 1842 and was succeeded by William Tarrant. Another appointment by Elliot was that of J. R. Bird as Clerk of Works, which marked the beginning of the Public Works Department. After Elliot had left, a beginning was made with a Medical Department, but the appointment of a Colonial Surgeon was disallowed. Samuel Fearon became Clerk of the Magistrate's Court and Interpreter and then was appointed Coroner; in January 1846 he was made Registrar-General and Collector of Chinese Revenue for Hong Kong while he was home on leave, but he did not take up the post, as in December of this same year he was appointed Professor of Chinese at King's College, London, and did not return to the Colony.

The next appointments were made, still on a temporary basis, by Sir Henry Pottinger in the summer of 1843, after the proclamation of 23 June 1843 declaring Hong Kong a British Colony. Caine, Pedder, Lena, and Fearon all kept their appointments; C. B. Hillier, who has already been mentioned, became Assistant Magistrate. The first Colonial Secretary to be appointed was Lt.-Colonel G. A. Malcolm, a member of Pottinger's staff who had taken the Treaty of Nanking to London for approval and returned with the ratification. Malcolm soon returned to England, and in November 1843 Pottinger wrote that he had intended to make J. R. Morrison the Colonial Secretary but for his untimely death; R. W. Woosnam, a military medical man, was pressed into service as Pottinger's official secretary.

A beginning had already been made with a Public Works Department, and this was amalgamated with the Land Department. Bird did not last long and by April 1843 had been replaced by A. T. Gordon, who became Land Officer and Colonial Engineer; in August of that year an assistant was appointed, Captain de Havilland, who died shortly after, and Charles St. George Cleverly succeeded him as Assistant Surveyor. Gordon and Cleverly were confirmed in their appointments when Sir John Davis came out in March 1844, and they were then joined by J. Pope as Civil Engineer. Gordon, Cleverly, and Pope were responsible for the early public works of the Colony.

Gordon came from the same place as Pottinger, to whom he owed his appointment. He was the first official to attempt to plan Hong Kong, and he gave the Colonial Secretary a report on this subject dated 6 July 1843. He recommended that Queen's Road should be continued around the island, and that the new town should be sited in Happy Valley, and linked to the harbour by a canal with numerous branches deep enough to admit large junks. This canal proposal originated with Jardine, Matheson & Co. He reported that the site of the church had been selected, "a flat place at the front of Government Hill". He proposed a *praya* to the east and west of the sea-front facing Government House, a proposal that had to wait many years for fulfilment. He left on sick leave in 1844, and Davis reported that he was incompetent and that improvement in the progress of the public works had resulted from his departure. Cleverly was employed chiefly on the roads; Pope appears to have done only routine work.

Davis reported in March 1845 that there was no one in the Colony capable of getting out plans for a church, government offices, and other public buildings required, and entrusted the work to Major Aldrich, the army engineer commanding officer who had been sent to Hong Kong especially to deal with military works. The Governor and Gordon quarrelled. Gordon complained to the Colonial Office, while at home, that Davis had stopped his private practice, and had ordered all plans to be submitted to Major Aldrich for approval. He asked for an increase in salary or the right of private practice, and that the Public Works Department be placed "on a proper footing". Gordon was a close relative of Pottinger, who had supported him, but Davis refused to agree to his requests. Gordon returned and produced plans for the Anglican church (soon to be the Cathedral), after his proposals for a more elaborate building had been turned down on the ground of expense. In November 1846 he resigned because of "domestic misfortunes", but it was the Governor who had made his continuance in office virtually impossible.

Cleverly became Surveyor-General in his place; he remained in charge of public works in the Colony for nearly twenty years, and built up the department after the early difficulties. After Davis left, the habit of submitting all plans for public works to Major Aldrich was dropped. Cleverly became a member of the Legislative Council in October 1857, and was chairman of the important Committee of Enquiry into Anstey's complaints against Caldwell in that year. He asked to resign in December 1864 and left the following March having served twenty-two years, nearly twenty of them as Surveyor-General. He built Government House, completed in 1856, and was responsible for laying out streets and roads, for the rebuilding of the Bonham Strand area after the fire of 1851, and for laying out the new district of Bowrington, and he began the central reclamation and *praya* under Bowring. He was under-staffed and over-worked, but the bad drainage, paving, and sewage which were so scathingly criticized later, remained a most serious blemish on his record of service to the Colony.

Among the appointments made by Pottinger at the time of the proclamation of the Colony was that of Charles E. Stewart as Treasurer; he was not confirmed in this post, and so remained in the Colony for a short time only. Another was R. Burgass, as Legal Adviser and Clerk of the Councils. He was a barrister in practice at Bombay, and in reporting his appointment the Governor referred to him as "happening to be in China". In fact he was a friend of Pottinger, and there can be little doubt that he had been sent for and promised a post, as had Gordon, and for the same reason. On the appointment of an Attorney-General from home, he returned to Bombay. A Dr. A. Anderson was appointed Colonial Surgeon by Pottinger.

It was not until 1844 that the first permanent appointments were made by the Secretary of State, following the normal practice of filling the senior posts from England and the junior grades locally, subject to confirmation from home.

The most distinguished official to arrive in the Colony with Sir John Davis was the Honourable Frederick William Adolphus Bruce (1814–67), son of the Earl of Elgin. He went to America with Lord Ashburton to assist in the boundary negotiations with the United States in 1842, and in January 1844 was appointed Colonial Secretary of Hong Kong. He had good political connections, and served in the Colony only fifteen months before being promoted to be Lieutenant-Governor of Newfoundland. He soon left that post, and various Foreign Office appointments followed. He joined his brother, the Earl of Elgin, on his mission to China, 1857–8 and 1859–60, and the next year became the first British Resident Envoy to China. He left in 1865 to be British Ambassador to Washington. His successors as Colonial Secretaries, Caine, 1846–54 and Mercer, 1854–67, have been mentioned above.

An official who served in a junior post in the Hong Kong Government and then went on to a distinguished career was Thomas Francis Wade (later Sir), who rose to be British Plenipotentiary at Peking for twelve years, 1871–83. Wade was born in London in 1818 and after one year at Trinity College, Cambridge, left to follow his father in a military career. He came to China with his regiment, the 98th Regiment of Foot, arriving in June 1842, and saw active service in the closing stages of the campaign at Chinkiang and Nanking. During the long voyage out to the East he had beguiled the time learning Chinese. When the campaign was over he studied Chinese under Charles Gutzlaff as a student-interpreter and then was appointed Chinese Interpreter to the garrison in Hong Kong, to which numbers of troops had been withdrawn on the conclusion of active operations in the north. Following a short period of sick leave in England, he was appointed Interpreter to the Supreme Court in the Colony[1], and in 1844 he was Acting Interpreter on the consular staff[2] at Amoy. Then, in 1846, he was promoted to be Assistant Chinese Secretary to the Superintendent of Trade. He spent the next six years at Hong Kong in the post, but when Sir George Bonham became Governor in 1848 with special instructions to enquire into all branches of the Hong Kong Government expenditure in order to make proposals for a thorough-going retrenchment, Wade was appointed especially to assist him in this arduous and responsible task.

In 1852 he left the Colony on appointment as Vice-Consul at Shanghai. He played a leading part in forming the Foreign Maritime Customs Service and was the British representative on the interna-

---

1 *Almanack and Local Directory of Hong Kong*, 1846.
2 *Chinese Repository*, January 1844.

tional committee which controlled it. In 1855 he returned to Hong Kong as the Chinese Secretary to the Superintendent of Trade. He was specially nominated to assist Mercer and May, the Colonial Secretary and Superintendent of Police, in their enquiry into the bread poisoning case in the Colony in 1857. When the Second Anglo-Chinese War came, he was appointed to the staff of Lord Elgin and played a vital part in the negotiations leading to the Treaty of Tientsin in 1858. He was appointed to the chief post on the staff of the proposed legation to China under the Hon. F. W. Bruce and was with Bruce when the latter, making his way to Peking in 1859, was repulsed at the Taku Forts at the mouth of the Peiho River. Wade's services were much in demand on the consequent renewal of hostilities in 1860. When the legation was finally installed in Peking in 1861, Wade took up his post as the principal assistant to the Plenipotentiary, and was promoted to be Plenipotentiary in 1871. He retired to Cambridge in 1883 and became the first Professor of Chinese there. He died in 1895. While at Hong Kong he wrote *A Note on the Condition of the Chinese and the Government of the Chinese Empire,* in 1849, and he published two other books in Hong Kong in 1859, the *Hsin Ching Lu (Book of Changes,* 尋津錄) and the *Peking Syllabary.*

One of Wade's predecessors as Chinese Secretary to the Superintendent of Trade was John Robert Morrison.[1] He was born in 1814 at Macao, the second son of Dr. Robert Morrison, first Protestant Missionary to China. After being taken home to Britain from 1815 to 1820, and again for schooling from 1822 to 1826, he returned in the latter year. At the age of eleven he began the study of Chinese, and later went to the Anglo-Chinese College at Malacca (founded by his father), where he spent over two years. He then returned to Canton and continued to study Chinese under his father. In 1830 he was employed as translator to the British merchants in Canton and was temporarily employed by the United States Government on a mission to Cochin China.[2] In 1833 he published *The Chinese Commercial Guide* and next year, on his father's death, succeeded him as Chinese Secretary and Interpreter to the British Superintendent of Trade, being then only twenty years of age.

Charles Gutzlaff, the other competent Chinese linguist in Canton was eleven years his senior, but being non-British, was employed in the more junior post as "joint interpreter". Morrison helped to found and was secretary of three important societies set up at Canton, the Medical Missionary Society, the Society for the Diffusion

---

1 See *Dictionary of National Biography* under Robert Morrison.
2 *Chinese Repository,* September 1843, the funeral sermon by The Rev. S. R. Brown, tutor in the Morrison Education Society scheme.

of Useful Knowledge, and the Morrison Education Society. All official Chinese correspondence passed through his hands, and when hostilities came and he was attached to the armed forces, his duties became heavy. Elliot tended to use Gutzlaff in field negotiations, but Sir Henry Pottinger used Morrison for personal negotiations, Gutzlaff being stationed in Chusan and then earmarked for the post of British Consul at Foochow. Pottinger came to rely on his young Chinese Secretary, and nominated him a member of the Hong Kong Executive and Legislative Councils in the summer of 1843, and to the position of Acting Colonial Secretary, with the substantive post in view. A few days later Morrison fell victim to malarial fever, and he died at Macao on 29 August 1843 on the first anniversary of the Treaty of Nanking in the negotiation of which he had played such a notable part, aged only twenty-nine. Pottinger referred to his death as "a positive national calamity".

Another figure who spent a comparatively short time in Hong Kong and yet who deserves more than a passing mention is Robert Thom. He was born in Glasgow in 1807, and entered on a business career which took him to North and South America. He went to China, probably in the employ of one of the commercial houses, and quickly showed an aptitude for the Chinese language, coming into some prominence with a Chinese translation of *Aesop's Fables*. On the outbreak of hostilities against China in 1840 he entered government service as an interpreter serving with the armed forces. On the fall of Chinhai in 1841 he was placed in charge of the city as civil administrator, and at the conclusion of the war, when the city was handed back, he returned to Hong Kong. J. R. Morrison and Thom were entrusted with the task of preparing the Chinese version of the tariff schedules, which were subsequently embodied in the Supplementary Treaty of the Bogue (or Hu Men Chai) of October 1843. On 1 September 1843 Pottinger wrote home proposing Thom for the post of Chinese Secretary to the Superintendent, but Gutzlaff was preferred so as to liberate qualified linguists of British nationality for the consular posts in China. So in the *Chinese Repository* for January 1842 he is shown with The Rev. Charles Gutzlaff as Joint Interpreter on the staff of the Superintendent of Trade. In 1844 on the opening of Ningpo as a Treaty Port, Thom was appointed to the post of British Consul there; as this city is only a short distance up the river from Chinhai, which he knew well, he seemed the obvious choice. But the strain of the three previous years led to his premature death at Ningpo in 1846, cutting short a promising career.

The earliest Lieutenant-Governor, Major-General D'Aguilar, C. B., was one of the more interesting characters of early Hong Kong. He arrived in December 1843 to assume command of the land forces in China and to deputize for the Governor. His rather eccentric behaviour caused some amusement. On one occasion when a neighbour called Welch was having a party, the General ordered him to stop singing. When Welch threatened to horsewhip the policeman who brought the message, he was called before the courts and fined $20. He had another man fined for galloping along Gap Road because of an ordinance against "furious riding", and he had the "Bamboo Ordinance" passed, forbidding night watchmen to disturb what was regarded by all as his night's peace, by striking two pieces of bamboo together. But he became quite popular, particularly when he protested against Hulme being tried for drunkenness, an event which was alleged to have taken place in his own house, and which he justifiably claimed to be private matter. He was given a public dinner when he left. He became K.C.B., was promoted to Lieutenant-General, and died in 1855.

On the judicial side, the Chief Justice appointed in 1844 was J. W. Hulme, and an Attorney-General, Paul Ivy Sterling, arrived in July 1844. Norton Kyshe quoted the London *Observer* as saying that seven barristers were approached before Sterling accepted the post, such was the evil reputation of Hong Kong for ill-health, and that he had to be offered a salary of £2,500 before he would accept. His actual salary was £1,500, with the right of private practice. He went on sick leave two years later because of an "attack on the eyes threatening blindness" and his place was taken for a time by a local barrister, N. d'E. Parker[1] and then, in December 1846, by Charles Malloy Campbell. Sterling was made a member of the Executive Council, and after a period of service on the Legislative Council, was again nominated to the Executive Council in 1853. He became Acting Chief Justice in 1852 and again in 1854, and in October the following year was appointed Puisne Judge of the Supreme Court of Ceylon, a position he held until his retirement in 1863. He died in 1879 at the age of seventy-five. He did not make a great reputation in the Colony, and on his departure a local editor commented that both "the learned gentleman and the community were congratulated on his removal to a new and richer field of inaction!" At one period in 1851, while acting for the Chief Justice during his illness and taking cases under the summary jurisdiction, Sterling won some notoriety by a frequent repetition of the words, "I'll dismiss this

---

1 N. d'Esterre Parker was admitted as a solicitor in Hong Kong in 1844 and was soon appointed Crown Prosecutor and also became Coroner. In 1849, having received information that a junk anchored at a nearby island had pirated property on board, he took it upon himself to cross and conduct a search on his own authority. In subsequent proceedings he was himself accused of piracy for this act, and was lucky to have the case dismissed. Two months later, in September 1849, he left for California in the gold rush, but the ship in which he sailed was never heard of again.

case without prejudice".

He was succeeded temporarily by W. T. Bridges and then by Thomas Chisholm Anstey, and when the latter was suspended, by William Henry Adams. Adams was a self-made man from Lincolnshire who began life as a compositor, became a newspaper reporter, then an editor, and eventually a newspaper proprietor. He qualified as a barrister and was elected Member of Parliament for Boston. He was described as "a man of moderate abilities and a fair share of industry and energy". His arrival luckily coincided with Hulme's retirement, and he assumed the position of Chief Justice, at first in an acting capacity, and held it until May 1865 when he retired. He died a few months later at the age of fifty-six, to the regret of the Hong Kong community with whom his reputation stood high.

Charles Malloy Campbell arrived in the Colony in December 1846 from Calcutta, and some days later was made Acting Attorney-General, a post for which he had obviously been recommended. In reporting his appointment, Davis pointed out that he had been in great difficulty over the Compton case due to the absence of the Attorney-General on leave. Campbell conducted the case against Hulme, and upon the latter's suspension in November 1847, was made Acting Chief Justice. He was a very young man and had been called to the Bar only in 1844. He made himself intensely disliked, and was described in the Press at the time as "an over-bearing Anglo-Indian", "a pariah practitioner", and "a half-caste barrister". He was treated with contempt by the community until Hulme resumed his duties in June 1848, when Campbell disappeared quietly from the scene.

In 1844, Magistrates Caine and Hillier were confirmed in their posts. In 1846, when Caine became Colonial Secretary and Hillier Chief Magistrate, Charles Gordon Holdforth was made Assistant Magistrate. Holdforth was a rather disreputable character, an adventurer from Australia, where it was alleged he was a fugitive from justice on a charge of horse-stealing. He first secured a junior clerkship, became Coroner in October 1845, Deputy Sheriff the next February, and was promoted to Assistant Magistrate in June 1846. The next year he took on the offices of Sheriff, Provost Marshal, and Marshal of the Admiralty Court. From these posts he received an annual income of £700, which he supplemented by methods which excited the greatest criticism. He withdraw from the Government Auctioneer, Markwick, the right of holding "sheriff's sales" and awarded it to another auctioneer, Duddell, and it was alleged that he did so for a monetary consideration. He allowed debtors in and out of the debtors' prison if they or their friends could purchase this privilege, and was accused of setting convicts to work on plots of land which belonged to him, and which had been bought cheaply because they required much levelling. He was suspected of collusion with Duddell, particularly in connection with the latter's habit of knocking down cheap lots to himself. He went on sick leave in April 1850 and sailed to San Francisco.

It was widely known that he would not return, and the rumour was that he hid himself on board ship, being afraid that at the last moment proceedings might be taken against him. When his leave expired he resigned, having, it was thought, made a small fortune by his illegal practices. He was never accused of malversation, but his appointments were never gazetted.

Holdforth was succeeded as Assistant Magistrate by William Henry Mitchell. Mitchell had been appointed by Pottinger as Assistant to the Consul at Amoy, but had been superseded by Hertslet, an appointee from home. He then drifted to Hong Kong and became editor of the *Hong Kong Register*. His editorials supported the Government, in contrast to those of other editors and, indeed, of his own earlier ones, and Bonham thought highly of him. He was made Assistant Magistrate on Holdforth's departure in April 1850, and at Bonham's request he produced a full report on Hong Kong's trade prospects in December 1850, and soon after a full report on the China trade. The reports were competent, and even his critics agreed that he was an able man. In 1853 he secured a year's leave, and while at home divorced his wife, citing as co-respondent the same Prince of Armenia with whom Hillier had become embroiled.

Anstey's arrival caused trouble for Mitchell. The Attorney-General complained of irregularities in the Magistrates' Courts over the taking of evidence, and Mitchell came in for additional criticism for his proceedings as Coroner. These accusations resulted in a scene in the Supreme Court at which Hillier and Mitchell were subjected to some well justified criticism. In June 1856 Anstey brought criminal proceedings against Mitchell as Sheriff, for attempted extortion. This complicated case arose when, in accordance with custom, additional jail rations were supplied to eight condemned prisoners, six of whom were afterwards reprieved, or had their sentences altered to transportation. Mitchell refused to pass the bills for the additional food and suggested that the prisoners should get their friends to pay the additional sum. Anstey suspected extortion and made a full enquiry, from which Mitchell was excluded, and brought criminal proceedings against him. Mitchell appealed to the Secretary of State against the whole proceedings. In the event, Mitchell was acquitted.

In August Mitchell brought an action against Anstey for defamation. Anstey had also accused Mitchell of irregularity in dealing with cases under a recently passed Buildings and Nuisance Ordinance dealing with sanitation. Mitchell interpreted the ordinance in a manner contradictory to its obvious intention, and the Acting Surveyor-General, Captain Cowper, complained strongly to the Governor and the Secretary of State that the magistrates were judging cases under this ordinance while they were themselves interested parties and were engaged in building operations. This was another opportunity which the crusading Anstey was unlikely to miss. Mitchell had invited some unofficial Justices of the Peace to sit with him on the bench in dealing with these cases, being reasonably sure that they would uphold his view, which was favourable to property-owners. Anstey was given some incorrect information by the Acting Captain-Superintendent of Police, and made accusations against Mitchell in a communication to another Justice of the Peace, whom he approached with the object of forming a special court to hear these cases. Mitchell's court action was based on these events. Anstey was acquitted, and serious suspicion rested on Mitchell, who was known to be heavily involved in property transactions.

When Hillier left for Bangkok in 1858, Mitchell hoped to be made Chief Magistrate, but a barrister from England, Henry Tudor Davies, was appointed. The latter shortly afterwards went into the Chinese Imperial Maritime Customs Service and Mitchell was again disappointed when another barrister, T. Callahan, was appointed in 1860. Mitchell was passed over again when Callahan left within a year, having been appointed Governor of Labuan. He had the small satisfaction of acting as Chief Magistrate on these occasions. He went on leave in 1860 and while at home in 1862 was allowed to retire on pension. During this period he read for the Bar, returned to Hong Kong, was admitted to the Bar there in 1865 and proceeded to practise at Shanghai. The Governor complained that he had retired on pension for health reasons yet had now returned, but it was found that Mitchell was breaking no rule and he continued to enjoy both his pension and his legal practice.

One interesting character who arrived in 1844 was Adolphus Edward Shelley. He had been given no official appointment, but came armed with an introduction from Lord Stanley, Secretary of State. Davis, assuming that he was to be given a post, made him Auditor-General and Clerk of the Councils. When the Governor announced the appointment, Lord Stanley noted that he had "not desired the Governor to appoint him to anything". Shelley had obviously taken a chance and brought it off. He had lived in India and occasionally acted as interpreter in Hindustani. He was a bon viveur, and a friend of Hulme, and both incurred Davis's displeasure. In November 1846, in a private letter to Earl Grey, Davis accused him of being dissipated, in debt, negligent, guilty of falsehood, quite unfit for high office, and of exercising a bad influence on the Chief Justice. Shelley followed the military expedition of April 1847 to Canton, and Davis complained of his "mischievous industry" there in spreading the idea that Canton's foreign consuls were against the Governor's action. Soon after, to Davis's great relief, Shelley left on appointment as Assistant Auditor-General of Mauritius.

The Colonial Treasurers, Charles E. Stewart, Robert Montgomery Martin, and W. T. Mercer have already been mentioned. When Mercer became Colonial Secretary in 1854, his successor as Colonial Treasurer was his Chief Clerk, Rienaecker, a German, described as of "a doubtful antecedent who, like most early officials, was taken into the service without any previous enquiry as to his former career".[1] From Third Clerk in the Treasury in December 1845, he had risen to be Chief Clerk, and had made himself indispensable to Mercer who recommended him for the post of Treasurer in 1854, at a considerable saving in salary. He appeared from the financial reports to be a capable official. He and d'Almada, the Clerk of the Councils, applied for British naturalization, but were told that this was an expensive process involving a private act of Parliament, and that it would be easier to proceed by local ordinance which would give them British citizenship limited to Hong Kong. There is, however, no record of this being done. In December 1856 Rienaecker went on leave and was given a pension. It was then found that the financial accounts were in disorder, largely because the Colonial and Consular accounts had not been kept separate as had been ordered in 1853. Contrary to Norton Kyshe's account, however, there is nothing in the Colonial Office records to show that Reinaecker was guilty of any defalcations.

Rienaecker was succeeded by T. H. Forth, a former Captain of the 21st Fusiliers, who was sent out from England. He was incompetent, and in 1862 was described by Mercer, acting as Governor, as "this worse than useless officer". He became a member of the Legislative Council and voted against the payment of military contribution in 1865, for which he was reprimanded by the Secretary of State. He retired soon after, in 1871, and died at Leamington in 1876.

The first Registrar-General was Samuel Turner Fearon. He was succeeded in July 1845 by Andrew Lysaught Inglis, a clerk in the Marine Magistrate's Office who had become competent in the Chinese language and rose in the service. Inglis was confirmed in the appointment on Fearon's resignation to become Professor of Chinese

---

1 J. W. Norton Kyshe, *History of the Laws and Courts of Hong Kong*, London, 1898, Vol. 11, p. 107.

at King's College, London. When Bonham held his full enquiry into the public service to secure reductions, Inglis decided to resign, and in May 1849 he joined the gold rush to California. He soon returned, was made Deputy Sheriff, and became virtually Prison Governor, in which post his expert Cantonese was invaluable. In August 1858 he became Harbour Master and Marine Magistrate in place of Captain Watkins (successor to Lieutenant Pedder), and held this office until his retirement in February 1861. He was succeeded by Lt. H. G. Thomsett, R.N., who held the post for 27 years until 1888.

When Inglis resigned in 1849, the work of the Registrar-General was handed over to the Colonial Treasurer. In April 1850 the office of the Registrar-General was combined with that of Superintendent of Police, and Charles May held the combined posts until 1853 when he became Acting Assistant Magistrate and Caldwell took his place temporarily. In 1857, under Bowring's liberal Chinese policy, the office was again made an independent one, and Caldwell was appointed Registrar-General, with the additional title of Protector of Chinese. When he was dismissed from the service in 1861, he was succeeded by an official of the department, Turner, until one of the new cadets, C. C. Smith, filled the post in October 1864, six months before the period of his study of Chinese was up. This important office was henceforth held by cadet officers with a knowledge of Chinese.

It is not possible to deal with all the many junior officials of the Colony's early years. Three, however, deserve mention. There was Alexander Grandpré, described by W. T. Mercer as "a Portuguese of French extraction", who, on Caldwell's resignation in 1855 took his place as Assistant Superintendent of Police and Interpreter. A year later, when Hillier left and May became a magistrate, Grandpré became Acting Superintendent of Police. He was responsible for the experiment of enlisting some thirty Portuguese discharged soldiers from Macao for police duties. Next year, his post of Assistant Superintendent of Police was withdrawn because he was found unsatisfactory, and he became Collector of Police and Lighting Rates. He retired on pension in 1864 and died at Macao the following year at the age of forty-six. In 1862 Mercer reported that Grandpré had been tried in various positions and had failed in all, that he was genial and willing, but was always ready with some trifing excuse. As Collector of Rates he apparently invariably allowed them to fall into arrears.

Another prominent official was Leonardo d'Almada e Castro, who carved out a considerable reputation for himself, and whom Norton Kyshe curiously ignores. He first entered the service of the crown in 1836 as a clerk in the office of the Superintendent of Trade at

Macao. In 1842 he came to Hong Kong when that office was trans-ferred to the island, and on the establishment of the Colony, he became Chief Clerk in the Colonial Secretary's Office. In May 1847, on the departure of Shelley, he became Clerk of the Councils in addition, and on the comparatively few odd days that Caine was away, d'Almada acted for him. However, on one occasion in 1853, Mercer deputized for Caine, and d'Almada complained to Bonham that he had done so in the past and should have done so on that occasion. Bonham ruled that the office of the Colonial Secretary was quite different from that of the working staff of that office. D'Almada memorialized the Secretary of State in a letter of great length, and when Bonham refused to forward it, he sent it himself.

Bonham explained that he had not forwarded the memorial because it referred to Caine and Mercer in improper terms. He said d'Almada had acted for Caine for very short intervals on two occasions only, and now claimed to be Acting Colonial Secretary on all such occasions. Bonham objected that since d'Almada was not a British subject he was not eligible to sit on the Executive Council nor to act for the Governor if an emergency arose, and therefore was unable to act as Colonial Secretary. The Duke of Newcastle ruled that he had no claim to be Colonial Secretary, but added that the senior officers of the service "appeared to be set against him", contrary to the interest of the public service, and that Bonham should have forwarded the memorial in the usual way. At that moment a reorganization of the service was being devised, with Caine as Lieutenant-Governor, and the Duke of Newcastle proposed that d'Almada should become Colonial Secretary at a large saving in salary. This suggestion did not commend itself locally, and Bonham, Bowring, and Caine agreed to recommend Mercer, on the ground that d'Almada was not a British subject. D'Almada and Rienaecker then applied for British nationality, and d'Almada described himself as born in Goa of Portuguese parents, and his father as an artillery Colonel from Lisbon. After a number of applications for an increase in salary he secured an extra £200 per year in 1858. He could have retired on a pension in 1865 but chose to go on, and died in public service in January 1875, aged sixty-one.

After much pressure, the Secretary of State agreed that his widow and daughter should have a small pension. The Chief Justice referred to him as "a very dictionary of public events, transactions and correspondence received during an official career of thirty-four years". Mercer reported in 1862 that he was a "Portuguese of the better class", but "hardly eligible for higher appointment", but after the quarrel of 1853 it was not likely that Mercer would recommend him. J. M. d'Almada, a brother, who in 1841 also entered the British public service under the Superintendent of Trade at Macao, followed him as Chief Clerk, and Clerk of the Councils until his death in January 1881.

Of all the earlier junior officials, mention might be made of P. C. McSwyney, a graduate of Dublin and an adventurer from Sydney, who became Deputy Registrar of the Supreme Court on its establishment in 1844. The next year he had to resign and was permitted temporarily to practise as a "barrister, attorney, solicitor, proctor and notary public". In June 1846, he accepted the post of Coroner, but was removed the following November for incompetence, after which he became an opium dealer. He married a Chinese who assured him that she had property in Canton. This proved untrue and he turned her out of the house. He went to Macao, and when she took proceedings against him, he successfully pleaded that he was resident in Macao and so outside the jurisdiction of the court. In July 1849 he became an insolvent debtor, and was accused of gross dishonesty and fraud, but he died in the Seamen's Hospital at Hong Kong in December 1850, before further trouble came.

It must be concluded that manpower was inadequate to supply the public service in Hong Kong's early years, and that recourse had to be made to whatever local men were available. Many were able and made good, but many used the opportunity to enrich themselves, and they were not particular as to their methods. It was to be many years before a regular civil service was organized with adequate pay and status.

PART III

SOME HONG KONG PERSONALITIES

18

WILLIAM THOMAS BRIDGES

WILLIAM THOMAS BRIDGES came to Hong Kong in April 1851 and for the next ten years he was one of the Colony's leading figures. He was a barrister, and since a man with law qualifications was a comparative rarity in Hong Kong, he quickly came to enjoy a lucrative practice. He also held high official positions from time to time acting as Attorney-General, and Colonial Secretary, while the holders of these offices were on leave. He secured the honorary degree of Doctor of Civil Law while he was in England engaged on a case before the Privy Council in 1856, after which he was always referred to, and called himself, Doctor Bridges. He was evidently very proud of the honour. He was a thoroughly able lawyer and a strong, determined, but rather unscrupulous character. He was typical of the adventuring class of Englishmen of that period.

He had little professional competition and he exploited the opportunity to the maximum, unfortunately succumbing to the temptation of allowing Chinese ignorance of English law to serve his personal ends. It is related that he once boasted "that his principal luggage on landing consisted of a cricket bat and wickets"; ten years later he left the Colony a wealthy man, but not without being involved in considerable scandal.

There is not much detail available about his early life. He was an Oxford man, had been a friend of W. T. Mercer at Exeter College, and was called to the Bar at the Middle Temple. Mercer had been brought out to Hong Kong by his uncle, Sir John Davis, Governor from 1844 to 1848 as Davis's private secretary, gained rapid promotion and eventually became Colonial Secretary. It was through his agency that Bridges came out, and it was in part due to this influential friendship that he quickly flourished.

The same morning that he was enrolled in the Hong Kong Bar, he complained against the practice of solicitors appearing in court for clients, a practice that had grown up simply because few barristers were available. Bridges's protest was upheld, and solicitors were barred from acting as counsel in the Supreme Court. He had been in the Colony less than a year when he was made Acting Attorney-General as deputy for Paul Sterling, who became Acting Chief Justice in place of Hulme, on leave. He occupied this post again in April 1854 when Hulme was granted sick leave, this time with a provisional seat in the Legislative Council, and on Hulme's return he continued to act for Sterling, who went on leave. Sterling resigned during this leave, and Thomas Anstey was appointed in his place. Bridges anticipated that Anstey, who was due to arrive in January 1856, would very soon become Chief Justice because Hulme was frequently ill and expected to retire, and Bridges saw an opportunity of becoming Attorney-General with the succession to the bench.

He went home in January 1856, to urge his claims so it was thought. If this was his reason it was wasted effort, because Hulme did not retire. Bridges had no reason to be dissatisfied with his first five years in the Colony, however. Three other barristers had recently arrived, but for much of the time he enjoyed a virtual monopoly and for nearly four years of the five, he had acted as Attorney-General. While he was so acting, one of his decisions came in for criticism at home. He had advised that cases concerning property held by British subjects in China should be governed by English law and not Chinese, on the ground that the Chinese were uncivilized. This drew from the home Law Officers the unequivocal rebuke that, "We do not concur in the conclusion of the acting Attorney-General that the Chinese are to be considered as beyond the pale of civilized nations".

Bridges returned to the Colony before the end of 1856. A few weeks later Mercer went on leave, and he became Acting Colonial Secretary, and provisional member of the Executive and Legislative Councils. He was also given the right to continue his private practice. This led to difficulties, and was only defended by Bowring on the ground that he was the most suitable man for the post and that he refused to accept it on any other terms.

The Attorney-General, T. Chisholm Anstey, had been crusading against extortion and malpractice amongst officials since his arrival early in 1856, and though he caused trouble and became the centre of a series of libel actions, he undoubtedly uncovered some real abuses. Dr. Bridges did not escape his scrutiny, and the two men became bitter enemies.

Bridges unquestionably was not too scrupulous over the etiquette of the Bar where this limited the lucrative character of his practice. He advertised himself by two brilliantly coloured signboards in English and Chinese, "the letters and characters being brightly gilt on a black lacquer". They were placed outside his office in Queen's Road so prominently as to constitute a breach of the rule against advertising. Bridges was eager to accept briefs direct from the public and so eliminate the solicitor, yet he had been earlier opposed to solicitors being allowed to conduct cases in court on the ground that the two branches of the profession should be kept distinct. He and other barristers urged that the two branches be amalgamated, and in January 1858 a joint meeting was held. There had been much criticism over the costs of legal actions and the heavy fees charged, and on Anstey's advice, Bowring had caused an ordinance to be passed controlling legal fees, and limiting the retaining fee for a barrister to ten dollars. At the meeting the barristers were out-voted and the two branches remained separate. Bridges took occasion to declare that he intended to continue to charge a retaining fee of twenty-five dollars, ordinance or no ordinance.

He also engaged extensively in money-lending and notoriously charged high rates of interest. His offices were often full of miscellaneous goods which had been deposited as security. Bowring had objected to this side of Dr. Bridges's activities, and had consulted Mercer about it, but the latter advised against any action on the ground that it was impossible to interfere with Bridges in the conduct of his private business. The Acting Colonial Secretary combined ability with strong-mindedness, but he allowed his keenness to degenerate into avarice. Bowring had not been very anxious to employ Bridges in an official capacity, but had felt that his ability was too useful to ignore. Anstey's crusading attacks on the two men drove them into each other's arms. Anstey initiated two famous cases that involved Bridges in scandal and showed up some of the sharp practice of which the latter was capable.

In the spring of 1858 a man called Hoey was charged with a breach of the opium monopoly. During the case there were disclosures of financial dealings between Dr. Bridges and the holder of the monopoly. The suspicions were echoed in the local Press. To clear himself Bridges asked for an official enquiry and a Committee of Enquiry comprising Davies, the Chief Magistrate, and J. M. Dent, a local merchant, was appointed in May 1858. It was discovered that as the Opium Monopoly Ordinance was being passed in March 1858, Bridges had accepted "cumshaw" from the monopolist in the guise of a retaining fee, despite the fact that he was in charge of the measure as Acting Colonial Secretary. The Committee concluded that though Bridges had not done anything dishonest or dishonourable, his conduct in accepting a retaining fee at such a time was open to censure. In spite of this compromising report, Bowring regarded Bridges as having been cleared and blamed Anstey for fomenting trouble by a personal attack on Bridges.

In the same month came another enquiry, into the Caldwell case, and again Dr. Bridges was implicated. Caldwell was a brilliant linguist employed as Interpreter and Assistant-Superintendent of Police, and had just been given the responsible position of Registrar-General and Protector of Chinese. Anstey accused Caldwell of being unfit to hold the office of Justice of the Peace because of malpractices in ownership and licensing of brothels, and because of his notorious association with Ma Chow Wong, an informer against pirates who was proved to be a pirate himself.

A Commission of Enquiry was set up under the chairmanship of Cleverly, the Surveyor-General, and it reported that of nineteen charges brought by Anstey, Caldwell was guilty only of four, and that these did not constitute sufficient ground on which to dismiss him from his post, or deprive him of his commission as a Justice of the Peace. This verdict was held to exonerate Caldwell, and as a result Anstey was suspended for causing scandal by bringing unjustified charges against high officials. But the affair did not blow over so easily. It transpired during the enquiry that some papers found in Ma Chow Wong's home at the time of his arrest had definitely incriminated Caldwell. These papers had been burnt by order of Bridges, and Tarrant, editor of *The Friend of China,* had declared in commenting on the case that Caldwell had got off by a contemptible damnable trick. Tarrant was accused of criminal libel, and at his trial the facts came out. Bridges admitted being on intimate terms with Caldwell, who had recommended Chinese clients to him. It was clear that the incriminating papers had been taken to Dr. Bridges, and were burnt on his instructions. Tarrant was acquitted, and suspicion at once centred upon Bridges, who had been drawn into the scandal.

Bridges had resigned as Acting Colonial Secretary soon after the suspension of Anstey. His aim was to become Attorney-General, and Bowring recommended him for the post should Anstey's suspension be confirmed. This was in August 1858, and as a first step Bowring made him Counsel to the Superintendent of Trade. However, Bridges never held office in the Colonial Government again. The revelations in the Tarrant libel case soon afterwards created too unfavourable an atmosphere. Bowring resigned, and left in 1859. The new Governor, Sir Hercules Robinson, came out in September 1859 with instructions to make a careful enquiry into the whole government service. Since his suspension, Anstey had stirred up public opinion at home to demand that the Caldwell case be re-opened. Clearly Caldwell and Bridges were both on trial, and a Civil Service Abuses Enquiry was set up in June 1860, which recommended the dismissal of Caldwell.

Bridges was unwilling to face this new probe, and before the enquiry was completed he left the Colony by the P. & O. steamer *Bakar* on 15 April 1861. His departure was allowed to pass almost unnoticed, except for some hostile comment in the Press, in marked contrast to his leave in 1857 when a public dinner had been given in his honour by the legal profession. He had unmistakably forfeited the esteem of the community.

Norton Kyshe says that where he went and what happened to him is not known, and it is to be presumed that with the fortune he had made in Hong Kong and his mode of making it he was not unwilling to retire into the obscurity of private life.

19

WILLIAM TARRANT

IN JULY 1850 William Tarrant became proprietor and editor of a newspaper published twice weekly, *The Friend of China and Hong Kong Gazette,* and so could not but be a prominent Hong Kong man. By taking a strong editorial line on every issue and expressing it in pungent language, he made himself perhaps unnecessarily prominent. His self-assumed task of keeping an especially vigilant eye on the local government and its leading officials led to immoderate attacks upon them, and involved him in libel actions, fines, and even imprisonment. He courted martyrdom, but since he lacked the necessary personal idealism he achieved only notoriety, redeemed by a measure of public sympathy.

He spent thirty-two years in the Far East, mostly in Hong Kong. Like many of his countrymen, he had started his career by going to sea, and arriving in the East had resolved to try his fortune there. He had come from a humble family and so had served before the mast. Sir George Bonham described him as "having formerly been steward of a ship called the *John Layard*", and he was thereafter often contemptuously referred to by his enemies as "steward". The epithet must have had some sting because the version put out by Tarrant was that the steward of the ship fell sick, and since he, Tarrant, was the handiest boy, he was ordered by the captain to take the man's place. He arrived in China in the old Canton days, in 1837, and apparently spent the next four years sailing in Eastern waters.

On the cession of Hong Kong, he secured a government post in the Surveyor General's Department as Land and Roads Inspector, according to an official notification of 15 November 1842. He was thus responsible for supervising the work on many early Hong Kong roads, and the cutting from Queen's Road to Happy Valley, now called Gap Road, is particularly associated with him. As a junior government official he seems to have given every satisfaction. For example, when he fell sick twelve months later and became unfit for out-door work, it was arranged that he should be employed indoors because he was described by the head of his department as an "old employee having been very zealous and attentive in the discharge of his duties". He was then given the post of Registrar of Deeds, with the principal duty of preparing land leases. When police rates were introduced in 1845, Tarrant became an assessment and valuation officer in addition to his other duties. He seemed set for a useful career in the government service, and Cleverly, the Acting Surveyor-General, reported that "he devoted every possible attention to his duties".

In 1847 he was the victim of extraordinary proceedings which led to his suspension and dismissal, and since he regarded himself as having been unjustly treated, he became embittered and developed an enduring hostility against the local government. In July of that year Tarrant reported to the head of his department that Major Caine's compradore was demanding payments from the stall-holders in the Central Market, because of the influence he claimed his position gave him. A Chinese compradore in the Treasury Department was also implicated. The Governor instituted an enquiry by the Acting Attorney-General, Campbell, who reported that the charges were completely without foundation, and that Tarrant was guilty of bringing Caine's name into disrepute and should be committed for conspiring to injure him.

Tarrant was summoned before the Executive Council and censured for bringing charges that appeared to be based only on hearsay. He admitted that he had had the information some eight or nine months before reporting it, but that he had delayed only to be quite sure. The Council censured him for this delay. Campbell had refused to make his report public, and Tarrant was therefore given no chance of knowing the reasons for the Government's displeasure. In due course he was brought before a Justice of the Peace, A. R. Johnston, and committed to the Supreme Court for trial for conspiracy, on the information laid by Caine. In view of these criminal proceedings, Governor Sir John Davis decided to suspend Tarrant from his duties. So Tarrant's attempt to check suspected extortion had merely resulted in his own suspension, and in the distinct possibility of being found guilty of criminal conspiracy.

In writing to the Secretary of State about the case, Davis said that the charge against the compradores was ill-founded. They had received money, but as part-owners of stalls, and in any case, Tarrant's implication was that Caine had allowed his name to be used in this so-called extortion. It further appeared that Tarrant was in debt to one of the compradores for a considerable sum, and he might therefore have had some additional motive in charging him.

The case against Tarrant was never heard. In December it was struck off the court calendar when the government prosecutor admitted in court that there was no evidence which would justify proceedings. Tarrant quite naturally asked to be reinstated and to receive his salary from the date of his suspension. He had already appealed to the home authorities, who withheld judgement pending the result of the trial.

In September 1847 Davis had amalgamated the office of Registrar of Deeds with that of Book-keeper and he refused to agree to Tarrant's re-employment on the ground that his old post had been abolished as redundant. Davis also told Earl Grey that Tarrant had taken private work "in the lower occupations of an attorney, and there is much reason to apprehend that his superfluous leisure was conducive to the disreputable course of proceeding which the late proceedings served to indicate".

In the spring of 1848 Bonham arrived as the new Governor, and Tarrant, who quite justifiably considered himself badly treated, wrote to him to request a government post. Bonham sent the letter home with the remark that there was no post available. Grey, however, had now learnt that the proceedings against Tarrant had been dropped. He felt that Tarrant had been made the victim of political persecution, and told Bonham to make a full enquiry into the case. The Governor did so, and a great deal of detail came out, but the main fact seemed to be that Davis had thought Tarrant unfitted to hold any post, and Bonham, though he admitted he did not know much about Tarrant, wrote that "from what he had heard" he would not be inclined to offer him a post. He described Tarrant as "a bustling, active kind of person, but at the same time one over which it was judged proper to keep watch". The result was that Bonham recommended no action, and Tarrant got no more than the salary due from the date of his suspension to the date of the abolition of the office. But there is no doubt that Grey considered that he had been harshly treated.

Tarrant became a man with a grievance, and no wonder. He continued to protest for some years, and even petitioned the Queen. He had a family to support in Hong Kong, and in July 1850 he was assisted by friends to purchase a bi-weekly newspaper, *The Friend of China and Hong Kong Gazette* and become its editor.

He became aggressively hostile towards Government, as indeed was only to be expected, and pursued a vigorous editorial policy based upon what he conceived to be the public interest. This of course only brought more trouble, and it is a tribute to his honesty if not to his tact, that he made little effort to avoid it. Bonham reported, soon after Tarrant had assumed control of his paper, that "it has levelled all sorts of abuse and scurrility against the local officers", and predicted, incorrectly, that "its days will not be many". Tarrant continued to attack Caine, with results that will be seen.

In 1857 he ran into unexpected trouble. In January of that year, an attempt was made to poison the European community in the Colony; the bread supplied by a Chinese bakery was found to contain arsenic. The attempt was very clumsy, the amount added to the bread being so excessive as to be quite noticeable, and so, fortunately, little harm resulted. The proprietor, Cheong Ah Lum, fled to Macao, but was brought back and tried in the Supreme Court. There was no proof, however, that he was personally implicated, and he was acquitted by a British jury much to the disgust of the European community, many of whom wanted him executed without the formality of a trial. Tarrant made himself the spokesman of their indignation by bringing an action against Cheong Ah Lum for damages, and he was awarded $1,010.

The baker was liberated by order of the Home Government, and was released so suddenly that he was able to get away leaving his debts unsettled. Tarrant blamed Dr. Bridges who was acting as Colonial Secretary. Bridges prosecuted him for libel, and Tarrant was found guilty and fined £100. This fine was paid for him by some sympathizers, who supported the stand he had taken, and a later issue of *The Friend of China* contained the names of the subscribers. He repeated the charge against Bridges a few months later, but avoided another libel action by an apology.

The next year, in August, Tarrant became involved in the Caldwell case. Caldwell was then Registrar-General, and he was accused by Anstey, the Attorney-General, of misbehaviour and malpractices which made him unfit to hold high office. An enquiry was held which exculpated Caldwell, and as a result Anstey was suspended. It was, however, known that certain incriminating papers were burnt at the order of Bridges who was anxious to shield Caldwell, and Tarrant entered the fray with the forthright editorial comment that Caldwell had escaped by means of a "contemptible damnable trick on the part of Government". For this he was charged with libel against the Government but was acquitted, to the applause of the Europeans in court.

For more than ten years, ever since the Caine compradore case in 1847, Tarrant had not ceased to attack Caine in private conversation and in his paper. He used to refer openly to Caine's "compradoric methods" as being synonymous with "squeeze". Caine ignored all this, holding that if he brought a libel action it was probable that a jury would refuse to convict. When Caine was due to retire in 1859 he decided to clear his name of Tarrant's implied charges. A particularly harsh comment about Caine in the paper of 24 August 1859, led to libel proceedings against Tarrant. Caine retained every barrister in the Colony, and Tarrant was forced to conduct his own case. He was found guilty, sentenced to one year's imprisonment, and fined £50.

This was a crushing blow, because it meant suspending publication of the paper, at least while he was in jail. While imprisoned he was given the disciplinary treatment of an ordinary felon until illness forced his removal to hospital. He was very soon ordered back to the cells by the visiting Justices of the Peace, a proceeding which was thought by many to be unnecessarily vindictive. Prominent members of the community, including members of the jury which had condemned him, now petitioned the Governor to have Tarrant confined in the debtors' section of the jail, in which conditions were less rigorous, but this request was refused. Agitation continued, and eventually brought about an enquiry into jail conditions. In addition, the British Press took up the case, and questions were asked in Parliament. This induced the Colonial Office to intervene, and Tarrant was released after serving six months of his sentence. The £50 fine was paid by public subscription.

No sooner was he at liberty than Dr. Bridges claimed $2,263 as costs of the trial, and Tarrant, who had lost everything and was unable to pay, found himself back in the debtors' prison. He appealed against the costs, and petitioned the Colonial Office at home. Bridges admitted he was out to drive Tarrant from the Colony, and offered to waive the claim if Tarrant would leave. Tarrant, however, refused his freedom on these terms. After four more months in jail, the money for Bridges was raised by another public subscription, and on 4 August 1860, Tarrant found himself at last a free man. Though public sympathy had shown itself unmistakably on his side, he was not able to make a fresh start in Hong Kong.

He moved to Canton where he attempted to start up *The Friend of China* again. The venture was not successful, and in 1862 he moved to Shanghai and published his paper there. Seven years later he sold out and retired to England in a poor state of health from which he never recovered, and which resulted in his death some twelve months later, on 26 January 1872. He bequeathed to the Hong Kong City Hall Library a complete file of *The Friend of China*.

Thus passed from the scene one of the characters of early Hong Kong. He may have been "more honest than politic", as one commentator said, but he was certainly the victim of persecution. He had the temerity to challenge the powerful, and the penalty was disproportionate to his deserts.

20

JAMES LEGGE

THE REV. JAMES LEGGE achieved fame as one of the great sinologues of the nineteenth century, and that sufficiently justifies his place in this account of early Hong Kong personalities. He also has other claims to inclusion, for he was an influential resident of the Colony for nearly thirty years and closely identified himself with its daily life and its social problems. As Minister of the Union Church, he was prominent in the religious life of the community, and those in authority sought his advice on problems relating to the Chinese, by whom he was highly respected. He was an all-round man: scholar, missionary, minister, chaplain, educationist, and public-spirited citizen.

He was born in 1815 at Huntley in Aberdeenshire. After a brilliant scholastic career, he won a bursary to Aberdeen University where he secured the Huttonian Prize. This award marked him out as a probable future Professor of Humanity there, but membership of the Presbyterian Church was an essential qualification for the post. The Legge family, however, was not Presbyterian but Independent, because the Huntley minister had been expelled from the Presbyterian Church as a deviationist and had been followed by most of his congregation. From this man, who was intensely interested in foreign missions, Legge received his first impetus to become a missionary. He refused to be converted to Presbyterianism to qualify for the professorship, and became a schoolmaster at Blackburn for two years before going to London in 1837 to join the London Missionary Society's Theological College at Highbury.

The Society sent him to Malacca and he and his wife arrived there in January 1840. He assumed the post of Principal of the Anglo-Chinese College, founded by Robert Morrison, and devoted himself to learning Chinese, to teaching, and to continuing the work of printing and distributing translations of religious tracts and portions of scripture. He had very close relations with the Religious Tract Society and with the British and Foreign Bible Society, both of which assisted the work of the College.

On the cessation of hostilities between Britain and China in 1842 which resulted in the acquisition of Hong Kong as a British Colony, the London Missionary Society decided to move the College to the island, and to devote more attention to the training of suitable Chinese for the work of spreading Christianity in China.

It was decided that Legge should remain as Principal, and so he found himself in Hong Kong with his family in 1843. The College was opened in November of that year. Attached to the College were a preparatory school, from which it should be supplied with pupils, and a seminary. The change was made not without difficulty. The London Missionary Society applied for assistance in the form of a free grant of land, but Pottinger refused the request because the Morrison Education Society, of which he was patron and a keen supporter, had just set up a similar institution in the Colony and he thought there was not room for two. The London Missionary Society then appealed to the Secretary of State, who supported their request. Help also came from Sir John Davis, who was critical of the Morrison Education Society because it had become dominated by Americans. He was, therefore, strongly opposed to giving it a monopoly. Legge was given a suitable plot of land, and the College was transplanted without further obstacle.

Legge was first of all a missionary; other activities were subordinate, and he never allowed them to interfere with his proselytizing work. Supervision of the London Missionary Society's mission occupied much of his time. To those who doubted the efficacy or necessity of missionary work, he replied that it was a fact that any valuable principles which heathen religions might have had, had been obscured by superstition and overlaid by undesirable social customs, and that some action was necessary. He lost no opportunity of preaching to the Chinese both in his chapel and outside, or of personally persuading those whom he came to know. He emphasized education because he believed, as others did, that successful conversion of the Chinese could be achieved only if Chinese themselves were trained and used. Yet he proved his sincerity as an educationist by advocating education for the Chinese for its own sake, and he was instrumental in secularizing the government schools.

The Society's printing press and founts had been brought up from Malacca, and the work of printing tracts and portions of the Bible went on, with the help of the Religious Tract Society. Legge paid several visits to Canton, in spite of the many difficulties a missionary faced there. Travel in China was restricted, and entry to the city itself was denied to foreigners. Much anti-foreign feeling was manifest, and Chinese converts were subject to persecution. On one occasion, while visiting the island of Honan in the river opposite Canton, he and his friends were stoned. After the Second Anglo-Chinese War, travel inland for missionary work was permitted, and Legge set out in 1861 to visit some of his proselytes in Kwangtung Province. This was dangerous because of T'ai P'ing rebels, and before setting out on one occasion to visit Pok-lo, which at that time was a particularly disturbed area, Legge stipulated that if he were murdered, no gunboat should be sent to avenge his death.

He became a sinologue and was famous for his translation and annotation of the Chinese classics, which he published with the Chinese text. This great task sprang from his missionary zeal. He believed, in common with missionaries generally, that it was essential to be able to speak to people in their own language. He saw that much of Chinese life was regulated by principles contained in their classical literature, and believed this literature had to be mastered in order to understand the Chinese people well. He was eager to understand Chinese thought and philosophy, and so grasp the principles underlying China's moral and social life. In this way he hoped to build the missionary effort on a firm base. The appeal was to be a rational one, based on understanding. His great task of translation occupied him much of his life. He began in 1841, and it was twenty years before the first fruits appeared, the *Analects of Confucius*, in 1861. The publication was assisted by Joseph Jardine, who had been impressed on one occasion by hearing a Chinese boatman declare that Legge's Chinese was better than his own.

Legge was also occupied at intervals in translation of the Scriptures. To fundamentalist dissenters the Bible assumed a much greater importance than it did to Anglicans and other denominations to whom liturgy and doctrine were more essential sides of their faith. It is no accident that Nonconformists have produced some of the greatest missionary sinologues. Legge assisted in a new translation of the Bible, and entered into the controversy over the Chinese translation of the term "God", supporting the characters standing for *"Shang Ti"*, as against those for *"Tien Chue"*.

His great gifts as a Chinese scholar brought him a world reputation in making Chinese classical thought available to the West, but in this brief account the emphasis must be· on Legge as a Hong Kong man and on his special contribution to the Colony rather than on his immeasurably greater contribution to Western scholarship.

Successive attacks of fever compelled him to leave the Colony for home in 1845, and he was accompanied by his family, and three young Chinese students. He rapidly recovered, and sailed again in the spring of 1848 to resume his Hong Kong post. The next year he took charge of the Union Church which had become the responsibility of the London Missionary Society. Legge accepted his call on condition that he could continue to reach to his Chinese converts in Chinese on Sundays. He also became Presbyterian Chaplain to the Forces. This demanded additional church services on Sundays, attention to the welfare of the troops, and the entertainment of soldiers in his home. In one letter, his wife referred to twenty soldiers coming to tea as if it were a normal occurrence. His ministry at the Union Church was successful, and in 1863 a new Chapel became necessary. It was completed in 1865 as a result of his successful drive for funds.

There were years of sorrow too, for in 1852 his wife died, and he had already lost four of his six children, all under the age of three. In 1858 he went home on a visit and married again. In 1865 his wife and three children were sent home for health reasons, and two years later he resigned his pastorate to rejoin his family in Britain. The new minister at the Union Church did not last long, and in 1870 Legge was approached to return to Hong Kong and again take over the church. He accepted for a period of three years, and finally left Hong Kong in 1873.

He impressed his personality on the Colony's education system. Like his Anglican and Catholic confrères, he was at first anxious to use the school as an instrument of missionary work, to introduce the Bible, and to make his college supply students for his seminary. Yet not a single preacher was produced, and eventually, in 1856, the Anglo-Chinese College was closed. Standards were low, for the successful organization of primary education was the first need. Legge believed that the Government should give more assistance to Chinese education on a comprehensive and systematic level. Bowring, who arrived in 1854, was a secularist in education and was very keen to improve the whole education system. He discussed many reform projects, but in fact maintained existing church control and concentrated on expanding the school population, explaining that the religious bodies were the only ones on whom he could depend.

In 1853 Legge was invited to join the Education Committee which had been set up by Davis in 1848 to administer grants to the Chinese vernacular schools. It was presided over by the Anglican Bishop, Smith, after his arrival in 1850, but Legge quickly became one of its most influential and active members. Perhaps it was fortuitous, but the Education Committee's 1854 Annual Report, the first after Legge became a member, contained pungent criticisms, and suggestions for reform including the building of new schools, the introduction of a system of apprentice teachers, the employment of additional teachers, and the appointment of an inspector. In May 1856 a German missionary, Rev. W. Lobscheid, was appointed Inspector of Schools.

Bowring retired in 1859. The next Governor, Sir Hercules Robinson, was more receptive, and changes followed. In January 1860, the Education Committee gave way to a Board of Education, and its first duty was to consider a comprehensive scheme of reform proposed by Legge, details of which were given in the Board's *Annual Report* for 1860. Lobscheid had resigned from the Board, and Legge proposed that he should not be replaced. He thought that as the number of schools had grown to twenty, the Inspector could give only two or three hours a month to each and that this lack of adequate supervision made progress impossible. He suggested that schools in Victoria should be concentrated in one building, the Central School, and placed under a European master who was also to be responsible for inspecting the outlying village schools. Legge thought that such a headmaster, who was actually engaged in teaching the Chinese, would raise the standard of teaching and make the Central School the model. He proposed that the Central School in Victoria should concentrate on teaching English, since English education would be more efficient. Legge also proposed that as English teaching was in demand for its economic value, fees should be charged. This would make the teaching of English more prominent in the Colony and, Legge added, "it ought to be so". He further remarked that he had placed these same ideas before Davis when the first education grants were made in 1847. His scheme made no mention of Bible teaching.

The Board resolved that "Education in English should in its opinion enter more largely into the conduct of the principal schools than it has yet done", and accepted Legge's scheme. In 1862 Frederick Stewart arrived as the new headmaster, and gradually Legge's ideas were implemented. The Board was abolished in 1865 and Stewart was able to begin the process of secularization, but he maintained the fabric of vernacular education in the village schools, and insisted that Chinese occupy half the curriculum of the Central School.

Robinson, and his successor MacDonnell, had a high opinion of Legge, and consulted him on matters relating to the local Chinese community. Robinson submitted a draft of his cadet scheme to him for his comments, particularly regarding the proposal to give the cadets two years of Chinese language study. The first recruits, C. C. Smith, W. M. Deane, and M. S. Tonnochy, were placed under Legge's tutorship. Robinson was about to leave at the time these first cadets qualified in Chinese, and he paid warm tribute to Legge in a function at Government House, presenting him on behalf of the Government, with a silver tea and coffee service.

In 1851 Legge urged that the solemnization of marriage should be permitted in the Union Church, describing himself as a Presbyterian Congregationalist Dissenter. Bonham refused these urgings, but the Home Government agreed to Legge's request, which was supported by Bishop Smith. An ordinance was passed to allow such marriages, but Legge refused to be Registrar of Marriages under it.

Legge became prison visitor, and took an exceptional interest in prisoners, and in jail preaching, regarding it as an essential part of his missionary activity. He was consulted by MacDonnell over his legislation of 1866 and 1867 providing for closer supervision over the Chinese ashore and afloat. He was opposed to MacDonnell's plan to license gambling, and in 1871 organized a widely signed memorial against it, and also induced the Chamber of Commerce to make a strong protest. Legge gave evidence before the Police Commission of 1872, and advocated the recruitment of more Chinese into the police force, arguing that the police must know the Chinese habits and language, and must have the respect of law-abiding Chinese. This suggestion was to result in the solution of the police problem. In these various ways, Legge left his imprint upon Hong Kong.

In 1870 he was honoured with an LL.D. by the University of Aberdeen, and the University of Edinburgh soon followed suit. Shortly after his arrival home in 1873, merchants and others associated with the Far East proposed to endow a Professorship of Chinese at Oxford, on the understanding that Legge should be the first to occupy the position. A committee under the chairmanship of Sir Rutherford Alcock made the arrangements, the University accepted the plan and the nomination, and in 1875 Legge became the first Professor of Chinese at Oxford, and was elected a Fellow of Corpus Christi College. He remained at Oxford until his death in 1897. There, with the assistance of Max Muller, he was able to complete his translations of the Chinese classics, and to produce other works including a *Life and Teachings of Confucius* in 1875 and *The Nestorian Movement* in 1888.

What stands out about this great man is his astonishing vitality, his devotion to the Chinese, his deep religious convictions, and his interest in the daily affairs of the Colony. Almost to the time of his death his devotion to his work and his tireless industry drove him to begin his day at three a.m.

21

GEORGE CHINNERY

LITTLE ENOUGH is known about George Chinnery, the artist who found inspiration in the scenes and people of India and the Canton River area, and whose reputation has grown with the years.[1]

He was born in 1774, the son of William Chinnery of Gough Square, Fleet Street. The Chinnery family was artistic and it is not surprising that he became an artist at an early age, and sent miniatures to the Royal Academy in 1791. The family was of Irish extraction, and the next year Chinnery went to Dublin, possibly attracted either by the patronage of the Earl of Lansdowne,[2] or by members of the family remaining in Ireland. He spent the next ten years in Dublin, living at College Green in the house of a friend of the family, whose daughter he married. He is said to have contributed eleven pictures to an exhibition in Parliament House, Dublin, in 1801.

In 1802 he came back to London and took ship for Madras. There has been considerable conjecture as to the reason for this move to India. He left his wife in Ireland, and it is generally supposed that the marriage had failed, and that he wished to escape. He used later to say that he had married the ugliest woman he had ever met, and he certainly spent a great many years afterwards trying to escape from her, and in continual fear that she would follow him to Macao. The disintegration of the marriage was probably Chinnery's fault, for he was a difficult person—temperamental, capricious, casual, careless over money, and too completely absorbed in his art and whatever momentarily attracted him, to be capable of a normal domesticity. The American merchant, Gideon Nye, who came to Canton in 1833 and spent some forty years there, referred to him in a book of reminiscences as "the gifted genial artist, George Chinnery—of Irish birth, who in his youth had been compromised in the rebellious movement of Lord Edward Fitzgerald—but was allowed to live in India and China".[3] This may have been so, but is unlikely, because if Chinnery had been implicated in the 1798 rebellion in Ireland and forced to

---

1 The fullest account of his life is by E. W. Bovill in *Notes and Queries*, New Series, Vol. 1, Nos. 5 and 6. There is also an account by Montalto de Jesus in *The China Journal*, Vol. 8, No. 6, June, 1925.
2 See *Dictionary of National Biography*.
3 Gideon Nye, Jr., *The Morning of my Life in China*, published privately, Canton, 1873, p. 30.

leave on that account, it is probable that he would have taken his departure in that year and not delayed it until 1802 as he did.

Quite possibly the voyage to India was forced on him by those financial difficulties which so permanently beset him. His family was reasonably well off, and was connected with the merchant house of Chase, Sewell & Chinnery of Madras, and the trip to India may have been a business venture rather than a voluntary or enforced exile. One account[1] says that he first became interested in the East as a member of the Macartney Embassy to Peking in 1793. This is doubtful, as he would have been too young, and presumably he was still in Ireland at that time; his name does not appear in the list of persons who accompanied that mission, as given in A. Anderson's account, for example.[2] Thomas Hickey is mentioned there as the portrait painter of the party, and it is unlikely that there was a second, though the young Chinnery may have served in some other capacity.

He lived at Madras from 1802 to 1807, and made a name for himself as a portrait painter, then a useful social occupation similar to the present-day photographer. An important commission, the painting of the Chief Justice of Bengal, took him to Calcutta in 1807, and he remained there until 1825. He became a popular painter with many clients: "In Calcutta Chinnery painted the portraits of everyone from Governor-General to the three-year-old William Makepeace Thackeray".[3] He was still casual and unreliable, lacking in methodical habits, and was energetic only when inspired. Despite these defects of character, he seems to have done well financially, for his income, presumably entirely derived from his painting, was estimated at £500 a month.

In 1817 his daughter sailed from England to join him, and next year Mrs. Chinnery followed; in 1821 his son came out to India, and Chinnery was thus reunited with his family after a separation of some twenty years. In the meantime, his domestic responsibilities had been increased by the birth of two sons in India. The resumption of family life was unsuccessful. In 1822 Chinnery was in debt and fled from Calcutta to the shelter of the Danish factory of Serampore, and three years later he sought voluntary exile on the China coast.

William Hickey, in the fourth volume of his *Memoirs*, covering his life in Calcutta from the year 1790 until he left in 1808, referred to Chinnery as an excellent Persian scholar[4] and gave the following description: "Mr. Chinnery, like many other men of

---

1 The *Dictionary of National Biography.*
2 A. Anderson, *Macartney's Embassy to China 1792–94.*
3 E. W. Bovill, *Notes and Queries,* May 1934.
4 *Memoirs of William Hickey,* 4 volumes, London, 1925, Vol. 4, p. 361.

extraordinary talent, was extremely odd and eccentric, so much so as at times to make me think him deranged. His health certainly was not good; and he had a strong tendency to hypochondria which frequently made him ridiculously fanciful, yet in spite of his mental and bodily infirmities, personal vanity showed itself in various ways".[1] Hickey also mentioned a report that Chinnery became insane: "I have lately heard that soon after my departure, Mr. Chinnery became determinedly insane and has ever since been kept under restriction, being now pronounced a confirmed and incurable lunatic".[2] This is plainly hearsay and since it is without corroboration, cannot be accepted as a statement of fact.

So began the last phase of his chequered life. From 1825 until his death in 1852, he made his home in the Portuguese Colony of Macao. One of the American residents of Canton and Macao who knew him well, W. C. Hunter, has given an amusing picture of the artist as he was in these Macao years in his book *Bits of Old China*.

He was very popular in Macao and Canton, and a very good talker, and was not averse to talking about himself with a sense of humour, a readiness to tell a joke against himself, and an apparently unlimited supply of anecdotes. "As a story-teller", says Hunter, "his words and manner equalled his skill with the brush". He has also given a brief description of his appearance: "While to one of the ugliest of faces were added deep-set eyes with heavy brows, beaming with expression and good-nature". Hunter says that he "took himself a wife" in Calcutta, and mentions the birth of a daughter there, but says nothing about the arrival of Mrs. Chinnery in 1818. He says that he left Calcutta because of "serious troubles" and "being tied, as he would say, to the ugliest woman he ever saw in the whole course of his life". This wife evasion became a staple of Chinnery's conversation and humour.

It was at Canton that Hunter first met him, for on his arrival on the China coast, Chinnery, in his anxiety to shake off Mrs. Chinnery, went from Macao direct to Canton where residence in the factories was forbidden to European women under the Chinese regulations controlling foreign traders. Chinnery used to refer to this regulation "that forbids the softer sex from coming and bothering us here" as "a kind providence"; he was grateful to the Chinese and praised their wisdom. But he was capable of making a good story out of any material, and probably his debts alone were a sufficiently compelling motive to drive him to China. Hunter describes one painting, which he says no one had seen,[3] and which

---

1 ibid., p. 385.   2 ibid., p. 387.
3 But Gideon Nye describes the same picture, which must therefore have been known to others.

illustrated his departure from Calcutta. It portrayed a European about to leave by ship, with the caption "200°: Too hot for me".

Chinnery became, as he had been at Calcutta, a general favourite with the foreign community at Macao.[1] He was himself "fascinatingly ugly", and an acute observer of human nature. He seemed quite uninhibited and made himself a popular guest wherever he went. He was an agreeable companion and "a much-sought-for guest", according to Hunter. He never had any money, and was unable to afford clothes which would enable him to appear at dinner conventionally dressed, but that was not allowed to limit the flow of invitations or deter his acceptance of them. He was eccentric in an attractive way and was notorious as a large eater. He totally abstained from alcohol. He took snuff, smoked, and snorted, which alarmed the ladies, though they found him "really polite", and an American lady, Miss Low, noted that "he speaks well of everyone".

Chinnery's artistic genius included the stage. He was "a welcome accession in the private theatricals of those days and I remember took the part of Madame Malaprop in the 'Rivals' ".[2]

He sent regular remittances to his wife, but was always afraid that she would follow him and on occasion he would come rushing up to Canton as a result of some rumour that his wife was on her way, much to the amusement of all his friends and not least of himself. Chinnery's relations with his wife were part of the diversions of society at Macao and Canton, and his treatment of the topic seems to have remained perennially fresh. A Calcutta newspaper announcement referring to "George Chinnery, an absconding debtor" annoyed him not because of the allegation that he was a debtor, but because the word "Esquire" had been omitted.

In 1839, on Elliot's refusal to resume trade at Canton, Commissioner Lin Tse-hsu tried to drive the British out of their refuge in Macao, and created such difficulties for the Portuguese authorities there that the British community was withdrawn to Hong Kong harbour on board merchant vessels. Chinnery was one of the very few who refused to leave. He regretted his boldness, and wrote to James Matheson saying that he was "living in the greatest misery I assure you",[3] expressing a wish to paint or attempt to paint a few good pictures before he was "put to the sword", and displaying the greatest anxiety as to his safety. He even contemplated a return

---

1 It may be noted that E. W. Bovill makes some errors regarding the foreign community at Macao; e.g. he refers to Dr. James Morrison as interpreter to Jardine, Matheson & Company, as one of two noted missionaries. This should be Dr. Robert Morrison, interpreter to the East India Company. The other, Charles Gutzlaff, is incorrectly referred to as a medical man.
2 Gideon Nye, op. cit., p. 32.
3 Quoted by E. W. Bovill, *Notes and Queries*, June, 1934.

to Calcutta, and to the society of Mrs. Chinnery, so unattractive did his existing plight appear.

He remained in Macao until his death from apoplexy on 30 May 1852 at the age of seventy-eight, Hunter and other friends being with him at the last. His sketches and paintings were sold in the absence of any will bequeathing his property. He died in comparative poverty. As his many friends of the old Canton days left the coast, the circle of his friendship had narrowed. The passing of the Honourable East India Company from Canton in 1834, and the arrival of the free-trading merchants gave him a different clientele. He opened an art school and one of his former pupils, Lamqua, began painting portraits at the cut price of $25, a competition not to Chinnery's advantage. Another pupil, Marciano Baptista, carried on his tradition, and has left behind many views of Hong Kong and Macao, said to be notable for accuracy of detail.

Chinnery remained a portrait painter and painter of miniatures to the last, but he did many sketches and colour drawings of scenes and life in the Canton area. Macao continued to attract him, and he did comparatively few drawings of Hong Kong. There are some, however, as proof that he came to the island but the local records make few references to him, and there is nothing about him in the official government records. Hong Kong was busy, bustling, and commercial, and his preference for Macao, mellow with age, Mediterranean in character, peaceful, and relatively well-ordered can be readily understood. Chinnery was happy there.

Possessed of the true artistic outlook, money did not interest him or worry him. He remained to the last a casual spendthrift, devoted to his art, and the art of living, and seeking the society of friends. He was at home in a predominantly male society, yet had ease of manner in social intercourse with all. People admired him partly because he devoted himself to his art and did not choose to seek the wealth which was within his reach. He was conscious of his skill, sent paintings to the Royal Academy, and did not consider it immodest to compare himself with the painters of his day. He took particular care to mix his colours himself and that is probably the reason for the continued freshness of his paintings. He was not much influenced by the Chinese style of painting, but he did do his miniatures on ivory, and this form seemed particularly to suit him. His forte was pencil and pen-and-ink sketches. He was assiduous, and went regularly by chair every morning to sketch, but he was in the habit of stopping and working at any subject that took his fancy, to the interest and amusement of the Chinese. Montalto de Jesus, in his brief note on Chinnery in the *China Journal of Arts and Sciences*, No. 6, June 1928, relates that Chinnery painted an oil lamp on the door of his house which was so life-like that the Chinese tried to handle it. Certainly his paintings have enriched the records of that time.

Gideon Nye has left us his impressions: "His ample fund of anecdote will soon be utterly forgotten; but his works of Art—being the emanations of a real genius will outlive us all, ... Chinnery had also some of the, so-called, characteristic weaknesses of genius, with his geniality of disposition; and such an exuberance of imagination and fancy that there was gusto in much that he did approaching the grotesque. He wielded a vigorous and facile, though somewhat wayward pencil—it was Nature's self in conveying action...".

The Chinese thought highly of him partly because he was one of the few foreigners to make his home in China, and his memory remained alive for many years.[1] He finds a place in this portrait gallery, though he can hardly be called a Hong Kong man, because he left a permanent record of the Hong Kong of his day and so earned the gratitude of the lover of beauty and of the historian. Part of his tragedy was that he, the most friendly and sociable of men, outstayed his friends, as most retired from the East, very few electing to live there as Chinnery did. He attempted to work almost to the last. *The Friend of China* of 2 June 1852 gives a touching account of his last days, when he was dependent on the generosity of others.

He was buried in the Protestant Cemetery at Macao, and the British residents there, by public subscription, had a memorial placed over his grave in the form of a stone slab with pillars in relief against a wall of the cemetery. There was some delay and Nye mentioned (1873) that it had not yet arrived from England.

---

1 E. W. Bovill, loc. cit.

22

Some Other Foreigners

IN THIS chapter an attempt will be made to describe more briefly some other characters of Hong Kong's early years. Among those of the foreign community who came to the Colony to trade or to government service or who merely drifted to the island, were many adventurer types. They were frequently interesting characters, and naturally so, because only the enterprising or the fugitive ventured as far as Hong Kong.

One who earned a doubtful reputation for himself was James Summers, a young schoolmaster appointed by The Rev. Vincent Stanton, the Colonial Chaplain, to the staff of his English school, and who afterwards taught in St. Paul's College. In June 1849 Summers went to Macao and, in that very Catholic city, fell in with a religious procession celebrating the feast of Corpus Christi. He was apparently a bigoted Protestant and refused to kneel, raise his hat, or show any mark of respect, although asked to do so. His discourtesy caused resentment, and he was taken into custody, partly for his own protection, and placed in the common jail. He managed to get letters sent out to make his imprisonment known. The Senior Naval Officer, Captain H. Keppel, was at Macao at the time with H.M.S. *Moeander,* but was on the point of sailing for Manila. Keppel called on Amaral, the Governor of Macao, and personally requested the liberation of the prisoner, but without success. He then wrote a formal application, and when that produced no result, landed a naval party and forcibly removed Summers from the jail, killing one Portuguese and injuring others in the process.

The Portuguese properly protested. In the diplomatic exchanges which followed it was clear that Lord Palmerston approved of this daring and spectacular rescue. He defended Keppel's action by the specious argument that Macao was not properly a part of the Portuguese dominions but was still under Chinese sovereignty, and so, under the Treaty of the Bogue, which granted extraterritorial rights, a British subject should have been handed over to the British authorities for trial. Palmerston also thought there was some doubt whether Summers had committed any criminal offence at all. Some amends were eventually given to the widow of the Portuguese soldier.

It was this incident which partly determined Amaral to declare

Macao a free port and close the Chinese customs office there, setting in train events that were to lead to his assassination. Summers remained unrepentant, and considered his attitude quite justified. Such truculence was not an unusual characteristic of the British of that time, and of the determination with which they forced their way into every part of the world, supported by Palmerston, who won the hearts of his fellow-countrymen by matching their audacity in the diplomatic field. Summers remained in the Colony only a short time, and then returned to England and became Professor of Chinese at King's College, London, succeeding another former Hong Kong resident, Samuel Fearon.

It must not be concluded that all who were associated with St. Paul's College were as foolishly bigoted as Summers. The first Colonial Chaplain and founder of the College was The Rev. Vincent Stanton. He came to Macao as a student and acted as Chaplain at Macao. He was kidnapped in August 1840 while bathing, and taken to Canton, where he was kept in chains until liberated in December of that year through Captain Elliot's intervention. He returned to England, and shortly afterwards was appointed Colonial Chaplain, arriving in Hong Kong in time to preach his first sermon in the mat-shed church on the military parade ground on Christmas Day 1843. He founded a free school for English children, which did not last long, as the Secretary of State refused to allow it a grant from public funds. Stanton set about organizing a seminary for the training of Anglican ministers, which he named St. Paul's College. He obtained a site, but it is difficult to know what progress had been made with the actual building before Bishop George Smith arrived in March 1850. The bishopric had been endowed by private gifts and a grant from the Society for the Promotion of Christian Knowledge, and there was money from the same sources for the endowment of St. Paul's College, which Stanton handed over to the Bishop.

Stanton left in the same summer due to ill-health, and did not return. He resigned the colonial chaplaincy and took a living in Middlesex which he soon had to resign because of illness, but he lived until 1891. St. Paul's College was built in 1851 and became entirely associated with the Bishop, so that the work of Stanton in founding the Cathedral and College was forgotten, to his disappointment.

Sufficient has been said in the chapter on William Tarrant to indicate that Hong Kong had an aggressive and vituperative Press. One editor who looked for and found trouble was Yorick Jones Murrow. A Welshman born in 1817, he came to China in 1838 and joined the old Canton firm of Jamieson, How & Co. He later set

148

up in commerce on his own account in Hong Kong and Canton, but did not flourish, and the Second Anglo-Chinese War further affected his business. In 1858 he took over the *Hong Kong Daily Press* which had been founded in 1857 under the editorship of a man named Ryder. The *Hong Kong Daily Press* gradually displaced *The Friend of China* when that paper declined owing to the misfortunes of William Tarrant. Murrow edited the *Hong Kong Daily Press* until 1867 when he retired from the Colony, but he remained its proprietor until his death in Jersey in March 1884.

Murrow was able, energetic, and public-spirited. He was vigilant over suspected public or private corruption, and subjected the actions of the Government to unceasing examination and criticism, quite undaunted by the fate of Tarrant.

Like most people in Hong Kong, he fell foul of Anstey. This happened in 1857 over the latter's defence of Cheong Ah Lum in the poisoned bread case, when Murrow considered that aspersions on his character had been made. No names had been mentioned in Anstey's speech, and the objectionable remarks concerned "a dilapidated individual" which Murrow said everyone knew meant himself. Later in the same year, a long letter abusing public officials in Hong Kong appeared in *The Straits Times*; Murrow was suspected of being the author, but denied this. In the course of defending himself, Murrow accused the Hong Kong Government of increasing his land rents out of spite for a letter he did not write.

In one article attacking the Government, Murrow accused Bowring of favouring the merchant house of Jardine, Matheson & Co., of which his son was a partner. The Governor instituted proceedings for libel, and Murrow was found guilty, fined £100, and sentenced to six months' imprisonment. At Bowring's suggestion he was treated indulgently and was allowed to serve the sentence not in the common jail, but in the debtors' prison, where the freedom normally allowed would enable him to continue. to produce and edit his paper. Murrow remained bitter and vindictive, and continued to attack Bowring in spite of this lenient treatment. On his liberation at the end of the year (1858), Murrow brought an action against the Governor for false imprisonment, but the Chief Justice ruled that Bowring was not involved, and Murrow lost his case.

Murrow's desire to expose abuses showed no sign of abating. In the Civil Service Abuses Enquiry of 1860, he was the only member of the general public to respond to Sir Hercules Robinson's appeal to supply information, but Murrow was a known enemy of Caldwell, and the Governor privately did not welcome so prejudiced an intervention. Late in 1861 Murrow wrote to the Secretary of

State, the Duke of Newcastle, and charged the Hong Kong Government with irregularities. He alleged that the Registrar of the Supreme Court was receiving half the court fees for his own private advantage. These fees were received not as Registrar but as Acting Official Administrator, Assignee, and Registrar of the Admiralty Court and were collected for the holder of those offices who had gone on leave, and who received the remaining half. The old rule that each received half fees had been changed, and the Treasury ought to have received half the fees, but Robinson explained this change had not been promulgated in the Colony. It was found that the information on this subject had been supplied by Forth, the Colonial Treasurer, who was reprimanded.

Murrow also charged that Robinson had suppressed the annual reports of the Colonial Surgeon for the years 1859, 1860, and 1861. The Governor replied that the first had been published, and that the second contained strictures which should have been brought up during the year and not in the annual report. The third report, that for 1861, had only just been received and again contained serious charges which made its publication undesirable.

Murrow then offered to prove charges against Caldwell, Bridges, and Mercer regarding the lorcha *Kee Lung Poo Oan* which had figured in the enquiry into the Caldwell affair, if the Government would open its archives to him. The Duke of Newcastle refused to reopen the enquiry and ruled that Murrow should present any facts he had in his possession with a view to a criminal prosecution against the men he named, or should be allowed to bring a specific charge if he wanted to, but that he should be given no other assistance. Murrow wrote to the Duke repeating his charges, but again without bringing any evidence. Mercer ignored Murrow completely, though he felt it necessary to explain to the Duke that he was not on such friendly terms with Bridges as Murrow suggested. The Duke warned Murrow that as he had failed to substantiate his charges, further communications from him would not have the same consideration they had had in the past.

Murrow continued to make accusations and complaints. He accused Judge Ball of the Summary Court of submitting cases to the arbitrament of Caldwell, and sent home three photos showing rocks and rubble lying in the Chancery Lane and Old Bailey Road, near the jail, to show the difficulties of access to his office. When he failed to retain the interest of the Secretary of State his attacks became less violent. He left Hong Kong in 1867 and retired to Jersey, where he died in 1884.

The newspaper with the longest history in the Colony and which still exists, is the *China Mail*. It was founded by Andrew

Shortrede, who arrived in the Colony in March 1845 with a letter of introduction from the Colonial Office. He was welcomed by Sir John Davis as a man of better education and "a fitter subject of patronage than the others [editors]" and the contract to publish the *Government Gazette* was given to him. A Colonial Office minute on Davis's letter announcing Shortrede's arrival gave the information that "Mr. S. has been long and zealously connected with the Conservative Party and is well known both in Edinburgh and in this country. His father, Mr. Shortrede, was a great friend of Sir Walter Scott's in early life...".

The *China Mail,* which he owned and edited, became an influential paper, though it later passed through lean times in competition with Murrow's *Daily Press,* but Shortrede himself proved a disappointment. He quickly got into trouble with Major Caine, whom he accused anonymously of receiving money levied on prostitutes. In fact, a voluntary lock-hospital had been set up on a basis of voluntary payments; the mistaken view was traced to Shortrede and the matter was closed by an apology to Caine.

Bonham sent home a report on the local Press in August 1850 which curiously did not mention the *China Mail.* In 1853 he reported again; the *Hong Kong Register* and the *China Mail* were described as appearing weekly, and *The Friend of China* twice a week. He remarked that "none of these is remarkable for being well-conducted" and said they all had much the same circulation, and were often vexatious to the public authorities, but did little harm. He complained that the *China Mail* "lately has virulent malicious and ill-founded attacks on myself and others" and said that the *Hong Kong Register* " had been employed to print official forms because its prices for this work were found to be 60 per cent cheaper than the *Mail*" and he thought this had caused Shortrede's ill-will. The Governor then discovered that the *Register* would print official government publications 20 per cent more cheaply. He soon made the change, and in October 1853 Bonham decided to terminate all contracts with local newspapers and to publish a weekly *Government Gazette* with all official notifications. The *Hong Kong Register* undertook the printing for £150 per year; Shortrede had been getting £550 for the same work.

The change was not successful, and in April 1855 the printer was declared incapable; tenders were invited for printing the *Gazette* and the contract with the *Hong Kong Register* was terminated in June 1856. This was partly because Bevan, its editor, was guilty of scurrilous attacks on Bowring, and because as temporary Chief Justice's Clerk, he used confidential information to the advantage of his paper. Shortrede soon disappeared from the Hong

Kong story but the paper he founded still appears.

Henry Charles Sirr came to the Colony in May 1844 *en route* to one of the Treaty Ports to take up the post of Vice-Consul. Reaching Hong Kong, he decided to give up the appointment and remain in the island, and he became the first barrister to practise there. When the Supreme Court was set up later in the year, he was one of the first to be admitted to practice. He did not remain long. He took a government appointment in Ceylon, which proved equally temporary. Sirr was not interested in the law. He was in fact by inclination a journalist. His book, *China and the Chinese,* published in London in 1849, was brightly written, full of interesting detail, and designed to entertain; it was the work of an observant man interested in human beings and one who found life amusing. In a later age he would have become foreign correspondent of a leading newspaper or journal.

Something might be said of George Duddell, a resident of the Colony for some thirty years whose name is perpetuated in Duddell Street. It is impossible to give a full account of his activities. He did not belong to the official class or to the professions or to the influential merchant class, but to the humbler ranks of society whose comings and goings were considered less worthy of record. Yet his name crops up now and again in the Colony's records, generally when he was in difficulties. He is interesting because he typifies the Englishman of the early- and mid-Victorian periods who went overseas to make their way in the world and succeeded. They were often without capital or political or social influence or even much education; their great assets were personality, energy, enterprise, and the determination to "get on". Often such men either came with the forces and elected to stay, or had run away to sea, the conventional starting point of the career of a Victorian. Duddell became an auctioneer, and this remained his bread-and-butter occupation. There was much competition and heavy taxation; under Davis's financial arrangements, auctioneers had to pay a licence fee of $50 and a 2½ per cent levy on all sales. In August 1848, eight auctioneers, including Duddell, successfully petitioned the Governor to remove the 2½ per cent levy and increase the licence fee to $100 or $150 instead. He was the first holder of the opium monopoly set up for the sale of opium in Hong Kong in 1845.

He became friendly with Holdforth, Assistant Magistrate and Sheriff, and received from him the right of conducting the "Sheriff's Sales" which had been conducted by Markwick, the official Government Auctioneer. The general view at the time was that Duddell had bought this right. The two men worked together over the auction sales; Duddell used to knock down lots on the cheap to himself, or to Holdforth acting for him, hoping to resell at a profit. This practice came to light in 1850, when, as a result of proceedings in the Admiralty Court, of which Holdforth was Marshall, Duddell was employed to sell a ship at auction, and upon enquiry was discovered to have knocked it down to himself. The Chief Justice ordered a re-auction at which the ship fetched $400 more than on the previous occasion, and Duddell lost his profit. The partnership came to an end when Holdforth left in 1850. In 1857 the Government Auctioneer Markwick was murdered, and Duddell succeeded him as the official Government Auctioneer, despite irregularities which, fortunately for him, only rarely came to light.

Duddell turned to other methods of making money. He established a bakery which was burnt down in February 1857, just following the bread poisoning episode. In November 1849 he was reported as having taken the lease of the Western Market for five years at $225 per month.

In a new British Colony, speculation provided the great opportunity. In October 1846 a proposal was made to build an Ice House by public subscription, and Davis sent home a sketch showing the site and proposing to construct a road (now Upper Ice House Street) by convict labour. In this sketch, a road parallel to the proposed road is marked as Duddell Street, and while it does not follow that a street necessarily existed, it does seem to show that Duddell had considerable property there at that time. When the Ice House Company was dissolved in December 1851, Duddell was anxious to take over the house and plot and was allowed to do so at the usual upset price.

Unfortunately Hong Kong failed to develop economically as expected, land values slumped, and the speculators were hit. For a few years, beginning in 1848, lot-holders began throwing up their lots, to the detriment of the public revenue, and after some hesitation Bonham allowed them to do this provided they paid up all arrears of rent. Duddell was hard hit, and began giving up some of his land. He gave up one plot in January 1848, and another plot was described in January 1849 as having upon it "houses in ruinous condition". The problem became so serious that in 1849 the term of the leases which had been fixed at seventy-five years was extended to 999 years, to encourage the holders to retain their holdings. A Land Committee was set up to make a full enquiry into the land question and to remove any proved hardships. The Committee gave a list of landholders which showed Duddell as the third largest holder in the Colony, having twenty-five plots for which he paid an annual rent of £621. 17s. 10d., about half of which were in the areas reserved for Chinese habitation. All the holders were invited to state their claims for a reduction of rents on ground of hardship, but only eleven did so, ten foreigners and one Chinese, involving forty-three lots, twenty-two of which were owned by Duddell. Only seven lots were recommended for reduction. The Committee refused to reduce the rents of plots which had been bought from the original purchasers, often at low prices. On this point, reference was made to four plots held by Duddell which he had bought from the feckless and impecunious Auditor-General, Shelley, when the latter left the Colony in 1847. Duddell was stated in the report to have bought these four lots at public auction for the ridiculous sum of £1. 0s. 10d. When he was made to pay arrears of rent which Shelley had left unpaid, he asked for a reduction of rent, but the application was naturally not sympathetically received.

Duddell became an owner of substance as the Colony expanded and and land values improved. He was involved in the currency question which came to the front in 1854. By the currency proclamation of 1845, parities between various British and Indian coins, and the silver dollar had been established and given legal sanction. The Chinese preference for silver dollars put them at a premium in the market, and it became profitable to make payments in British coins which could be bought cheaply and which were legal tender. Duddell rented some property from a ship-owner, Lapraik, and insisted on paying his rents in British money. Lapraik demanded dollars in accordance with his contract with Duddell, and took the case to court, where the Chief Justice ruled that the rents should be paid in dollars and not in other currency even if it were of equal value.

Duddell appeared before the public eye in 1870. In June of that year General Whitfield, who was administering the Government at the time, bought from Duddell some land situated just above the Botanical Gardens, for the purpose of building a new civil hospital. Duddell raised great opposition to the purchase, claiming that his private interests were being sacrificed, with the apparent object of securing a greater amount in compensation by representing the lots as having great value to him. The General then changed his mind and decided not to proceed with the scheme or take over the land. Duddell, however, then insisted that the Government carry through the purchase which it had undertaken, and so the plots were bought, and added to the Botanical Gardens. Duddell was at least an inadvertent benefactor of the Colony.

This chapter ought not to be concluded without reference to a lady, Miss Harriet Baxter, who devoted herself to the cause of the education of Chinese girls in Hong Kong in the 1860's. It will hardly have escaped notice that she is the only person to appear in this collection to redeem it from its otherwise exclusively masculine complexion. This may be regrettable but cannot excite surprise because early colonial society in Hong Kong was predominantly male. In a typical year, 1854, there were 40,517 males out of a total population of 55,715, the discrepancy being more marked among the Chinese than among the Europeans. It is not that there were no able women capable of making a contribution to the community; it was simply that in a society in which convention was a powerful force, it was unconventional for a woman to seek the prominence of public life.

Harriet Baxter came to Hong Kong in 1860. She was an Anglican missionary, but was not sent out by the official Anglican missionary body, the Church Missionary Society, because that society did not at that date send single women out into the field. She worked for the Female Education Society and was possibly brought out from England by Mrs. George Smith, wife of the Anglican Bishop, who was at that time strongly advocating schools for Chinese girls. Eitel says that Harriet Baxter "beside much samaritan activity among all classes of the community and valuable zenana-work among Chinese women, commenced to labour for the education of the Eurasian children of the Colony", from which it appears that her work was not confined to the education of girls. He says, "She established schools in the Mosque Terrace and in Staunton Street which were subsequently amalgamated and located in Baxter House, Bonham Road [now No. 8 Police Station]."

The 1864 Education Report mentions this school in Bonham Road as being under her and as containing forty-eight boys and fourteen girls. Miss Baxter founded other schools, all subsequently known as the Baxter Mission Schools, certainly one in Hollywood Road, and probably others in Queen's Road, D'Aguilar Street, and West Point. The Hollywood Road School was destroyed by fire, and was re-erected in 1876 on the same site. This building still exists (1962) and was used as a Church Missionary Society Day School until 1958, and in it there is a tablet to Miss Baxter's memory. She died on 30 June, 1865, after only five years in the Colony, and her grave can still be seen in the Colonial Cemetery in the Happy Valley.

There is a letter in the local Diocesan records relating an incident which shows something of the hazards of the Hong Kong of her day. She was walking along Bonham Road after dark, and, being approached by an unrecognized acquaintance, she nearly shot him before she discovered that he was a friend.

The Baxter Mission Schools lasted some years under Miss Oxlad and then under Miss Johnstone, and became known as the Baxter

Vernacular Schools; in the 1883 Report of the Inspector of Schools, there were five, all girls' schools. By 1886, they were known as F.E.S. (Female Education Society) Schools, and later some, if not all, were taken over by the Church Missionary Society.

It must not be inferred that Miss Baxter worked alone in this field. The Daughters of Charity, were certainly similarly at work in the cause of girls' education, and in Miss Baxter's own day, the Misses Legge of the London Missionary Society and Miss Eaton, who came to Hong Kong in 1862 and subsequently became the wife of E. J. Eitel, the Colony's historian, were working in the same field. But she alone attached her name to a group of schools, and that of itself is tribute to her personality and influence.

23

THE PRINCELY HONG

IT is high time to mention the men who really mattered in Hong Kong, namely the merchants who played leading parts in the economic activities for which the Colony had come into being, and on which the interests of all other groups on the island were in the long run dependent. Hong Kong was established to protect and encourage British trade with China: "Hong Kong except for the security of British commerce is unnecessary", declared William Ewart Gladstone in 1846.

The difficulty facing the historian is the absence of those personal and intimate records by which members of the merchant class could be brought back to life, for it is in the nature of things that the merchant should prefer the privacy of his own counting-house, and that neither in business nor in private life would he normally welcome any publicity not of his own choosing. There is insufficient available material to permit the biographer to resurrect those men and bring them before the reader as living people.

In pride of place must come some of the men who guided the fortunes of Jardine, Matheson & Co., the "Princely Hong", often referred to as "Ewo", from its close business associations with a Hong merchant of the old Canton days, Howqua or Woo Haou Kwan, whose trade name this was. The House was founded in 1832 by Dr. William Jardine and James Matheson both of whom had been partners with H. Magniac, of Magniac & Co.

Jardine was born in 1784 at Lochmaben, Dumfriesshire. After qualifying in medicine, he joined the service of the English East India Company as a ship's surgeon, and went to the East in 1802. About the year 1819 he started a business on his own account in Bombay, in close association with some Parsee merchants, and he joined Magniac & Co. in 1827. His interests in the China trade became so extensive as to demand his residence in Canton and Macao from 1827. He was described by Magniac as "honourable and liberal beyond what we generally meet with in the general intercourse of business transactions".[1] W. C. Hunter in his book *The Fan Kwae at Canton* described Jardine as "a gentleman of great strength of character and of unbounded liberality" and he added, "As a peculiarity of his character, it may be mentioned that,

---

1 *Jardine, Matheson & Co. 1832–1932*, Hong Kong, printed privately, 1934, p. 12. Much of the information given in this chapter is taken from this source.

in his own private office in the Creek Factory, a chair was never seen—a hint to any who may be bothered with gossips or idlers during business hours".[1] He shipped the first cargo of "free" teas to London after the ending of the East India Company's monopoly, and one authority estimated that the Jardine House controlled one-third of the foreign trade at Canton during the first few years of free trade with up to seventy-five ships under his control in any one trading season.[2] He quickly became the most influential of the British merchants in Canton and was one of those who encouraged Lord Napier to take a strong line against the Chinese in 1834 by ordering up the two frigates to Canton. He retired from Canton in January 1839,[3] and the occasion was marked by a public dinner given by the community as a tribute to his influence and public-spirit. His name, "The iron-headed old rat", was apparently given him by the Chinese after he had unflinchingly endured a buffeting from them at the city gate. He retired from business in 1840 and the next year became Member of Parliament in the Whig interest for Ashburton, Devon. He thus fulfilled an ambition for a political career of which he had made no secret among his friends while in Canton, and which his commercial rival, J. M. Dent, had openly ridiculed as a pipe-dream.

In England he became more influential in the shaping of British policy in the Far East than he had been in Canton, for he was able to gain the ear of Lord Palmerston through a mutual friend, J. A. Smith. In a letter to Smith dated 26 November 1842, the Foreign Secretary acknowledged his debt to Jardine[4] in these words: "To the assistance and information which you, my dear Smith, and Mr. Jardine so handsomely afforded us, it was mainly owing that we were able to give our affairs, naval, military and diplomatic, in China, those detailed instructions which have led to these satisfactory results". The letter also paid tribute to the fact that the information supplied by Jardine "which was embodied in the instructions which we gave in February 1840, was so accurate and complete". In fact, the British demands and the mode of conducting hostilities followed very closely the proposals which Jardine had submitted. The concessions secured in the Treaty of Nanking, including the cession of Hong Kong, are in large measure due to Jardine. He never saw the Colony, though during his long stay in the Delta it is most improbable that he never saw the island, and yet he must be regarded as one of the founders of the Colony of Hong Kong, and must take his place as a matter of right in this

---

1 W. C. Hunter, *The Fan Kwae at Canton*, p. 135.
2 Gideon Nye, *Morning of My Life in China*, p. 26.
3 Hunter gives the date as November 1838, and Nye repeats this.
4 Maurice Collis, *Foreign Mud*, p. 262–6.

DR. WILLIAM JARDINE

Hong Kong gallery. He died shortly after the war was over, in 1843, in his fifty-ninth year. By general consensus of opinion his enterprise, strength of character, decision, public-spirit, and generosity combined to give him a position of accepted leadership in the Canton foreign community.

Jardine's partner was Nicholas James Sutherland Matheson (later Sir N. J. S. Matheson of the Lews, Bart.) who had joined the firm of Magniac & Co. in 1828, and with whom he founded in 1832 the famous commercial house that bears their names. Matheson was born at Lairg, Sutherlandshire, in 1796, and his mother was a daughter of the local minister. He went up to Edinburgh University from the local High School and went out to Calcutta in 1813 in the employ of his uncle's firm, Mackintosh & Co. The story is related that he forgot to deliver an important business letter to the captain of a vessel before it departed and as a result was told by his uncle to return home. While taking steps to carry out this probably unintended injunction, he was advised by a ship's captain to try his fortunes in Canton[1] and so he found himself in China in 1818.

He became Danish Consul in 1823, and this post put him beyond the reach of the East India Company's officials who for some years tried to prevent private English merchants from taking up residence in Canton. There he formed business associations with Jardine and Magniac which led to their entering into partnership, and eventually to the establishment of Jardine, Matheson & Co. in 1832. He became head of the partnership when Jardine retired, and he himself retired shortly after, in 1842. He succeeded Jardine as M.P. for Ashburton in 1843, and held the seat until 1847, after which he sat as member for Ross and Cromarty until 1862. He was created Baronet in 1851 for his work in relieving famine on the Island of Lewis, which he had purchased seven years before. He died at Mentone in 1878.

As head of Jardine, Matheson & Co. during the war against China, 1840–2, he was responsible for the firm's early move to Hong Kong and its establishment at East Point, and for pushing on with the development of the site before the outcome of hostilities could have been known for certain.

One early partner may be briefly mentioned here, though he can hardly be called a Hong Kong man. He is Henry Wright, a partner from 1829 (Magniac & Co.) until his retirement in 1841. Referred to as "Old Wright", Gideon Nye says of him that he "had not left their Hong for seven years, and who, on looking around found he had no hat!"[2]

---

1 *Jardine, Matheson & Co. 1832–1932*, p. 4.
2 Gideon Nye, op. cit., p. 28.

James Matheson was succeeded as head of the firm by his nephew, Alexander Matheson,[1] who joined Lyall, Matheson & Co. in Calcutta, and in 1835 became a partner of Jardine, Matheson & Co. He left China in 1846 but remained head of the firm until 1852. He became a Director of the Bank of England in 1848, sat as M.P. for Inverness Burghs from 1847 to 1868, and then followed his uncle as M.P. for Ross County from 1868 to 1884. He is said to have "made a huge fortune in the East, and about 1851 bought large estates in Ross-shire, it being stated that his total possessions in that county had cost £773,000",[2] but that he had had to sell much of his estates in the last four years of his life because of pecuniary misfortunes. W. C. Hunter records that he was partly instrumental in founding the first foreign newspaper in Canton, The *Canton Register*, "which was printed on a small hand-press lent for the purpose by Mr. Alexander Matheson, of the then house of Magniac & Co. Its [the paper's] size was but a little more than that of a large sheet of foolscap".[3] Hunter added a footnote as if he were not sure of this, to the effect that, "The late Sir James Matheson was the reputed founder of the foreign press in China [the *Canton Register*]; but it was an open question whether it was he or Mr. Wood. I contributed to that paper … but in the consequent daily intercourse with Wood, he never hinted that he was not its sole founder. If my memory serves me Sir James was at the time on a trip up the coast. Nevertheless there is but one 'old Canton' who can decide the point, the present Sir Alexander Matheson". (Hunter was writing in 1882.) It is unlikely that the Mathesons would have supplied the press if they did not control or approve of the editorship.

Sir Alexander Matheson was made a baronet in 1882 and died in 1886. After his retirement it was mainly the Jardine family which supplied the members of the ruling dynasty of the Princely Hong.

David Jardine, a nephew of Dr. William Jardine, went to China in 1838 at the age of twenty, was made a partner in 1843, and became head of Jardine, Matheson & Co. on the retirement of Alexander Matheson. He became one of the first two unofficial members of the Hong Kong Legislative Council in 1850, and died shortly after returning to Britain in 1856. There is in the Colonial Office records a curious letter from Sir John Bowring, Governor from 1855 to 1859, in which he states that David Jardine did not attend the meetings of the Legislative Council very frequently, and indeed "had ceased to attend, because his time was too

---

1 Alexander Matheson was the son of James Matheson's sister; she had married John Matheson, who was apparently unrelated to the other Mathesons.
2 *Jardine, Matheson & Co. 1832–1932*, p. 52.
3 W. C. Hunter, *The Fan Kwae at Canton*, p. 109.

valuable to waste on trivialities". This is probably an exaggeration, as Bowring was arguing the case for a reformed Legislative Council and was anxious to discredit the existing one.

Joseph Jardine, brother of David, was born in 1822 and followed the family tradition by going to China in 1843 and being given a partnership in Jardine, Matheson & Co., in 1845. After David left he presumably became head of the firm and a member of the Legislative Council. He retired in 1860 at the age of thirty-eight, and died next year at Castlemilk, an estate which had been bought for him by his brother. He subscribed largely to the Sailors' Home at West Point in whose grounds St. Peter's Church was subsequently erected as a Seamen's Church.

The third brother, Robert Jardine, the youngest of the three sons of David Jardine, elder brother of Dr. William Jardine, was born in 1825. He came to China in 1849 and left in 1860, so that although he became head of Jardine, Matheson & Co. he never became a member of the Colony's Legislative Council. He was elected M.P. for Ashburton 1865–8, for Dumfries Burghs 1868–74, and for Dumfries County 1880–90. He was made a Baronet in 1895, and died ten years later, apparently with as great a reputation or perhaps greater in the sporting world as he had in the commercial.

Joseph Jardine was followed on the Legislative Council by two partners of Jardine, Matheson & Co., Alexander Percival and James Whittall. Percival (1821–66) was related to the wife of Sir James Matheson and came from County Sligo. He went to China in about 1846, became a partner in Jardine, Matheson & Co. in 1852, and followed Joseph Jardine as a member of the Legislative Council in 1860 until his retirement from Hong Kong in 1864. He was succeeded by another partner, James Whittall (1827–93). Whittall came from a family of Worcestershire yeomen, associated closely with the Turkey trade. He joined Jardine, Matheson & Co. probably in 1856, and from 1861 to 1864 looked after the firm's affairs in Shanghai. In 1864 he came to Hong Kong and became a member of the Legislative Council until he left in 1875, when he founded his own firm of J. Whittall & Co. Judging from such accounts of the Legislative Council meetings as we have, Whittall was extremely active in question and debate, and became in every sense a Hong Kong man.

Other partners of the house who lived in Hong Kong may be briefly mentioned. Andrew Jardine (1812–81), eldest brother of David, Joseph, and Robert, already mentioned (and all sons of David Jardine, brother of Dr. William Jardine), came out in 1832 and left in 1843; William Stewart, who came to China in 1835, became a partner in 1842 and died in Hong Kong in 1846; Donald

Matheson, nephew of Sir James Matheson, was a partner from 1843 to 1849, when he retired, though he lived until 1901. He was the founder of the Rio Tinto Company. There was Alexander Campbell Maclean, who was brought out in 1848 by Alexander Matheson, became a partner 1849, and left 1857. John Charles Bowring, 1821–93, the eldest son of Sir John Bowring, went to China in 1848, the year before his father, joined Jardine, Matheson & Co. and became a partner in 1854, remaining one for ten years.

William Keswick, 1834–1912, became a prominent Hong Kong citizen, but he can only be mentioned briefly here because the main period of his life in Hong Kong falls outside the period covered by this book. He was a grandson of Dr. William Jardine's elder sister Margaret Johnston. Coming to China in 1855, he became a partner in 1862 and went on to nearly twenty years' membership of the Legislative Council, retiring in 1886.

APPENDIX A

List of Governors of the Colony of Hong Kong, 1841–1882

Capt. Charles Elliot	Administrator	January–August 1841
Sir Henry Pottinger	Administrator	August 1841–June 1843
	Governor	June 1843–May 1844
Sir John F. Davis		May 1844–March 1848
Sir S. George Bonham		March 1848–April 1854
Sir John Bowring		April 1854–May 1859
Sir Hercules Robinson		September 1859–March 1865
W. T. Mercer	[Administered]	March 1865–March 1866
Sir Richard Graves MacDonnell		March 1866–April 1872
Sir Arthur E. Kennedy		April 1872–March 1877
Sir John Pope Hennessy		April 1877–March 1882

APPENDIX B

List of Secretaries of State for the Colonies, 1841–1885

Ministry		Secretary of State for the Colonies Note: Secretary of State for War and the Colonies until June 1854.	
Peel: TORY	1841–6	Lord Stanley	Sept. 1841–Dec. 1845
		W. E. Gladstone	Dec. 1845–July 1846
Russell: WHIG	1846–52	Earl Grey	July 1846–Feb. 1852
Derby: TORY	1852	Sir J. Pakington	Feb.–Dec. 1852
Aberdeen: COALITION	1852–5	Duke of Newcastle	Dec. 1852–June 1854
		Sir George Grey	June 1854–Feb. 1855
Palmerston: WHIG	1855–8	S. Herbet	Feb. 1855
		Lord John Russell	Feb.–July 1855
		Sir William Moles- worth	July–Oct. 1855
		H. Labouchère	Oct. 1855–Feb. 1858
Derby: TORY	1858–9	Lord Stanley	Feb.–May 1858
		Sir E. Bulwer-Lytton	May 1858–June 1859
Palmerston: WHIG	1859–65	Duke of Newcastle	June 1859–April 1864
Russell: WHIG	1865–6	E. Cardwell	April 1864–June 1866
Derby: TORY	1866–8	Earl of Carnarvon	June 1866–Mar. 1867
Disraeli: TORY	1868	Duke of Buckingham	Mar. 1867–Dec. 1868
Gladstone: LIBERAL	1868–74	Earl Granville	Dec. 1868–July 1870
		Earl of Kimberley	July 1870–Feb. 1874
Disraeli: TORY	1874–80	Earl of Carnarvon	Feb. 1874–Feb. 1878
		Sir M. Hicks Beach	Feb. 1878–April 1880
Gladstone: LIBERAL	1880–5	Earl of Kimberley	April 1880–Dec. 1882
		Lord Derby	Dec. 1882–June 1885

GLOSSARY

Bazaar	Native business area; native area.
Bogue	(From Portuguese *bocca*, mouth.) The mouth of the Canton River.
Cadet	Term used in Hong Kong for a government officer of the administrative grade until 1960.
Cash	A Chinese copper coin with a centre hole for stringing and having a nominal value of one thousand to the dollar.
Co-hong	A group of Chinese merchants in Canton who possessed a theoretical monopoly of the western trade.
Compradore	(From Portuguese *comprar*, to buy.) A buyer, a Chinese agent used in buying or selling.
Cumshaw	A gratuity.
Dollar	Silver coin worth approximately 4*s*. 2*d*., and at this period usually Spanish, Mexican, or of one of the South American States.
Foreigner	A term frequently used for all non-Chinese.
Godown	A warehouse.
Hong	A Chinese merchant house.
Joss	(From Portuguese *deos*, God.) Deity or idol.
Lorcha	A ship with a European hull and Chinese rigging.
Praya	A road adjoining the sea-front.
Shroff	Banker, or one who examined and valued silver for accountancy purposes.
Tien Wang	Heavenly King, the name adopted by the leader of the T'ai P'ing rebels.
Tepo	A native police official.

A SELECT BIBLIOGRAPHY

The following are some of the sources that have been used:

Colonial Office Records (Public Record Office, London)

Series 129	Governors' Dispatches and Replies by the Secretary of State.
Series 130	Hong Kong Ordinances.
Series 131	Minutes of the Hong Kong Executive and Legislative Councils.
Series 132	Hong Kong Government Gazettes.

Newspapers

Canton Register,	1829–43.
Chinese Repository,	1832–51.
The Friend of China,	1842–61.
China Mail,	since 1845.

Printed Sources

Belcher, Sir E.	*Narrative of a Voyage Round the World, performed in H.M.S. Sulphur,* 2 vols., London, 1843.
Benard, W.D. and Hall W.H.	*The Voyage of the Nemesis,* 2 vols., London, 1844.
Bingham, J.E.	*Narrative of the Expedition to China,* 2 vols., London, 1842.
Cunynghame, Capt. A.	*An A.D.C.'s Recollections of Service in China,* 2 vols., London 1842.
Eitel, E.J.	*Europe in China,* London, 1895.
Mackenzie, K.S.	*Narrative of the Second Campaign in China,* London, 1842.
Macpherson, D., M.D.	*The War in China,* London, 1843.
Norton Kyshe, J.W.	*The History of the Laws and Courts of Hong Kong,* 2 vols., London, 1898.
Sirr, H.C.	*China and the Chinese,* 2 vols., London, 1849.
Smith, The Rev. G.	*A Narrative of the Exploratory Visit to each of the Consular Cities of China, and the Islands of Hong Kong and Chusan,* London, 1847.

Reference Books

Allen, C.G. and Donnithorne, A.G.	*Western Enterprise in Far Eastern Development*, London, 1954.
Collins, Sir Charles	*Public Administration in Hong Kong*, London, 1952.
Collis, Maurice	*Foreign Mud*, London, 1946.
Costin, W.C.	*Great Britain and China, 1833–1860*, Oxford, 1937.
Endacott, G.B.	*A History of Hong Kong*, Oxford, 1958.
Endacott, G.B. and She, D.	*The Diocese of Victoria*, Hong Kong 1949.
Morse, H.B.	*The International Relations of the Chinese Empire*, London, 1918.
Orange, James	*The Chater Collection*, London, 1924.
Sayer, G.R.	*Hong Kong, Birth, Adolescence and Coming of Age*, Oxford, 1937.

INDEX OF PERSONS

SELECTED WORKS BY G. B. ENDACOTT

The Diocese of Victoria Hong Kong: A Hundred Years of Church History, 1849–1949. (With Dorothy E. She). Hong Kong: Kelly and Walsh, 1949.

An Eastern Entrepot: A Collection of Documents Illustrating the History of Hong Kong. London: Her Majesty's Stationery Office, 1964.

Fragrant Harbour: A Short History of Hong Kong. (With A. Hinton). Hong Kong: Oxford University Press, 1962. Rev. ed. Hong Kong: Oxford University Press, 1968.

A History of Hong Kong. London: Oxford University Press, 1958. Rev. ed. Hong Kong: Oxford University Press, 1973.

Government and People in Hong Kong, 1841–1962: A Constitutional History. Hong Kong: Hong Kong University Press, 1964.

Hong Kong Eclipse. Ed. and with additional material by Alan Birch. Hong Kong: Oxford University Press, 1978.